IMAGES
of America
COSTA MESA
1940–2003

*In memory of Karen Blumenthal
She loved books*

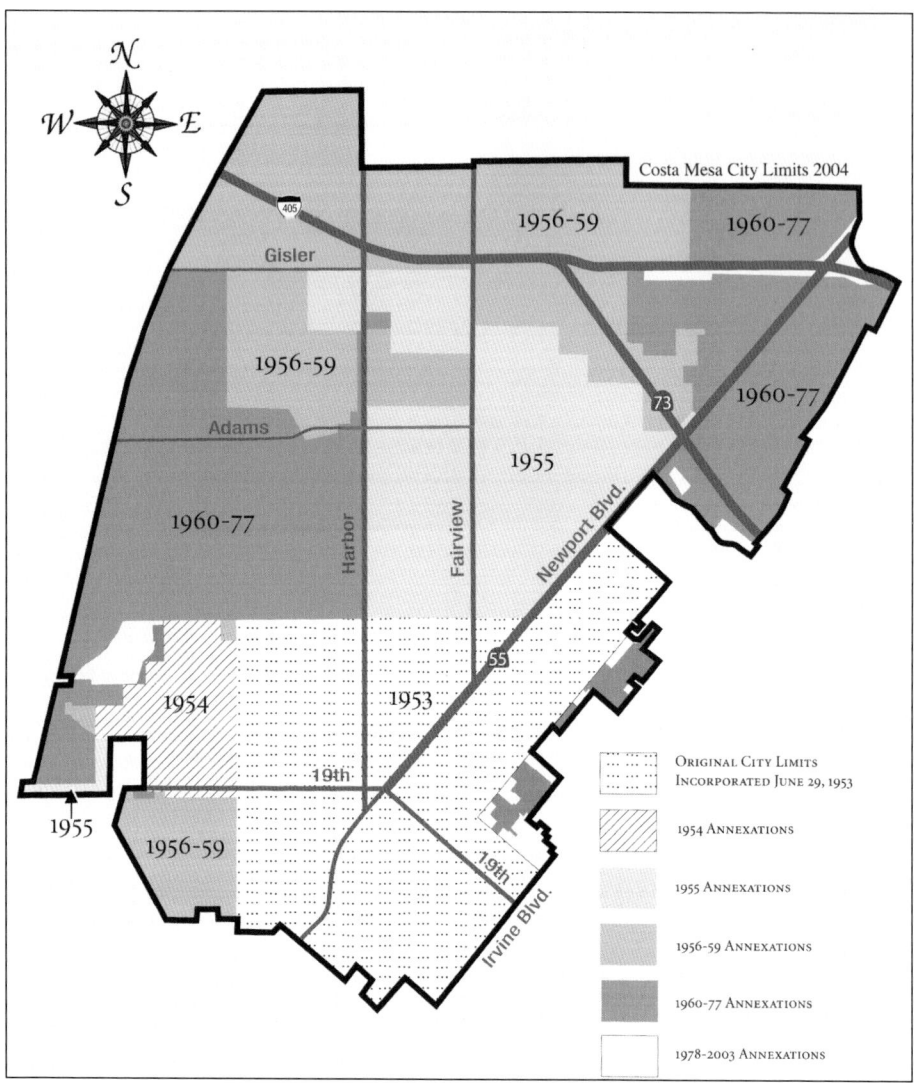

In 1953, Costa Mesa incorporated as a general law city covering a 3.5-square-mile area centered on the established downtown district at the intersection of Newport and Harbor Boulevards. Because the new city was surrounded by older, established cities, the race was on to reach critical mass via annexation. Over the 25-year period from 1953 to 1978, Costa Mesa more than quadrupled its area to 15.7 square miles. The new city encompassed world-class retail and commercial districts, performing arts venues, high-rise office buildings, redevelopment districts, housing of all types, a freeway crossroads, and an adjacent airport. By the early 1990s, Costa Mesa was at the center of an edge city known as South Coast Metro, according to Joel Garreau's *Edge City*. (Courtesy of Keith Hall.)

ON THE COVER: By 1948, Costa Mesa had grown into a bustling community of nearly 10,000 people. It had been just 40 years since the opening of the area's first business, Ozment's General Store, in 1908. This photograph shows the traditional downtown business district in 1948, looking northeast along the 1800 block of Newport Boulevard. From the photographer's vantage point on the rooftop of today's El Matador Restaurant, one could see a long distance, but Costa Mesa's destiny would lie beyond this horizon. (Courtesy of Costa Mesa Historical Society.)

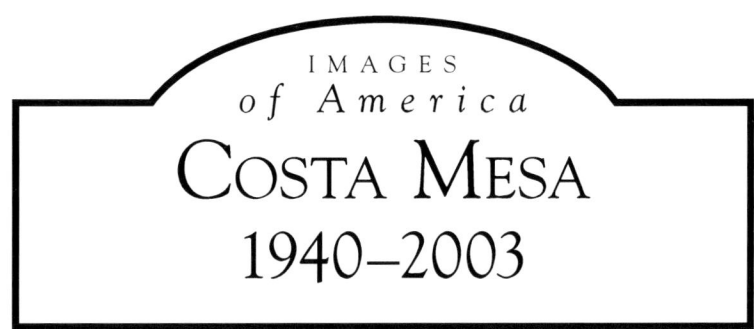

Costa Mesa Historical Society

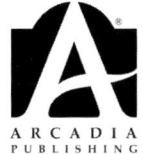

Copyright © 2016 by the Costa Mesa Historical Society
ISBN 978-1-4671-1576-6

Published by Arcadia Publishing
Charleston, South Carolina

Printed in the United States of America

Library of Congress Control Number: 2015955679

For all general information, please contact Arcadia Publishing:
Telephone 843-853-2070
Fax 843-853-0044
E-mail sales@arcadiapublishing.com
For customer service and orders:
Toll-Free 1-888-313-2665

Visit us on the Internet at www.arcadiapublishing.com

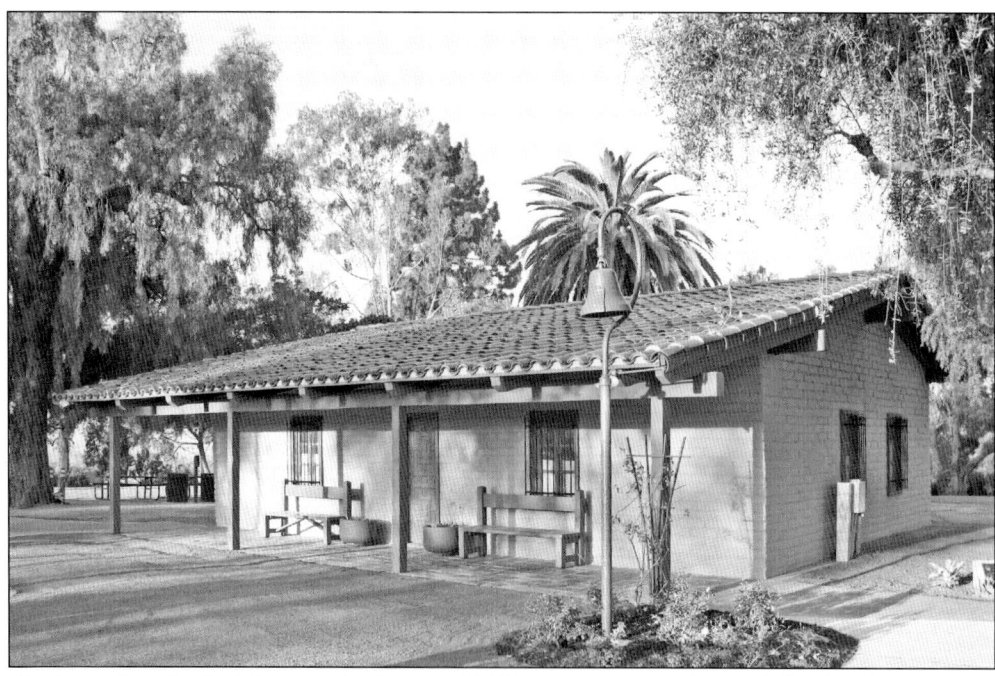

The Diego Sepulveda Adobe was built around 1820 as an outstation for cattle herders from Mission San Juan Capistrano. A subsequent property owner, Gabe Allen, enclosed the adobe walls within a wood-frame ranch house, incidentally assuring survival of the adobe brickwork. In 1963, the Segerstrom family donated the building and surrounding five acres to the city for use as a community heritage site and public park. Since the building's restoration in 1966, the Costa Mesa Historical Society has operated the adobe as a museum. A second restoration was completed in 2011. The Diego Sepulveda Adobe (California Historical Landmark No. 227) is located in Estancia Park at 1900 Adams Avenue, Costa Mesa. (Courtesy of Costa Mesa Historical Society.)

Contents

Acknowledgments		6
Introduction		7
1.	War and Peace	11
2.	Incorporation	31
3.	Annexation and Growth	47
4.	Coming of Age	69
5.	Redevelopment and South Coast Metro	89
6.	CostaMazing	111
Epilogue		127

Acknowledgments

Preparing *Costa Mesa: 1940–2003* for publication has reacquainted us with the city in which we live. We have revisited the events that defined and shaped the incorporation and subsequent development of Costa Mesa and have scoured the depths of our collections in search of images and documents that would tell the story clearly and succinctly.

The first of our acknowledgments goes to all those who have donated materials from their personal and organizational collections to the Costa Mesa Historical Society for preservation and promotion of local history. Without these donations from hundreds of community members and groups, this book would not have been possible.

For the years from 1940 to the mid-1970s, we have relied on our Edrick Miller Collection and upon Miller's seminal book, *A Slice of Orange*. Our community owes a profound debt of gratitude to Ed Miller for researching, collecting, and copying many original photographs and documents. The Costa Mesa Historical Society is privileged to be the repository for the Edrick Miller Collection.

The City of Costa Mesa is acknowledged for its partnership with the historical society since the society's founding in 1966. Our relationship facilitates the preservation and promotion of local history through museum exhibits, cataloged resources, public outreach, and educational materials. The Costa Mesa Historical Society is pleased to be part of the city's program for enhancing a sense of community among our residents.

Keith Hall created maps that we gratefully acknowledge. A number of images in this book have been used with permission of family members and organizations. Specific credits are provided in the captions for those images. Unless otherwise noted, images in this book are from the collections of the Costa Mesa Historical Society.

Also, we wish to thank Prof. Henry "Hank" Panian and past mayor Mary Hornbuckle for their review and constructive criticism of the manuscript. Finally, we thank our editors at Arcadia Publishing for their patience and guidance throughout the creation of this book.

—Art and Mary Ellen Goddard
Costa Mesa Historical Society

INTRODUCTION

In the times before 1940, Costa Mesa experienced successive transformations from Native American habitat to cattle ranching, to grain farming, to small-scale farming, and then to the formation of early communities. Along the way, Costa Mesa endured droughts, earthquakes, floods, annexation attempts, and the Great Depression. Equally as important, Costa Mesa built schools and infrastructure and, out of necessity, developed a tradition of local governance. By 1940, the unincorporated community of Costa Mesa had met all challenges that had come its way and emerged with its sense of community intact. With a growing population of more than 4,000, the stage was set for what would become the postwar miracle of Costa Mesa.

While the community celebrated its survival of the 1930s by holding scarecrow carnivals from 1938 to 1941, the winds of war were increasing in Europe and the Pacific. Just before the outbreak of war with Japan, Costa Mesa was selected as the site for the Santa Ana Army Air Base (SAAAB). During its run from 1942 to 1946, more than 125,000 cadets passed through the base. Many of them would remember the agreeable climate in Southern California and return to the region after the war. Along with the population influx, 1,337 acres of SAAAB land and buildings were converted to civilian use. The Orange County Fair found a permanent home on former base land, as did Orange Coast College, Southern California Bible College (now Vanguard University), Mesa Del Mar and College Park housing tracts, Costa Mesa High School, Costa Mesa Civic Center, parks, and schools. Base buildings were moved to become new apartments, churches, and meeting places—St. Joachim Church and the Costa Mesa Grange are two examples. Costa Mesa's service clubs continued their community support, including the Costa Mesa–Newport Harbor Lions Club, which held its first annual fish fry and parade in 1946.

As Costa Mesa was surrounded by older, established cities—Santa Ana, Newport Beach, and Huntington Beach—there was a growing realization that Costa Mesa could not continue indefinitely as an unincorporated community. Starting in the Great Depression and through the war years, there had been a 25-year hiatus during which no new cities were incorporated in Orange County. During this time, the City of Santa Ana opined that it should annex the former SAAAB land because, among other things, the base was named after the city. Apparently Costa Mesans were not swayed by such impeccable logic, as once again the wheels of home rule began to turn. In June 1953, the people of Costa Mesa voted to incorporate with original boundaries as shown in the map on page 2.

It is hard to imagine any city having more modest beginnings than Costa Mesa. The city council met after-hours in a local courthouse on West Eighteenth Street. Each council member contributed $20 to create a city treasury. The first city hall was located in a former auto parts store at 1998 1/2 Newport Boulevard. City officials felt that this street number lacked sufficient gravitas, so they flexed their newly acquired municipal muscle and changed the address to 111 East Twentieth Street.

Soon, Costa Mesa officials were introduced to the chess game of annexation, when, in times preceding the Orange County Local Agency Formation Commission (LAFCO), Newport Beach ran a "cherry stem" along the edge of the Banning Ranch property to annex a tract north of West Nineteenth Street. As later explained, Newport Beach had used this area as a city dump and felt obliged to clean it up. That justification notwithstanding, Costa Mesa officials saw the annexation as a shot across the bow and responded to protect the city's flanks by annexing a 200-foot-wide strip that went across the Santa Ana River to meet the city limits of Huntington Beach.

The race was on for Costa Mesa to annex enough land to achieve critical mass. The Freedom Homes tract was annexed in 1954. In 1955, an area comprising central Costa Mesa, including the College Park, Mesa Del Mar, and Halecrest tracts, was annexed. Between 1956 and 1959, most of North Costa Mesa was annexed, including the future site of South Coast Plaza. Also annexed during this period was a Westside area from Placentia Avenue to the Banning Ranch border, south of West Nineteenth Street. The bulk of Costa Mesa's remaining annexations occurred from 1960 to 1977. These areas included Mesa Verde, Fairview State Hospital, Fairview Park, and northeast Costa Mesa, including the airport industrial area and Sakioka Farms. (See map on page 2.) By 1978, Costa Mesa had annexed most of the land available to it. The size of the stage had grown to nearly 15.7 square miles. What would play on that stage over the next 25 years would be nothing short of amazing.

There was much more going on in Costa Mesa during those annexation years. Besides housing development and new retail and commercial districts, industry had found a home in Costa Mesa, mostly on the Westside. Boatbuilding and other businesses based on fiberglass were prominent, as was Cla-Val, Kingsley Manufacturing, and many others. Glasspar was poised to give Detroit some competition but then dropped its fiberglass auto body business to concentrate on boatbuilding. Eastside Costa Mesa saw the development of new retail businesses as East Seventeenth Street developed into a "Miracle Mile." Fairview State Hospital opened in 1959 and became one of the area's largest employers. Serendipity prevailed as Costa Mesa inherited a central greenbelt consisting of contiguous open space from Fairview Park, across the state hospital grounds and converted SAAAB land, to the Santa Ana Country Club—a greenbelt that to the present day encourages the flow of cooling ocean breezes across the city.

Of major significance was the formation of the Costa Mesa County Water District in 1960. By 1968, the district foresaw the rising cost and potential unreliability of imported water and embarked on a sustained program of water independence by drilling deep wells. The district was rebranded as the Mesa Consolidated Water District in 1978. Also during the 1960s, the Harbor Boulevard of Cars developed into a major source of sales tax revenue for the city. Costa Mesa High School opened its doors in 1958, followed by Harbor Shopping Center in 1959. South Coast Plaza began construction in 1965, just before the extension of the San Diego Freeway to Harbor Boulevard in 1966 and to State Route 55 and Jamboree Road in 1968. Changes in the educational system were debated, with an election in 1965 leading to formation of the Newport-Mesa Unified School District in 1966. Newport Beach voters opposed the merger but found themselves party to the shotgun wedding nonetheless. During this period, the original city hall was superseded by a second city hall on West Nineteenth Street and then by a modern civic center on Fair Drive.

From their viewpoint along Fair Drive, city leaders did not appreciate an event held across the street at the Orange County Fairgrounds in August 1968—the first annual Newport Pop Festival. Headliners included Jefferson Airplane, Tiny Tim, Eric Burdon and the Animals, the Grateful Dead, and Steppenwolf. Attendance totaled 140,000 young people. The city council disapproved and took action to preclude a second annual pop festival from taking place in Costa Mesa. The mid-to-late 1960s also offered more significant events such as the opening of Estancia High School, Mesa Verde Branch Library, Atlantic Research, Bethel Towers, and the Orange County Marketplace, originally known as Treasures 'n' Trash, to name a few.

The 1970s were not to be outdone by the 1960s. The Mesa Verde and North Costa Mesa areas flourished with the opening of Travenol Laboratories, Mesa Verde Center, Vista Del Lago,

FEDCO, Red Hill Industrial Complex, and South Coast Plaza Hotel, among others. Another type of construction took place as the tall ship *Pilgrim of Newport* was built in a residential yard. In 1972, Costa Mesa formed a redevelopment agency with city council members at the helm. Six years later, a statewide voter revolt led to passage of Proposition 13, adding a property tax revenue incentive to the city's redevelopment plans. Beautification became an issue, leading to the burying of electrical utilities underground along Harbor Boulevard. With beautification came a focus on city recreation and leisure services, as Lions Park was expanded and the Boys' Club was purchased to serve as a recreation center.

One new development did not sit well with the residents of the Mesa Del Mar and College Park tracts. In 1979, a pact was signed to build a Hollywood Bowl–style amphitheater on the Orange County Fairgrounds, an amphitheater second in size in Orange County only to the 43,204-seat capacity of Anaheim Stadium. The City of Costa Mesa objected, but a Superior Court judge ruled that the fair board did not have to submit its development plans to the city. The Pacific Amphitheater opened in 1983, thus triggering a 12-year battle over sound levels and traffic congestion that resulted in cessation of loud concerts in 1995. A kinder, gentler version of the amphitheater opened in 2003.

Another chain of events in the 1980s set the stage for the next 20 years. Private philanthropy by the Segerstrom family paved the way for land and buildings for the South Coast Repertory and the Orange County Performing Arts Center. Public art found places in what then became known as the Theater and Arts District. *California Scenario* was created by artist Isamu Noguchi and installed in Pacific Arts Plaza. Parcels of the Sakioka Farms were rezoned to accommodate high-rise office towers and upscale apartment buildings. Crystal Court opened in 1986. At this point, it was clear that the center of gravity of Costa Mesa was shifting from the traditional downtown area along Newport Boulevard northward towards Town Center. A "City of the Arts" was taking shape, and decades of Costa Mesa's attempts to hitch its star to the harbor area became moot. Costa Mesa had found its stride.

Not to be upstaged, the traditional downtown area was due for revamping with oversight by the Costa Mesa Redevelopment Agency. Fire Station No. 3, Casa Bella Apartments, Neighborhood Recreation Center, Pacific Savings Plaza, Costa Mesa Courtyards, Newport Boulevard Demonstration Block, Donald Dungan Library, and Triangle Square constituted the major projects.

As Costa Mesa rolled into the 1990s, regional issues took center stage. After years of delay, State Route 55 was extended from the fairgrounds south to Nineteenth Street. The extension became a holding ramp for motorists awaiting entry into the freeway-averse City of Newport Beach. Further extension of the freeway from Nineteenth Street to the city limits would prove to be a Gordian knot left for future generations to unravel.

In 1993, the federal government announced its intent to close El Toro Marine Corps Air Station (ETMCAS). Thus began a decade of wrangling to convert ETMCAS into an international airport serving Orange County. The anti-airport faction won that contest decisively in 2002, leaving the county residents with a giant balloon at ETMCAS and leaving Costa Mesa with an established airport, John Wayne International, close by. The area of north Costa Mesa, with its intersection of freeways and airport, had become an edge city known as South Coast Metro.

As the airport issue was unfolding, Costa Mesa resident John Moorlach pointed out the risks of Orange County's investment strategy. On December 6, 1994, one day short of Pearl Harbor Remembrance Day, Orange County declared bankruptcy and soon thereafter found it had lost $1.6 billion. Costa Mesa was lightly invested in the county pool and faced a potential loss of $3 million.

By 2000, Costa Mesa had reached a build-out exceeding 98 percent. In effect, there were vested interests covering every square inch of land within the city limits. New development and density became the topics of heated discussion as no-growth, slow-growth, and pro-growth factions duked it out in local elections. Such contests notwithstanding, Costa Mesa continued to benefit from an engaged city government, vocal residents, and broad support for livability, including the arts, recreation, amenities, education, economics, and infrastructure.

Heading into the 50th anniversary of its incorporation, Costa Mesa's transformation was nothing short of amazing. Population had grown 23 times, from 4,700 in 1940 to 109,000 in 2003. City land area had more than quadrupled to 15.7 square miles. The transition from agricultural land use to suburban and urban land use had been essentially completed. Costa Mesa had rebranded itself from "Hub of the Harbor Area" to "City of the Arts." Costa Mesa had become its own place.

According to a 1984 issue of Costa Mesa's local newspaper, the *Daily Pilot*, "It wasn't so long ago that a photographer, invited to immortalize the City of Costa Mesa on postcards, took one look at the town and declared flatly, 'You really don't have anything worth photographing.' " That quote highlights the purpose of this book: to tell the story of modern Costa Mesa and demonstrate that there is indeed much worth photographing!

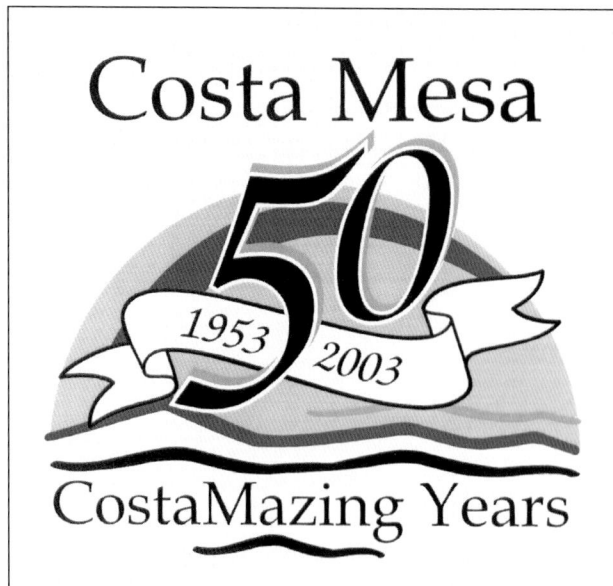

By 2003, the 50th anniversary of city incorporation, Costa Mesa was in a mood to party. It had been an epic journey from mission and rancho times to arrival at a place not long foreseen: a "City of the Arts" located at the center of the ultimate overlay zone, an edge city known as South Coast Metro. "CostaMazing" became the anniversary motto. Celebrations extended over a one-year period and included a kickoff barbecue, a new city flag, an anniversary party, an award-winning county fair exhibit, oral histories, a hoedown, a 5K fun run/walk, and a gala named Dining through the Decades.

One
WAR AND PEACE

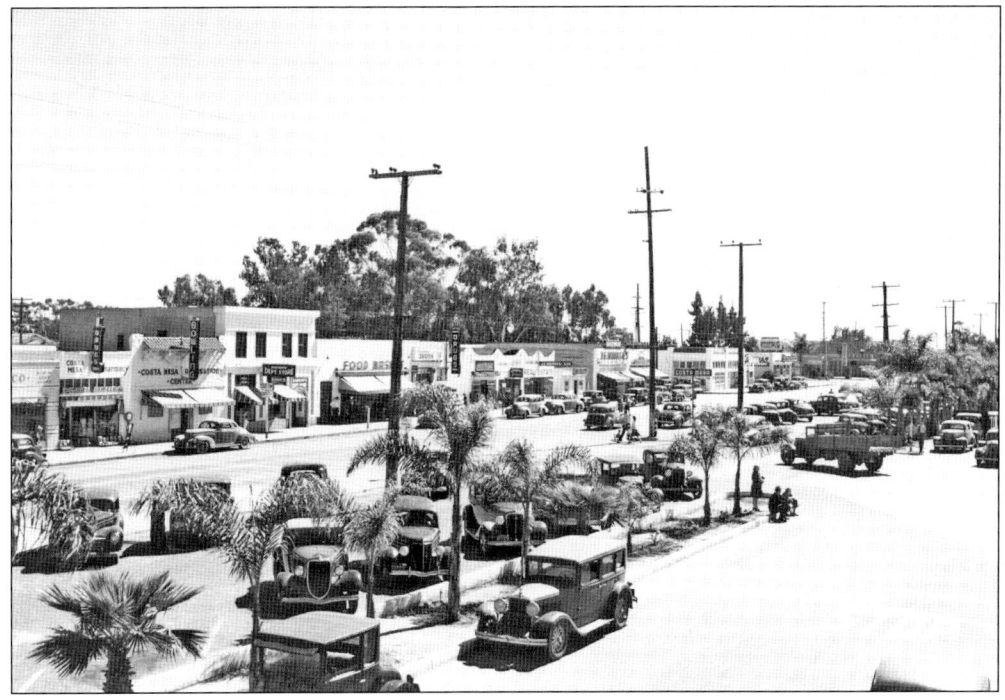

By 1940, Costa Mesa had become an established community with a downtown district centered at the junction of Newport and Harbor Boulevards. The community had developed a personality and cohesion, due in part to the establishment of schools, churches, service clubs, and the Costa Mesa Chamber of Commerce, which provided local services that had been overlooked by the county supervisors in far-off Santa Ana. During the war years, the downtown area appeared much as shown in this 1945 photograph.

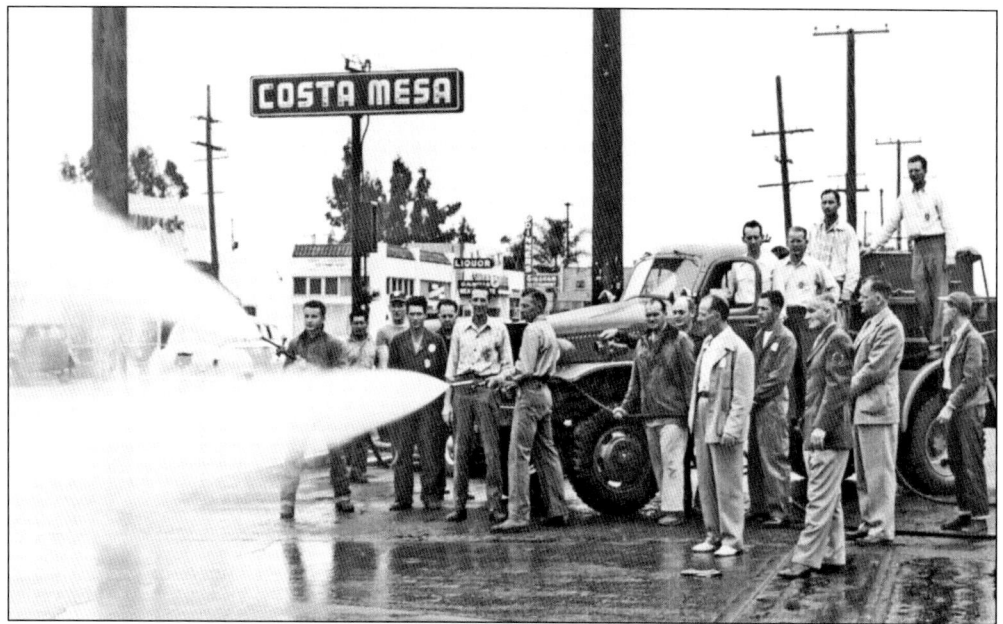

Costa Mesa's volunteer firemen staged this public demonstration in 1947 to show the department's latest acquisition, a surplus World War II high-pressure tank truck. Fire chief Bertren "Bert" Smith appears at the center of action, sixth from the left. Like many leaders in Costa Mesa, Smith was a local businessman. He served as fire chief for more than a decade and then as a member of the first city council. The volunteer fire department was formed in 1924 and continued to serve the community until the Costa Mesa Fire Department reached sufficient staffing in 1965.

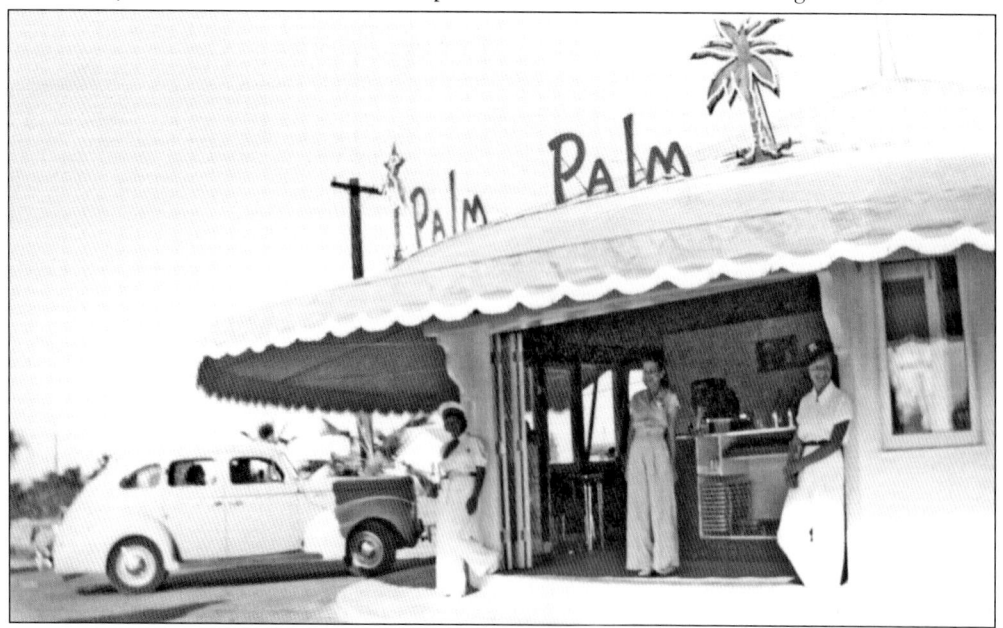

The Palm-Palm restaurant was a popular spot on Newport Boulevard at East Nineteenth Street. Carhops dressed in sailor suits served hamburgers and chicken dinners to drive-in customers. Inside seating was also available. The menu featured hot pork sandwich lunches for 25¢ and steak or chicken dinners for 50¢.

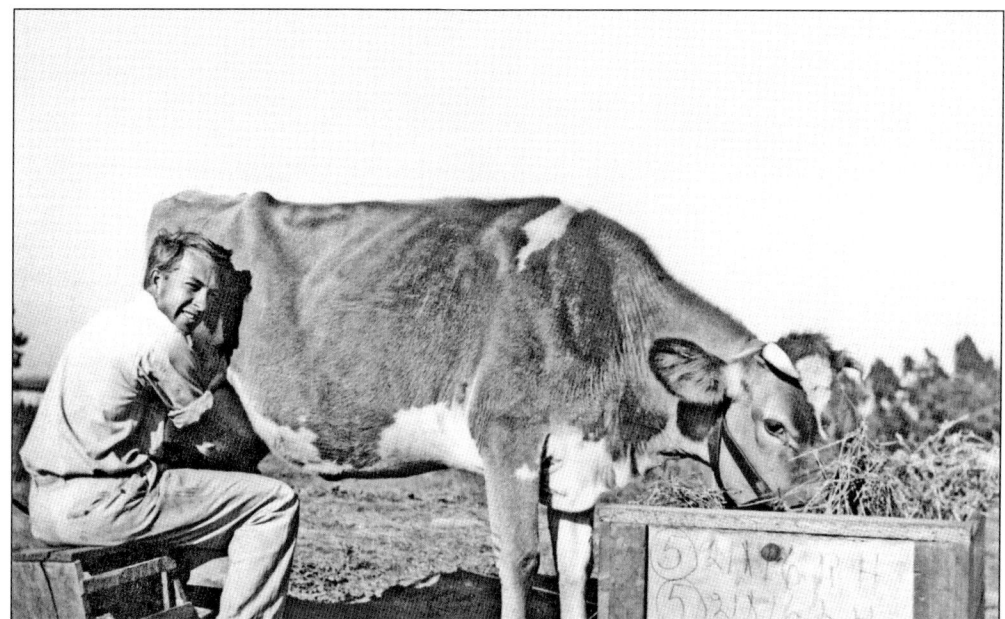

Costa Mesa's agricultural roots were evident not far from the downtown business and residential district. Here, Charles Beecher milks the family cow, Bessie, at his new property at 2039 Newport Boulevard. During World War II, Beecher worked in the marine hardware industry, then sold Fuller brushes, then became a postal clerk. In recognition of his civic generosity, the Costa Mesa City Council declared July 20, 1998, Charles Beecher Day.

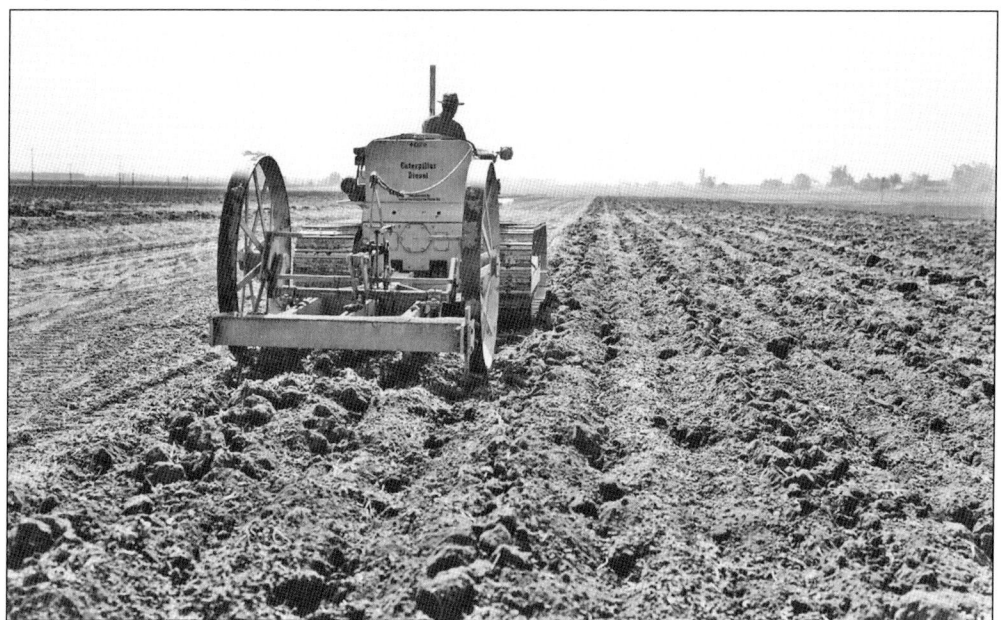

In addition to family-sized farming operations, much of the area in the northern part of what is now Costa Mesa was the site of large-scale farming by the Segerstrom family. In this 1940 photograph, a field is being prepared for planting lima beans. The family became the largest independent producer of lima beans in North America before turning its attention to development of shopping malls, office space, housing, and performing arts venues.

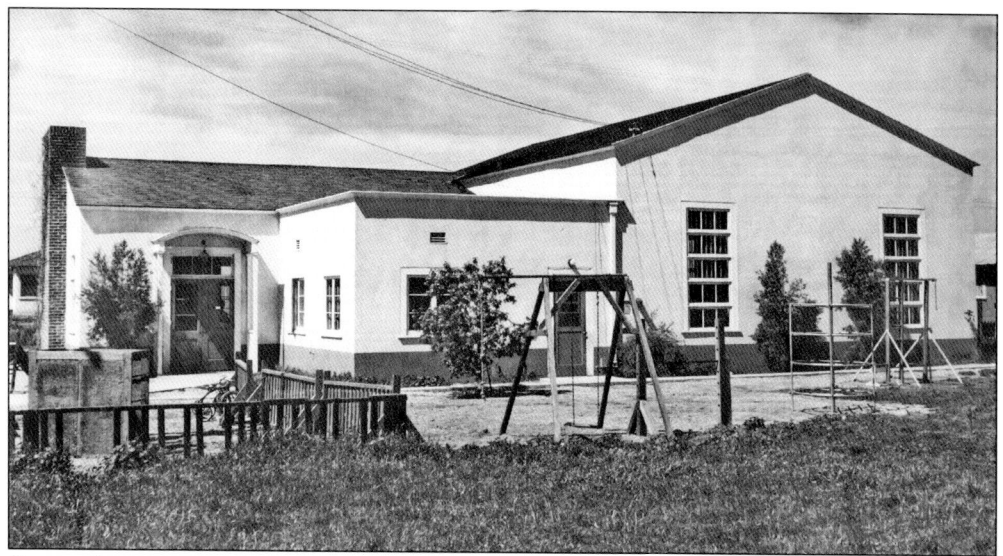

Originally a private residence, the building pictured here became a Boys' Club in 1941. During World War II, it served as a daycare center for mothers working in defense jobs. In 1947, the building again served local youth as the Boys' Club of the Harbor Area. The city purchased the building in 1970 and operated it as the Downtown Community Center until it was replaced by the new Downtown Recreation Center in 2002.

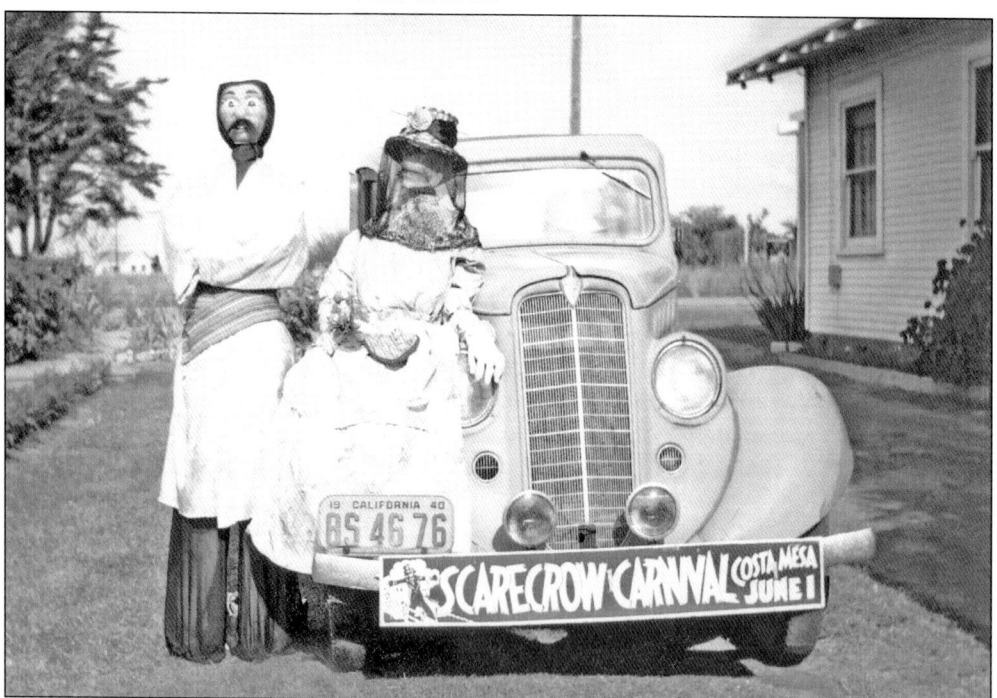

By 1938, Costa Mesa had survived earthquakes, floods, and the Great Depression. Community spirit was unbroken, and the chamber of commerce sponsored annual scarecrow carnivals that attracted thousands of attendees. On the morning of the third annual event in 1940, Nell Murbarger photographed her two entries, "Chinese Mandarin" and "Village Gossip," posed next to the Willys coupe that would transport them all to the carnival site.

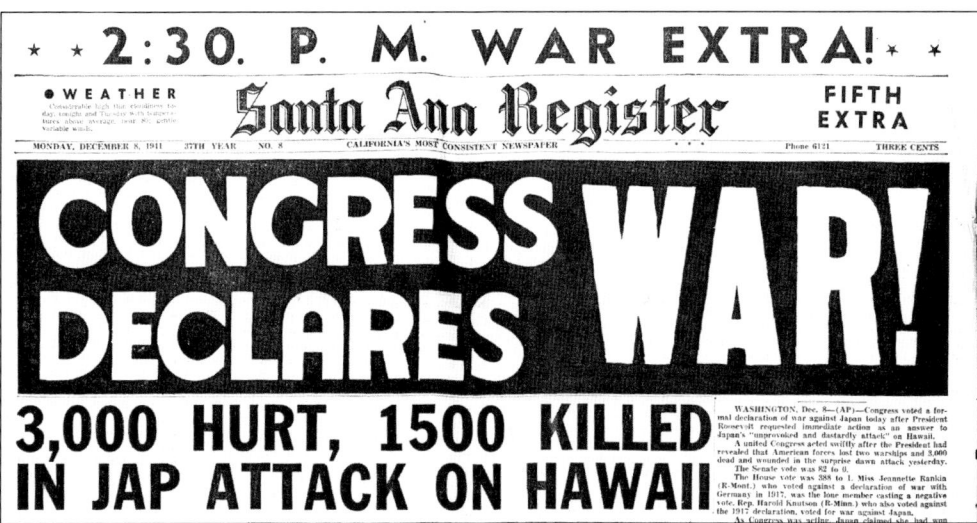

On Monday, December 8, 1941, newspaper headlines read the same all across the nation. But Costa Mesa was to experience extraordinary impacts. For one thing, Costa Mesa, with a population of about 5,000, hosted the 1,337-acre Santa Ana Army Air Base, an instant city that peaked at a population of more than 26,000. Also, as a West Coast community, Costa Mesa endured blackouts and civil defense drills and provided civilian volunteers to staff local observation posts of the Aircraft Warning System (AWS).

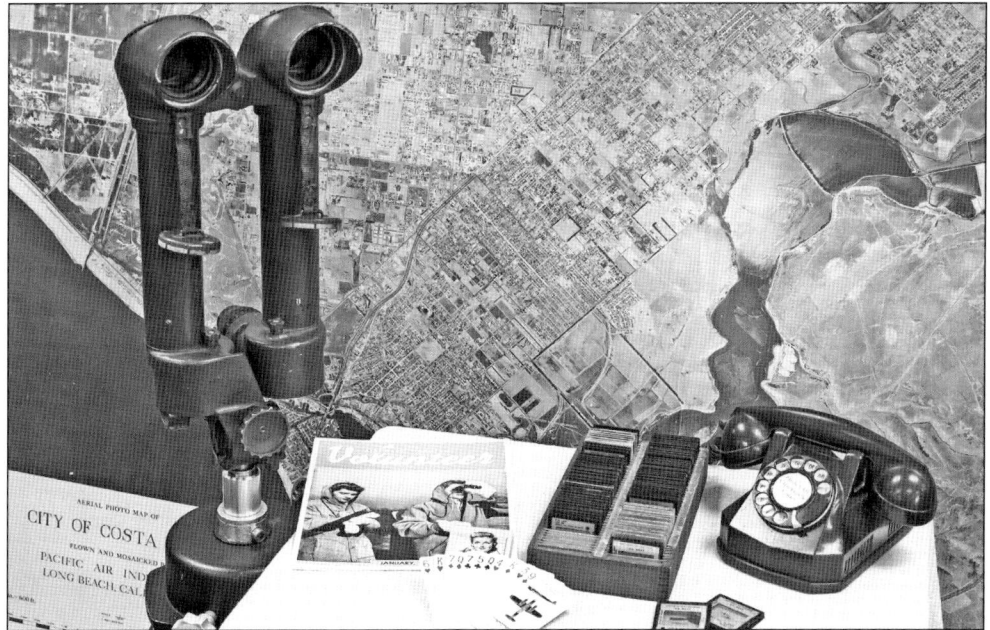

The newspaper front page pictured above carried a short notice activating all observation posts of the AWS. Costa Mesans staffed two posts, one at the Fairview Farms pumping station and one at the Irvine Salt Works. Local pharmacist Alvin "Al" Pinkley served as assistant chief observer at the Fairview Farms post. Components of the AWS pictured here include recognition training slides and playing cards depicting enemy aircraft silhouettes, an M65 telescope, an edition of *Volunteer Observer* magazine, and a telephone to call the regional coordination center. (M65 telescope courtesy of Christian Eric.)

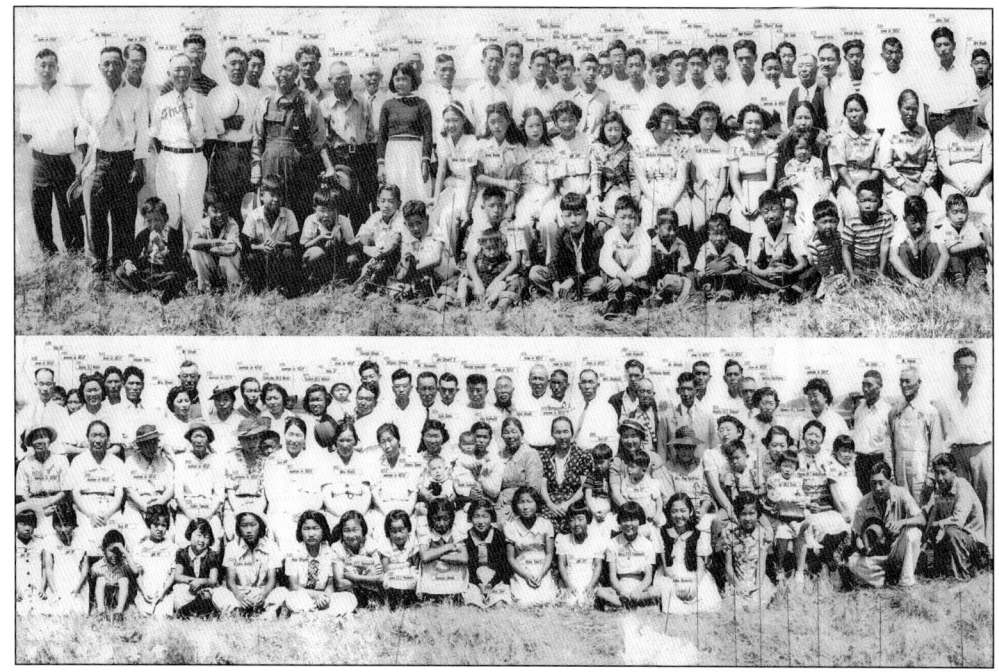

Another event in Costa Mesa's wartime experience involved its Japanese American community. The 1939 Costa Mesa Directory listed 22 families of Japanese descent. Several of those family members are pictured in this September 1940 photograph taken for the Japanese Schools of Orange County. By May 1942, Costa Mesa's Japanese American families had been sent to Poston War Relocation Center in Arizona or other internment camps. Those families would not be allowed to return home until early 1945.

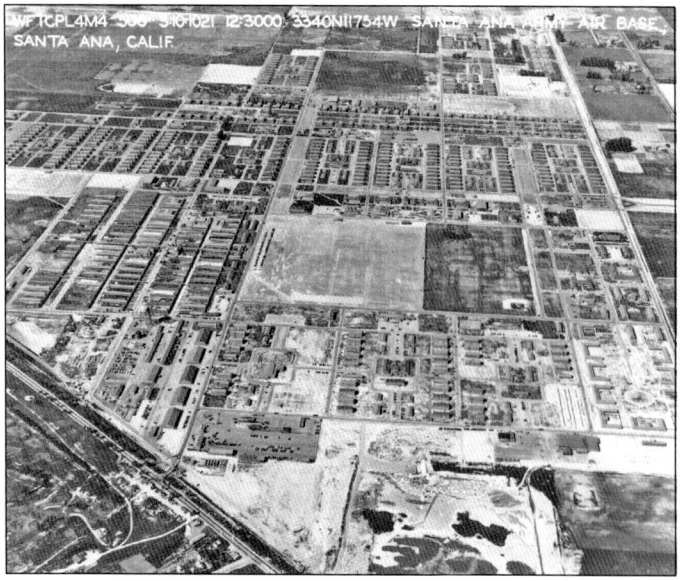

By March 1943, the Santa Ana Army Air Base was in full swing. The base was a city unto itself, consisting of 800 buildings, four chapels, four theaters, and approximately 30 miles each of water mains, electrical lines, and sewers. With an area of 1,337 acres, the base occupied nearly 15 percent of today's city footprint. In this aerial view looking west, Newport Boulevard and the northern tip of the Santa Ana Country Club appear at lower left.

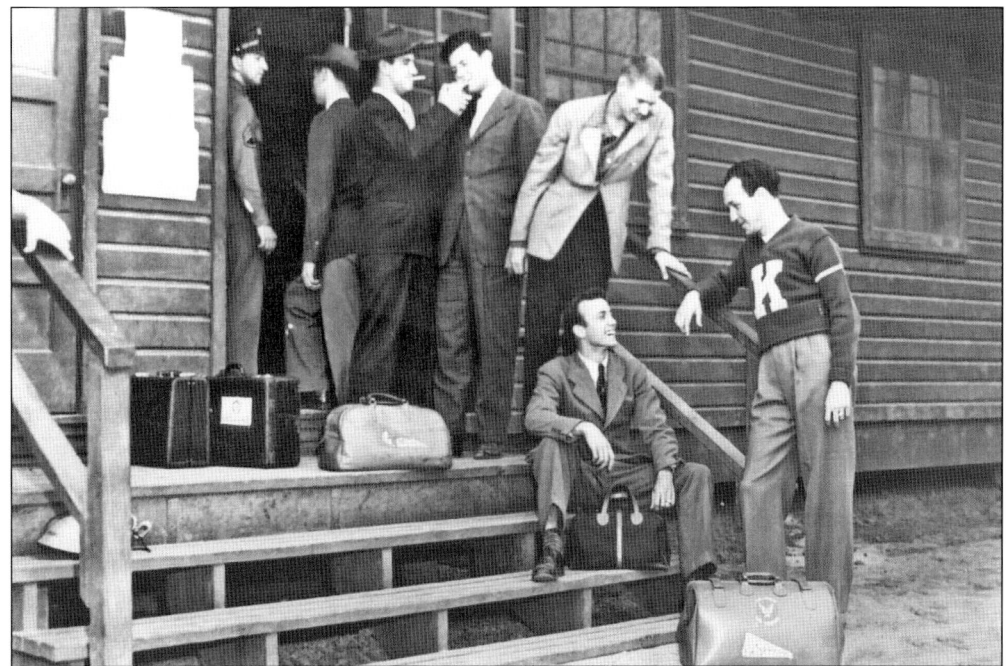

New recruits came to the Santa Ana Army Air Base (SAAAB) from all walks of life. Those cadets who passed the preflight training regimen would go on to Army Air Corps flight training schools and become pilots, navigators, or bombardiers. More than 125,000 cadets would pass through SAAAB during the war. Some of them would note the agreeable climate in Costa Mesa and return to the area after the war.

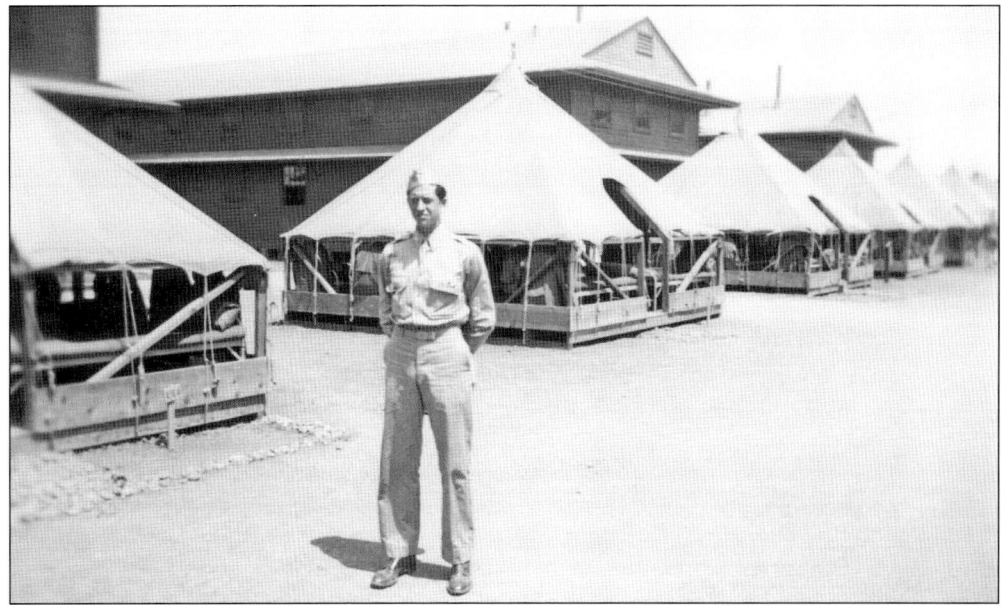

Aviation cadet Howard Nunn stands at parade rest in a barracks area of the Santa Ana Army Air Base. In early-to-mid-1942, the base was unfinished, and many cadets lived in Army tents, six to eight per tent. When the wall partitions were removed from the two-story barracks, the occupancy rose from 38 to 63 cadets per building and the need for tents decreased.

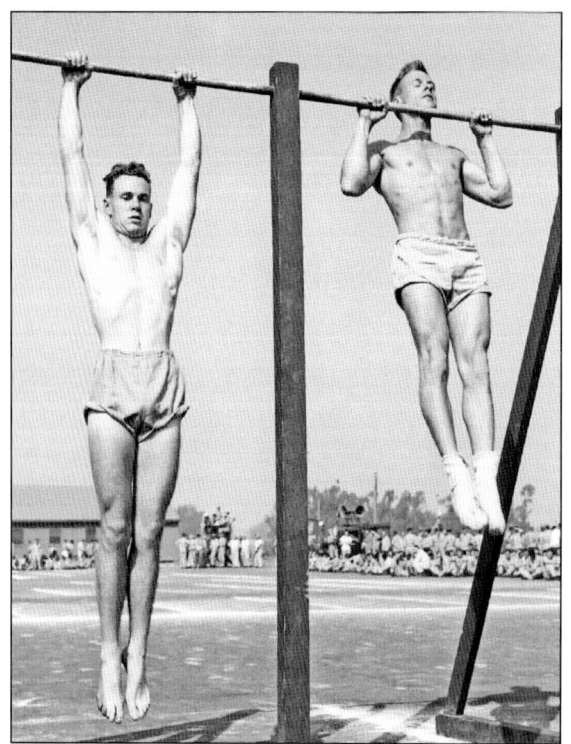

Base routine involved long hours and hard work. A cadet's day began at 5:00 a.m. and extended through 17 hours of physical and mental exertion. Leave time was rare and regulations stringent. Typical activities included 30-second formations, drills, bivouacs, and calisthenics such as chin-ups on the high bar.

Base chow was rated top notch by the cadets. Providing three meals a day to thousands of cadets and staff proved a formidable logistical challenge. In February 1943, construction was completed on a 3.4-mile standard-gauge rail spur to connect the base to the Pacific Electric railway at Greenville. A portion of that track ran along the east edge of Harbor Boulevard, across Baker Street, then south until it curved into the base warehouse area located along today's Village Way.

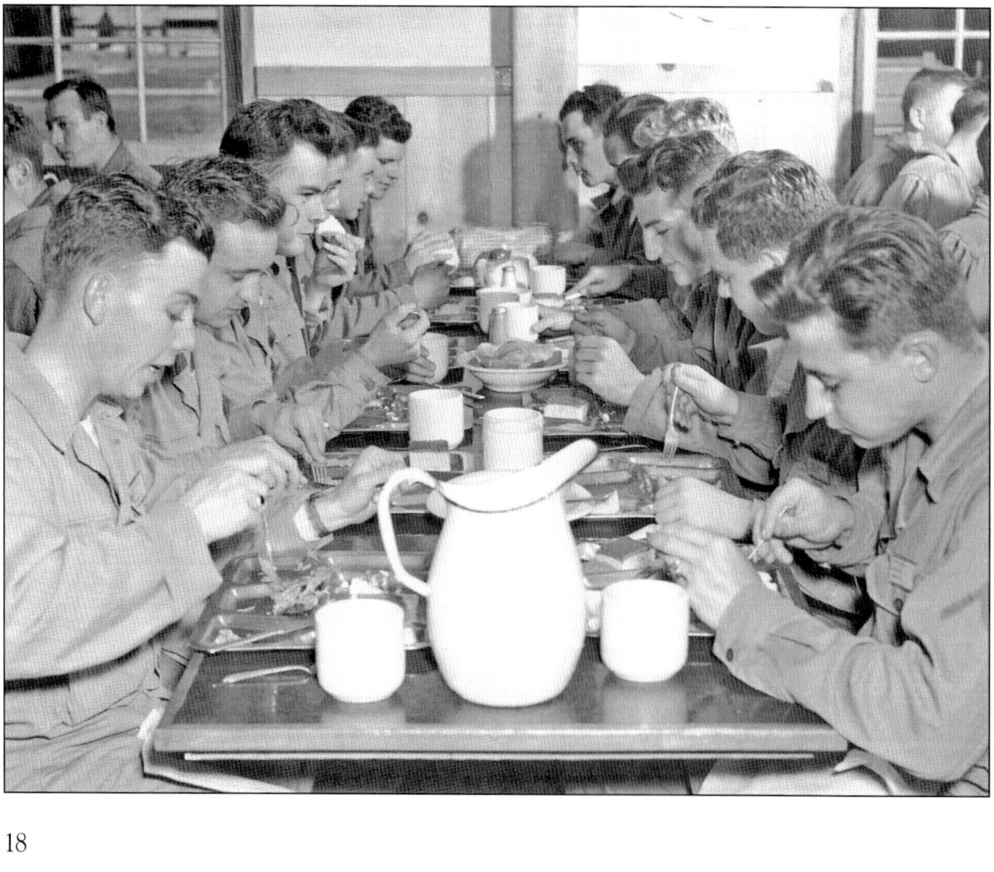

Physiological training was an important part of each cadet's preflight instruction. Here, cadets check their pulses in an altitude chamber in order to better understand the symptoms of hypoxia, a shortage of oxygen reaching bodily tissue.

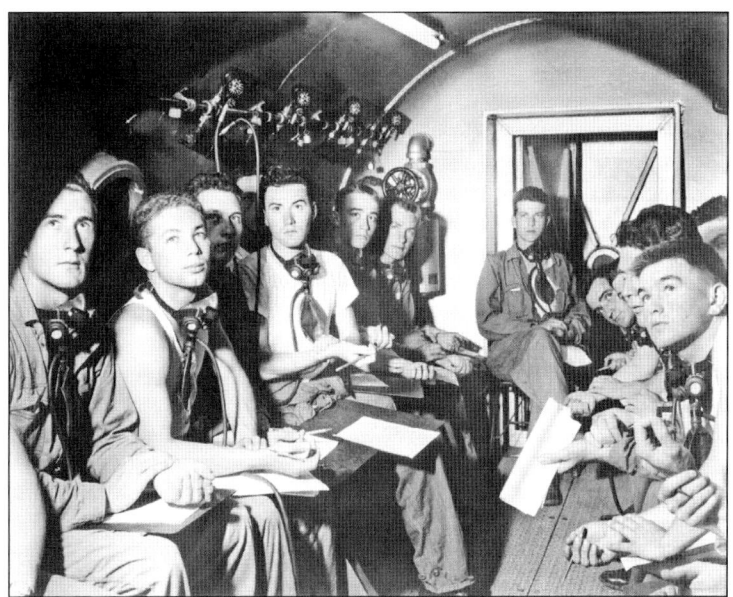

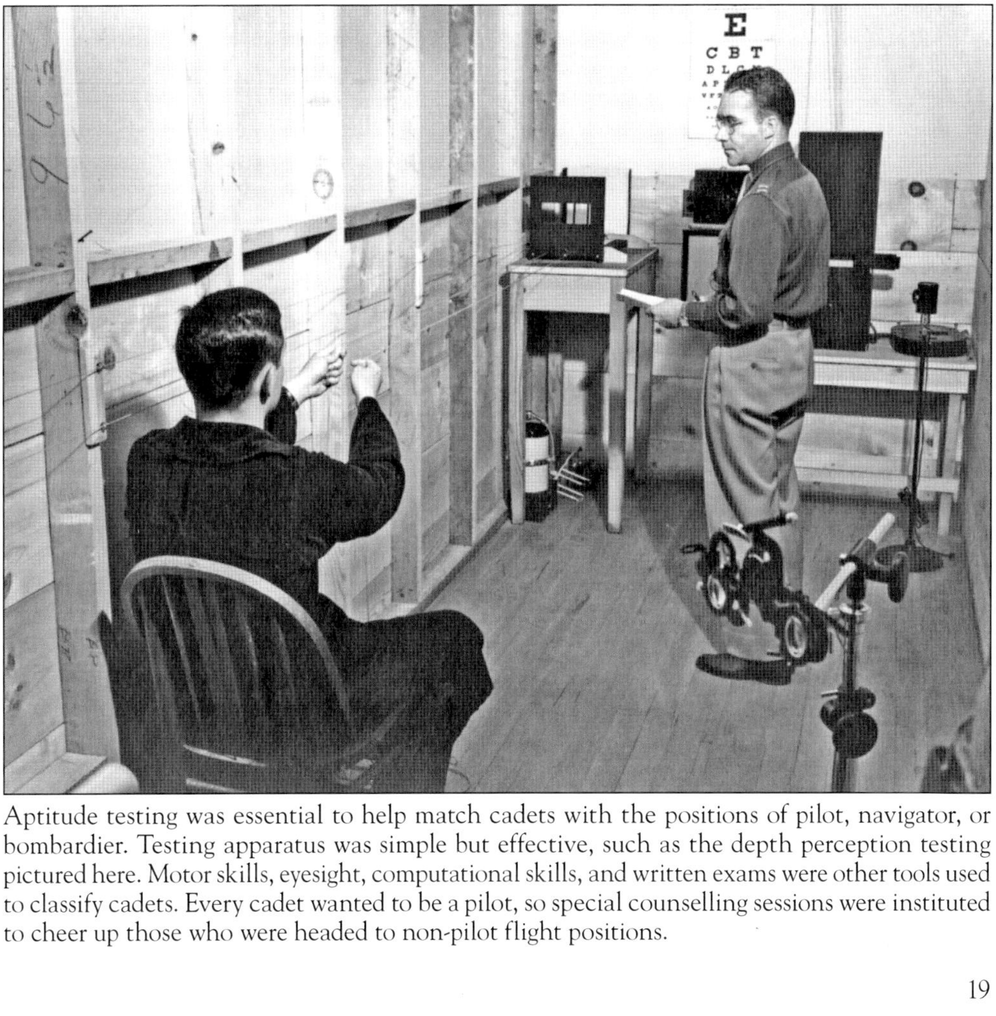

Aptitude testing was essential to help match cadets with the positions of pilot, navigator, or bombardier. Testing apparatus was simple but effective, such as the depth perception testing pictured here. Motor skills, eyesight, computational skills, and written exams were other tools used to classify cadets. Every cadet wanted to be a pilot, so special counselling sessions were instituted to cheer up those who were headed to non-pilot flight positions.

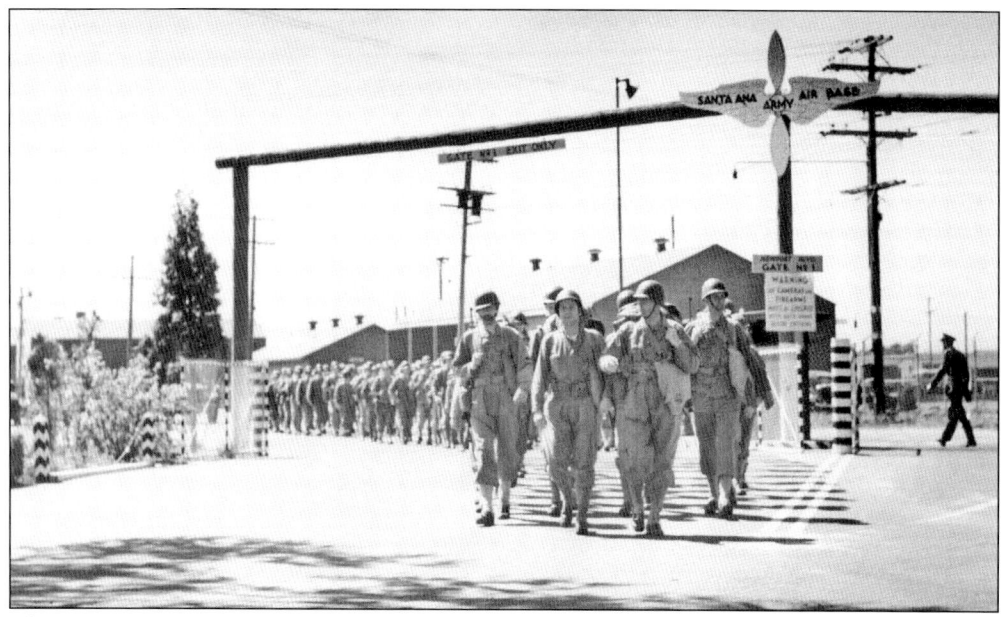

The 1941 movie *You're in the Army Now* likely was on the minds of these cadets on April 23, 1944, as they marched out Gate No. 1 to a bivouac area five miles distant. The Santa Ana Army Air Base had several entrances, notably Gate No. 1, shown here, on Newport Boulevard facing the Santa Ana Country Club, and Gate No. 6 on Baker Street near today's Mendoza Drive.

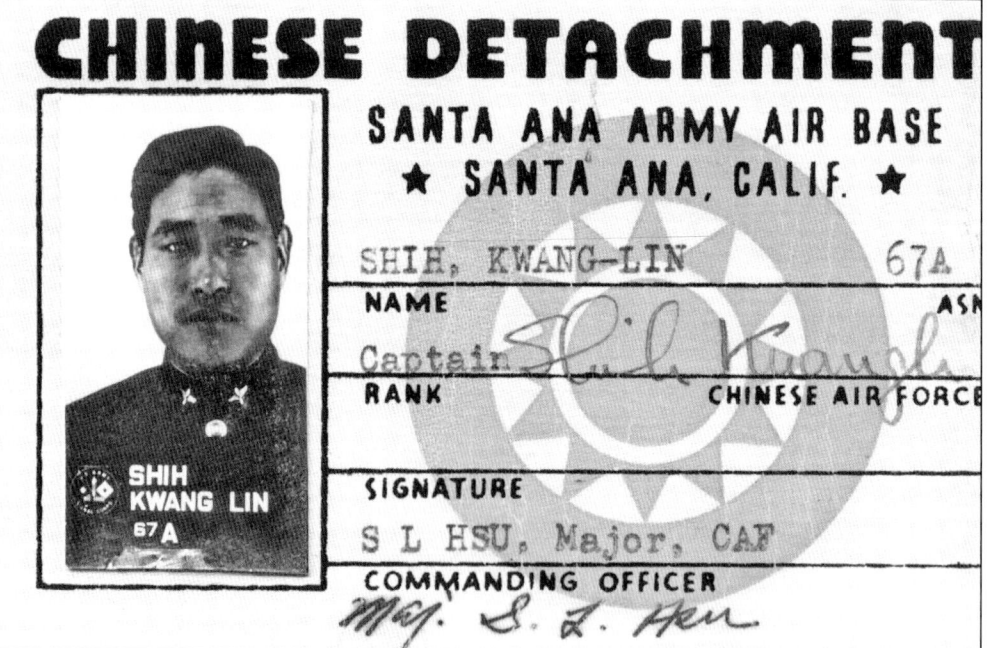

In September 1943, the first detachment of trainees from the Chinese Air Force was organized at the Santa Ana Army Air Base. Under a Lend-Lease arrangement with the Republic of China, the US Army Air Corps provided English language instruction, general military indoctrination, and preflight aircrew training. The Chinese detachment reached a total strength of 520 men by the summer of 1944.

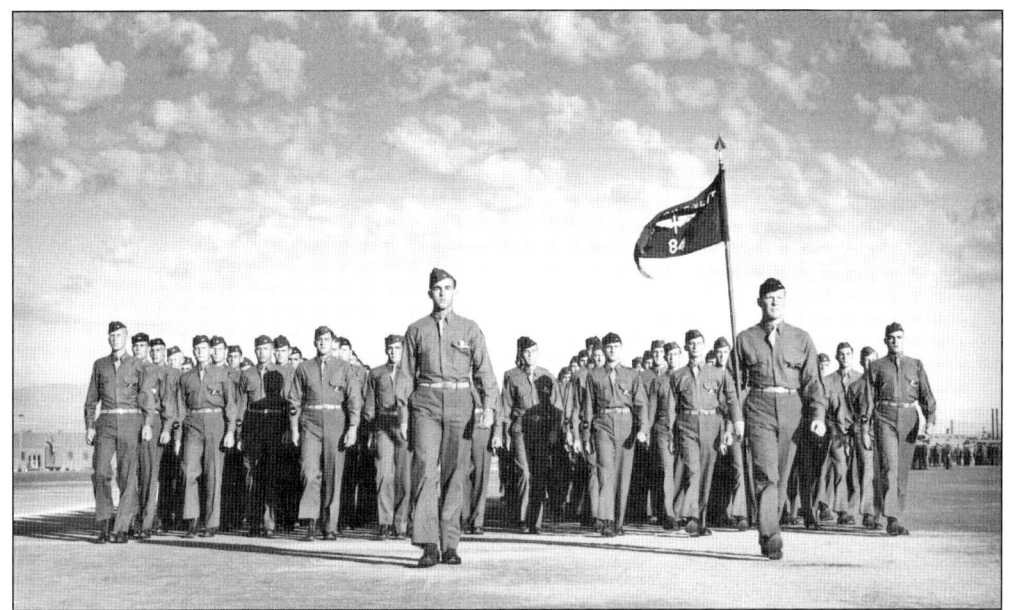

According to *The SAAAB Story* by Edrick Miller, "Without fail, Sunday reviews were held weekly on the huge blacktopped parade ground. It was quite a spectacle to behold. Here, squadron after squadron dressed in class 'A' uniforms passed in review to the music of the base band." In this photograph, Cadet Squadron 84 marches in a 1943 Sunday parade.

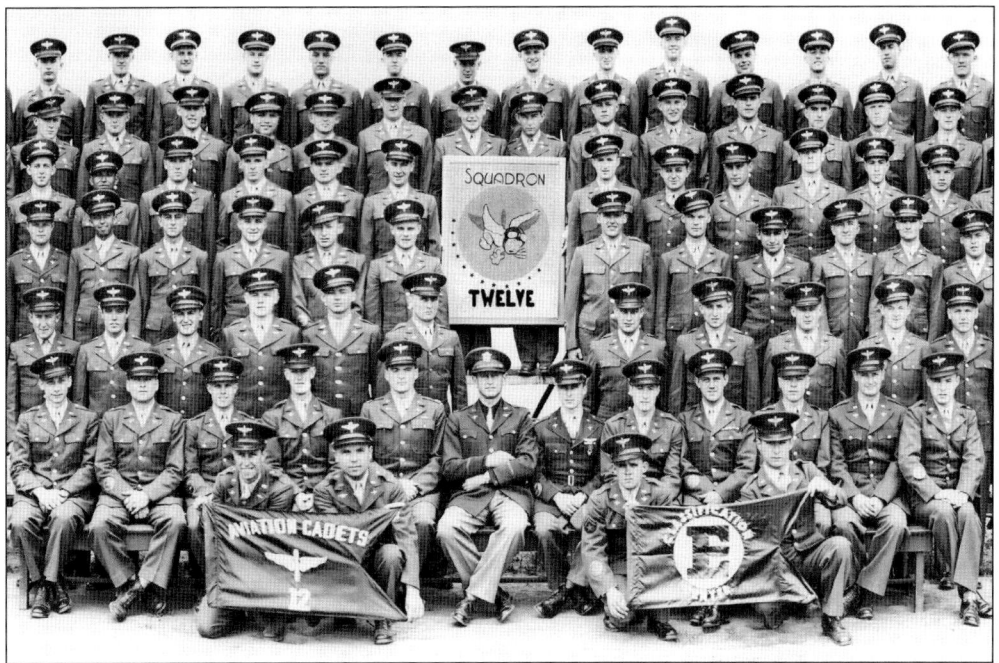

The need for wartime personnel was immediate, so training was intense. The average class duration was 10 weeks. Shown here is the center portion of the class photograph of the 183 aviation cadets of Honor Squadron 12. The Santa Ana Army Air Base graduated more than 125,000 cadets during the period from February 15, 1942, to November 1, 1944. More than 250 SAAAB class photographs are archived at the Costa Mesa Historical Society.

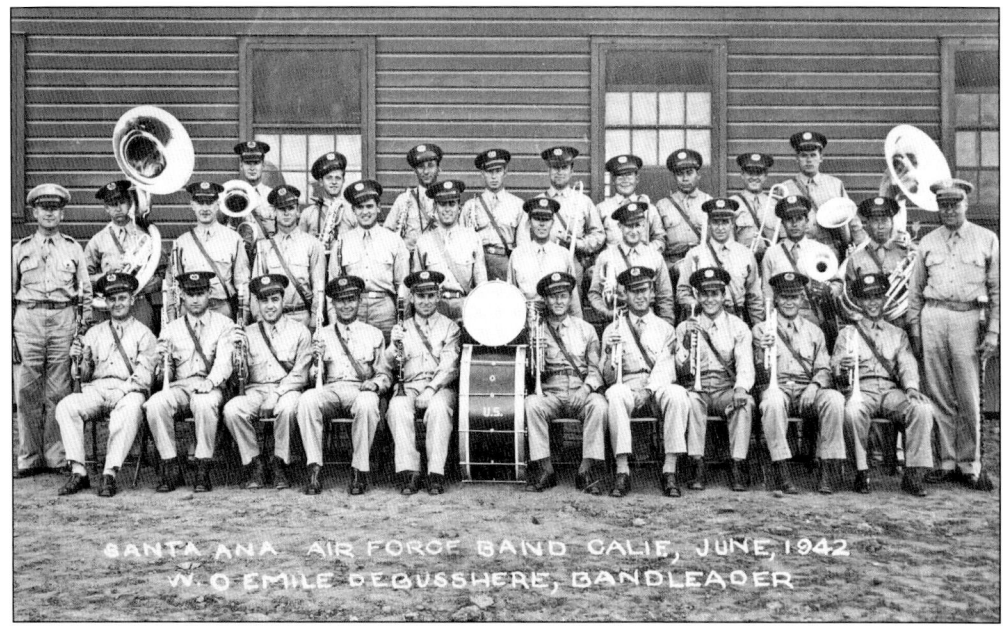

There was no shortage of musical talent at the Santa Ana Army Air Base. The band pictured here played at Sunday parades under the direction of WO Emile DeBusschere. Another band, under the direction of M.Sgt. Felix Slatkin, played on national broadcasts intended to recruit young people to join the Army Air Corps. Alex Hyde wrote sheet music such as the "Hubba Hubba March" while stationed at SAAAB.

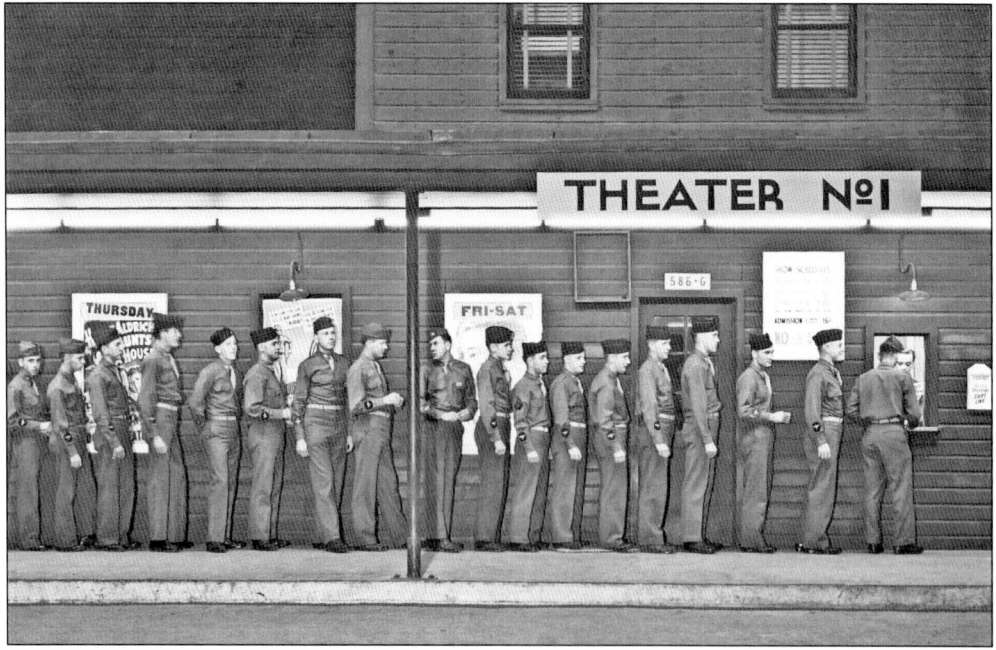

Given the intense training schedule and paucity of leave time, cadets took advantage of on-base entertainment. There were four theaters on the base, including Theater No. 1, pictured here around December 1943. Cadets lined up to pay a 15¢ admission fee to see the Thursday show *Henry Aldrich Haunts a House* or the Friday-Saturday show *Old Acquaintance*, starring Bette Davis.

Even in wartime, Christmas offered a break, albeit short, from the daily grind. Here, service members enjoy socializing at the Servicemen's Club in front of a large Christmas tree, and behind that, one of the two *Gremlins* murals. The murals were created in early 1943 by Hollywood art director John E. "Jack" Otterson while he was stationed at the Santa Ana Army Air Base. Each 9-by-16-foot mural depicted gremlins, those little spirits that were blamed for any foul-up, inserting themselves into all aspects of Army Air Force operations. In 1979, author Edrick Miller, with the help of Congressman Robert Badham, located the murals at the Air Force Museum at Wright-Patterson Air Force Base. The murals were returned to the Costa Mesa Historical Society and subsequently placed on long-term loan to Orange Coast College (OCC). The murals are on display in OCC's Arts Center.

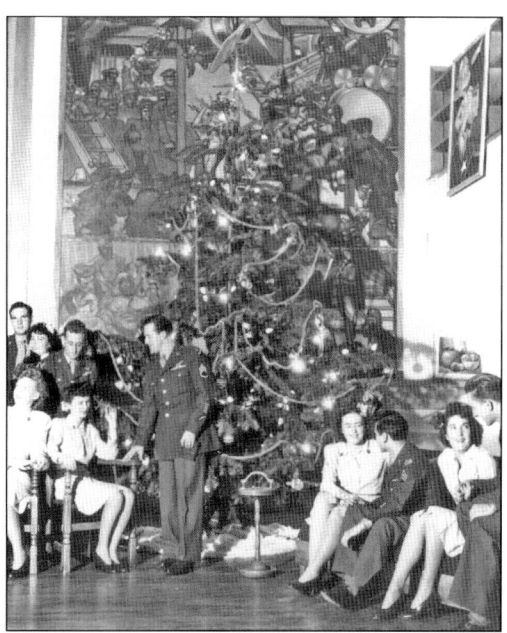

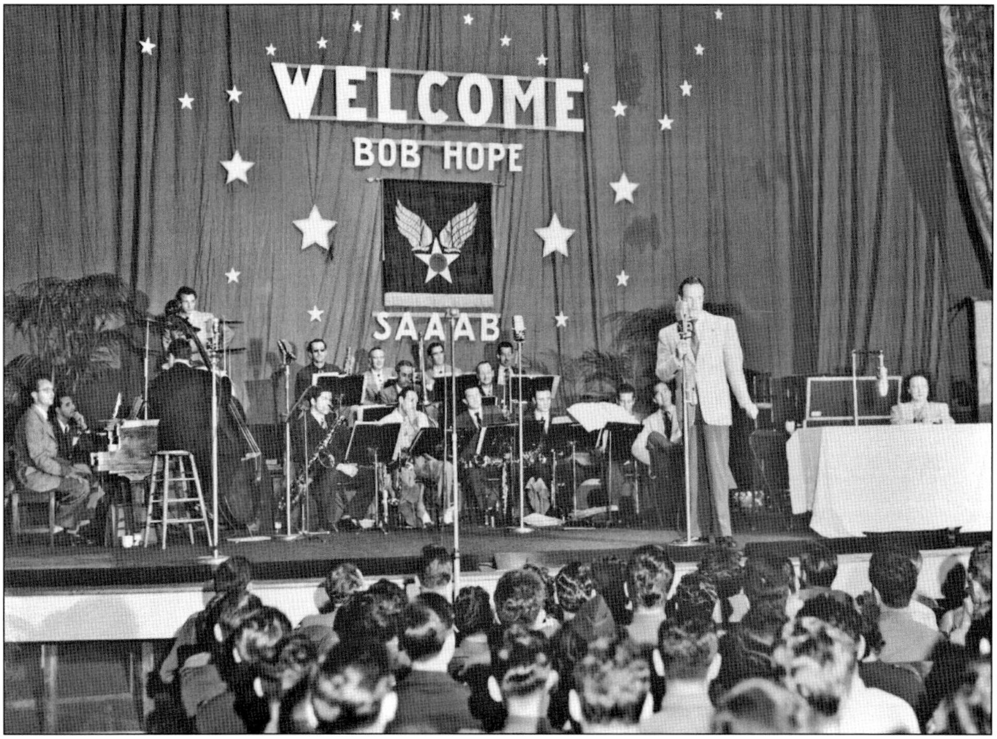

Hollywood celebrities certainly did their part to boost the morale of the troops. Here, Bob Hope (on stage, second from right) appears with Barbara Jo Allen (stage name Vera Vague, at right) at the Santa Ana Army Air Base Servicemen's Club in the spring of 1945. Other celebrities who visited the base included Bing Crosby, Jack Benny, Mary Livingstone, Eddie Anderson (Rochester), Burgess Meredith, Jeanette MacDonald, Jerry Colonna, Edgar Bergen and Charlie McCarthy, Duke Ellington, Spike Jones, Frances Langford, Adolphe Menjou, and June Allyson.

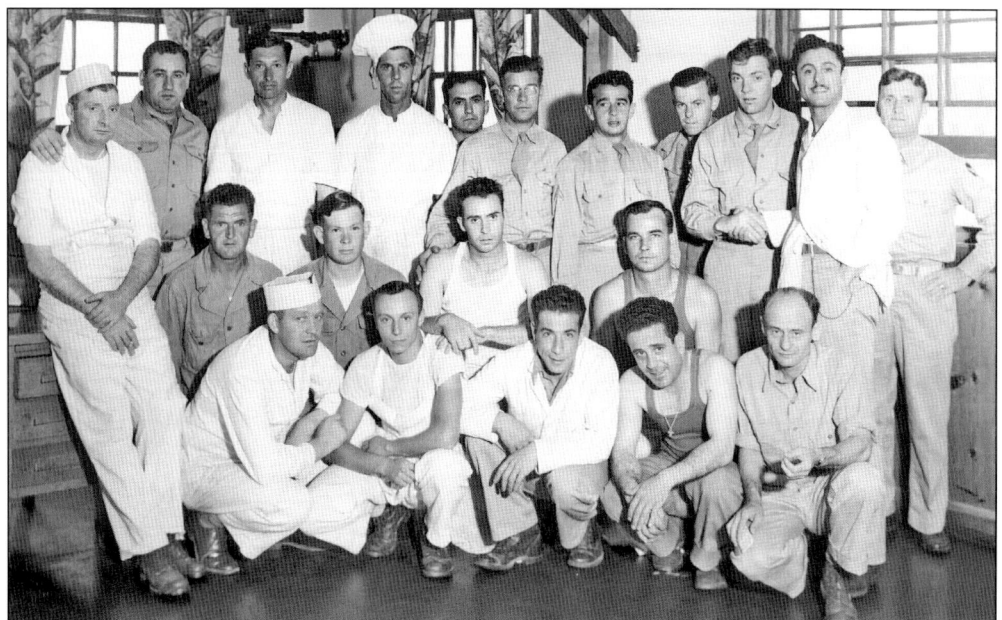

By May 1945, more than 10,000 German prisoners of war were working in Orange County farm fields. In November, more than 500 of those prisoners were relocated to a stockade on the Santa Ana Army Air Base to work as cooks, bakers, mechanics, janitors, and general duty helpers, thus relieving Army enlisted men of all duties not connected to redistribution and separation from service. Pictured here are POWs assigned to kitchen duty, together with US Army supervisory staff.

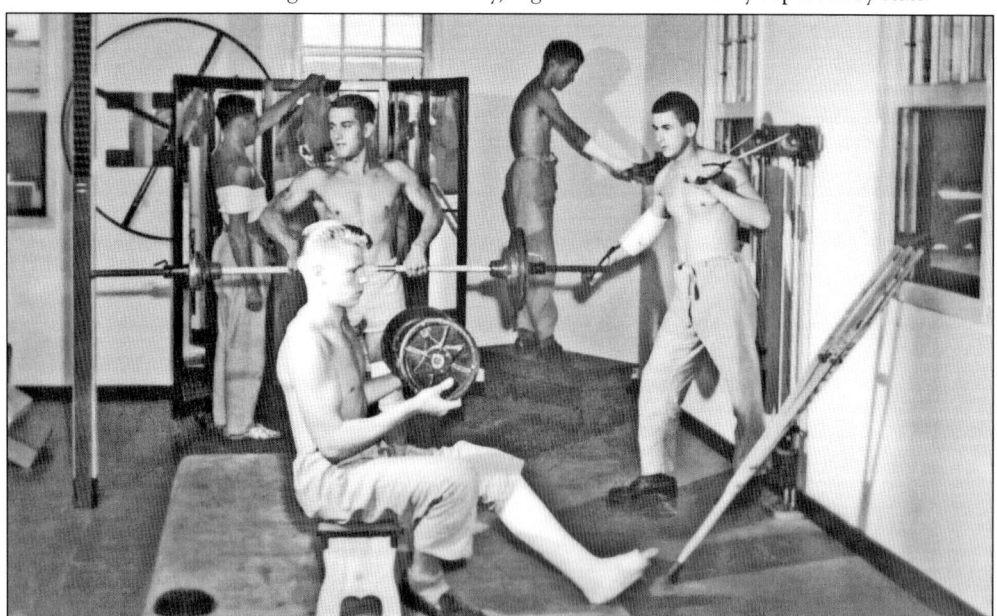

After nearly three years of preparing cadets for combat duty, the Santa Ana Army Air Base was re-tasked as an Army Air Force (AAF) convalescent hospital whose role was the physical and emotional rehabilitation of personnel. In this 1945 photograph, servicemen work out with weights and exercise equipment. Also in 1945, SAAAB served as an AAF redistribution center. Returning personnel were evaluated and either assigned to other AAF bases or separated from service.

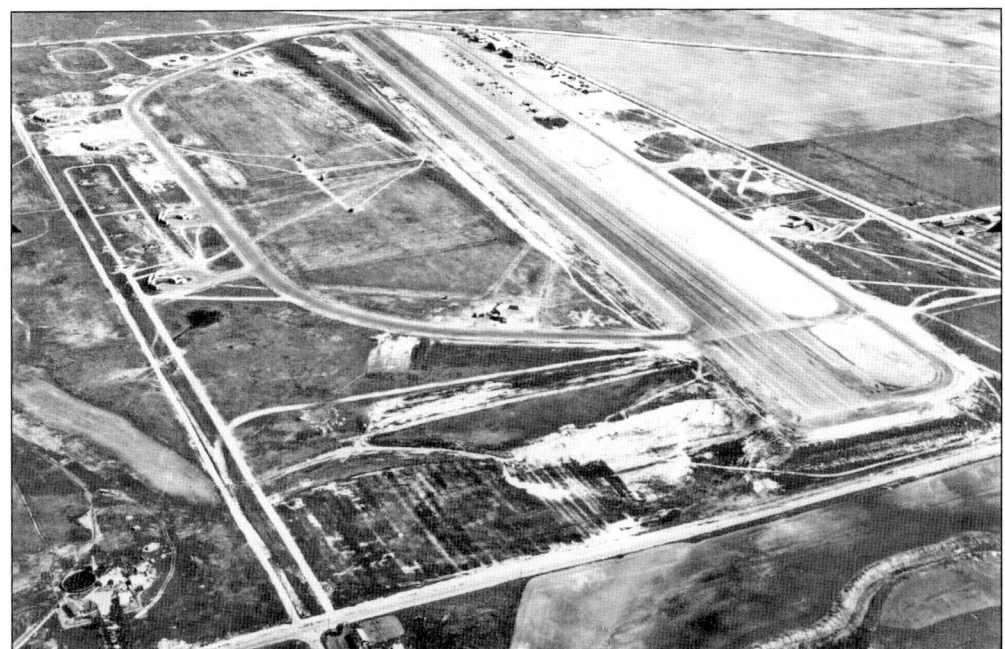

Soon after the attack on Pearl Harbor, the Fourth Air Force decided it needed to use the Orange County Airport, pictured here in 1942, as a dispersal field. By early 1943, a squadron of 16 P-38 fighter aircraft were established here. Orange County resumed civilian operation of the airfield in May 1946. Orange County Airport was renamed John Wayne Airport in 1979.

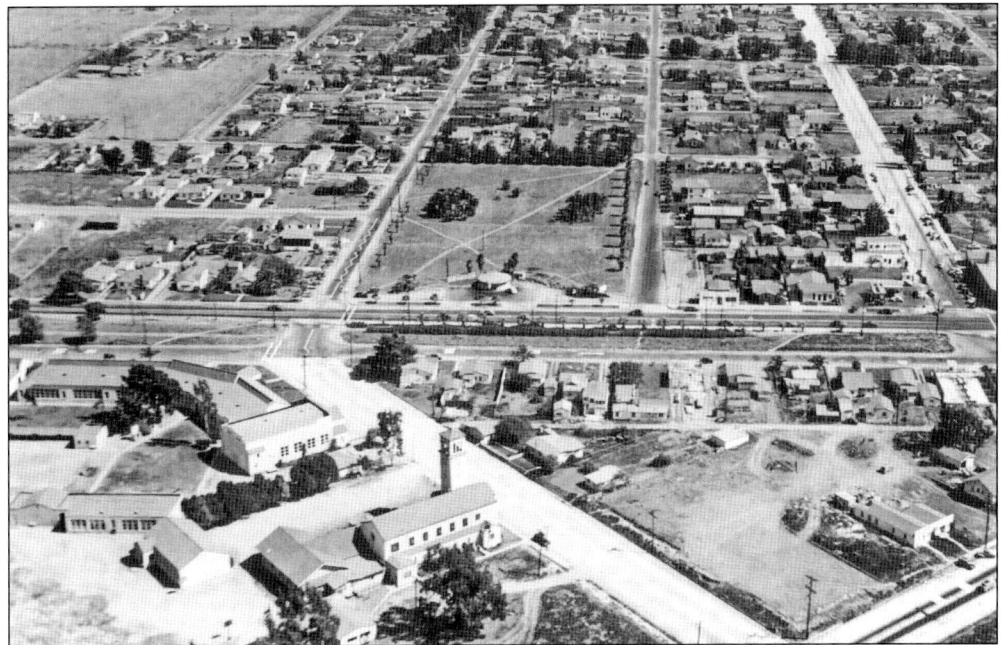

The war's end marked the beginning of a new era for Costa Mesa. This 1947 aerial photograph shows Newport Boulevard running horizontally at center, the Community Church and Main School on West Nineteenth Street at lower left, and the circular Palm-Palm restaurant in an open field near the center, across Newport Boulevard from the future site of Triangle Square.

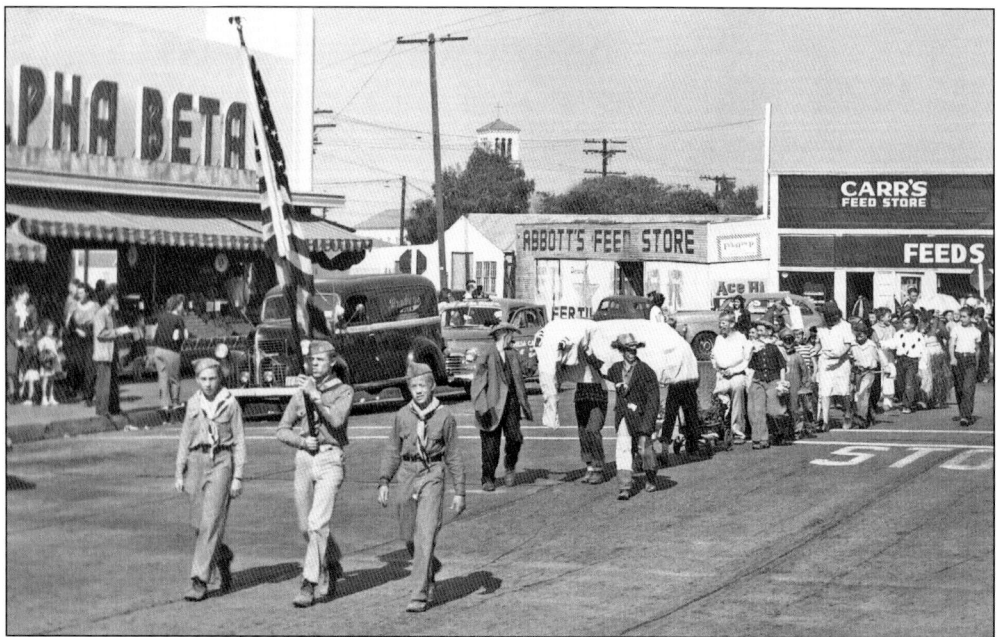

Life in Costa Mesa was getting back to normal after World War II. In 1945, a Boy Scout Circus Parade made its way along Newport Boulevard at the intersection with Harbor Boulevard. Alpha Beta was a popular grocery market, while Carr's and Abbott's Feed Stores continued to serve local small-scale farms.

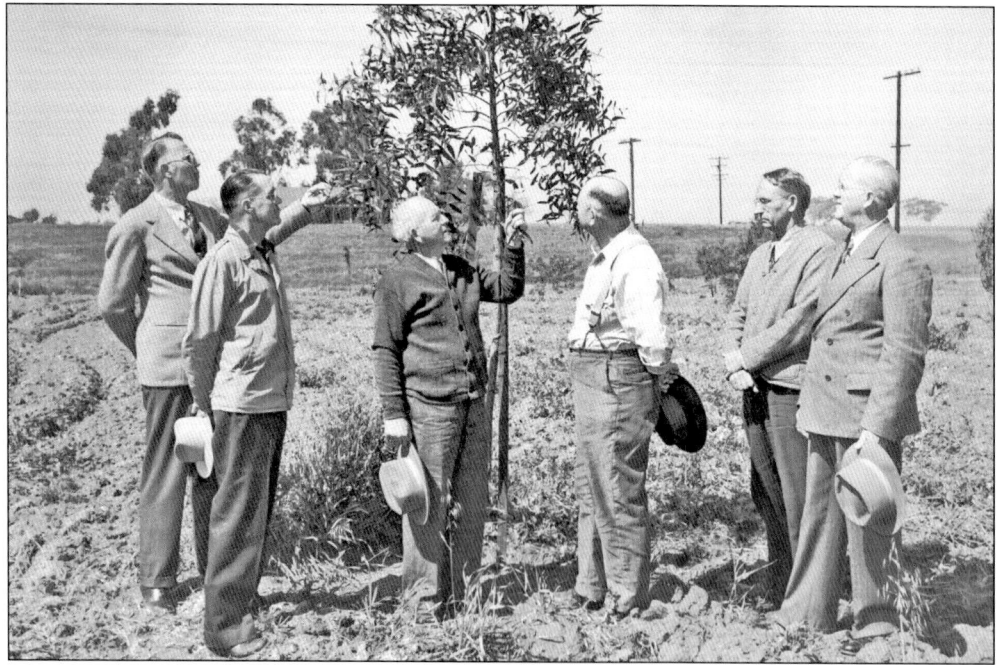

Costa Mesa Park, later named Lions Park, opened in 1943 and was the town's only public park before city incorporation. Once the town had a park, the chamber of commerce set out to improve it. Among those pictured here in 1945 planting a tree in the park are local businessman Charles TeWinkle (second from left) and municipal judge Donald Dodge (fifth from left).

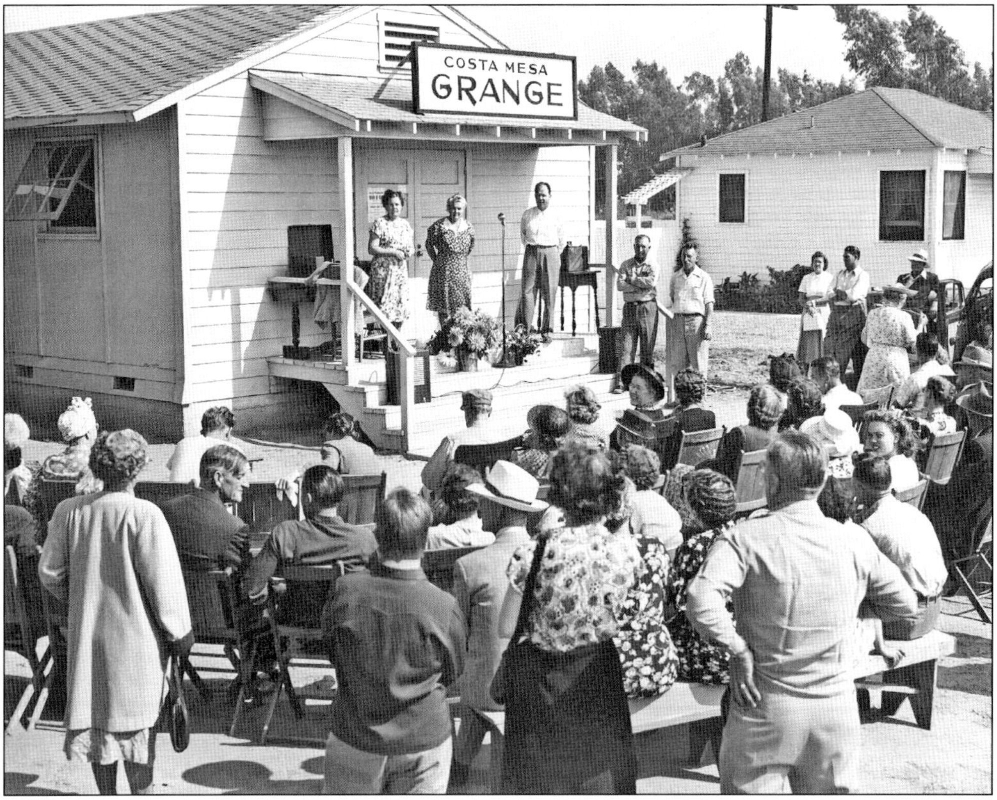

On March 31, 1946, the Santa Ana Army Air Base was deactivated, and soon thereafter, title to the property passed to the War Assets Administration for disposition. There was no shortage of schemes for the base site: World's Fair, Olympic Games, fairgrounds, GI university, housing project, and civic center were just a few of the proposals. Some of the SAAAB buildings were purchased and moved, including the Costa Mesa Grange building, located at the corner of Victoria and Thurin Streets. Shown here during the dedication ceremony on August 29, 1948, Costa Mesa Grange No. 612 was the first Grange in Orange County to own its own hall.

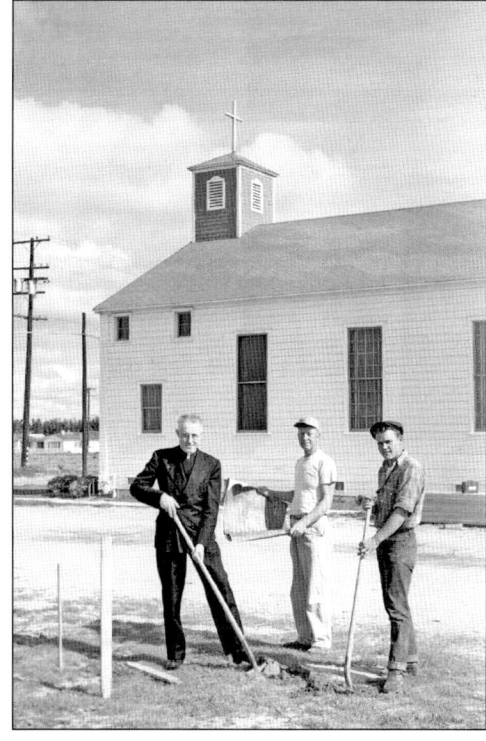

In 1947, one of the four base chapels was moved to 1964 Orange Avenue to become St. Joachim Catholic Church. In addition, a barracks building was moved to the site to provide school rooms and a social hall. Shown here in 1949 are Rev. Thomas J. Nevin (left) and two workers breaking ground for the parish rectory, with the church in the background.

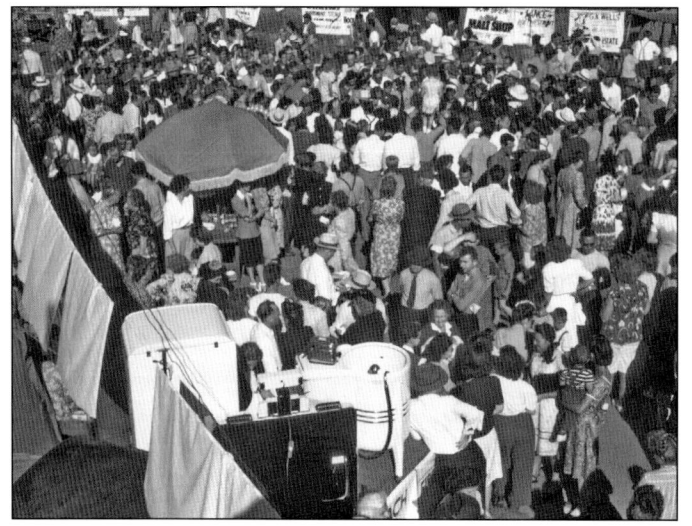

Costa Mesa's service clubs were active in promoting and improving the community. The Lions Club held its first annual carnival and fish fry in the summer of 1946. The event was attended by 5,000 people and raised $4,487. Evident in this photograph of that 1946 event are an enthusiastic crowd and a display of household appliances such as washing machines, refrigerators, and toasters that were unavailable during World War II.

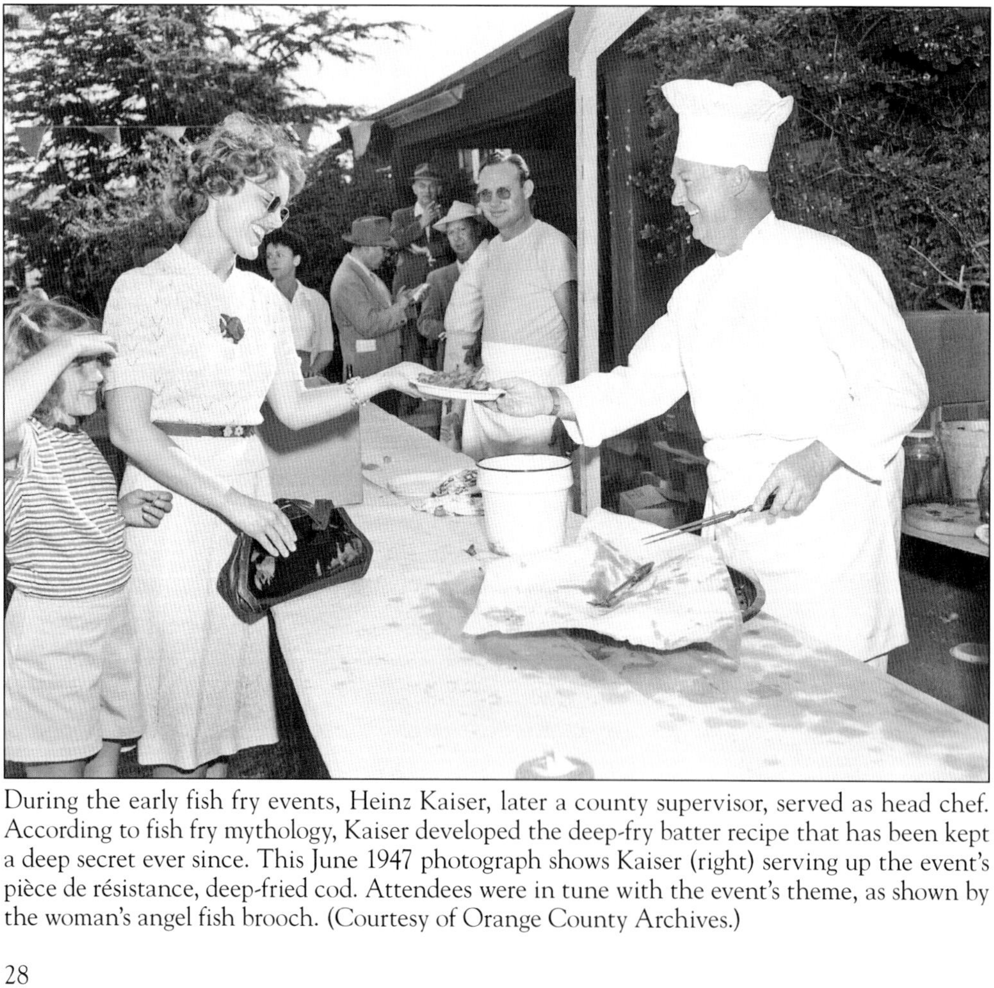

During the early fish fry events, Heinz Kaiser, later a county supervisor, served as head chef. According to fish fry mythology, Kaiser developed the deep-fry batter recipe that has been kept a deep secret ever since. This June 1947 photograph shows Kaiser (right) serving up the event's pièce de résistance, deep-fried cod. Attendees were in tune with the event's theme, as shown by the woman's angel fish brooch. (Courtesy of Orange County Archives.)

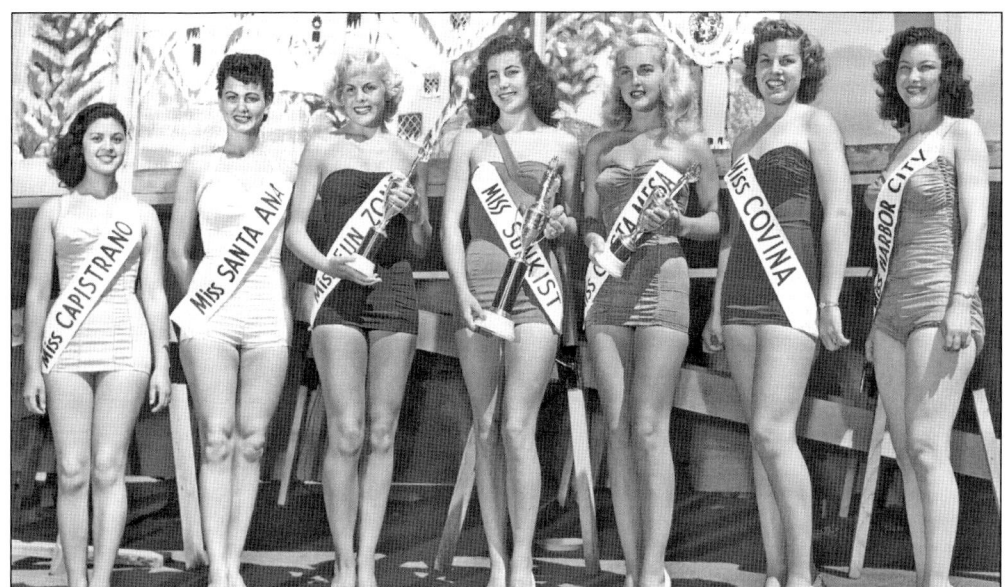

Over the years, contests have added spice to the annual fish fry event—for example, frog jumping, cutest baby, and beauty contests. The entrants in this 1947 beauty contest hailed from Costa Mesa and other Southern California cities, the Balboa Fun Zone, and Sunkist Citrus Cooperative. Miss Costa Mesa (third from right) reigned for one year.

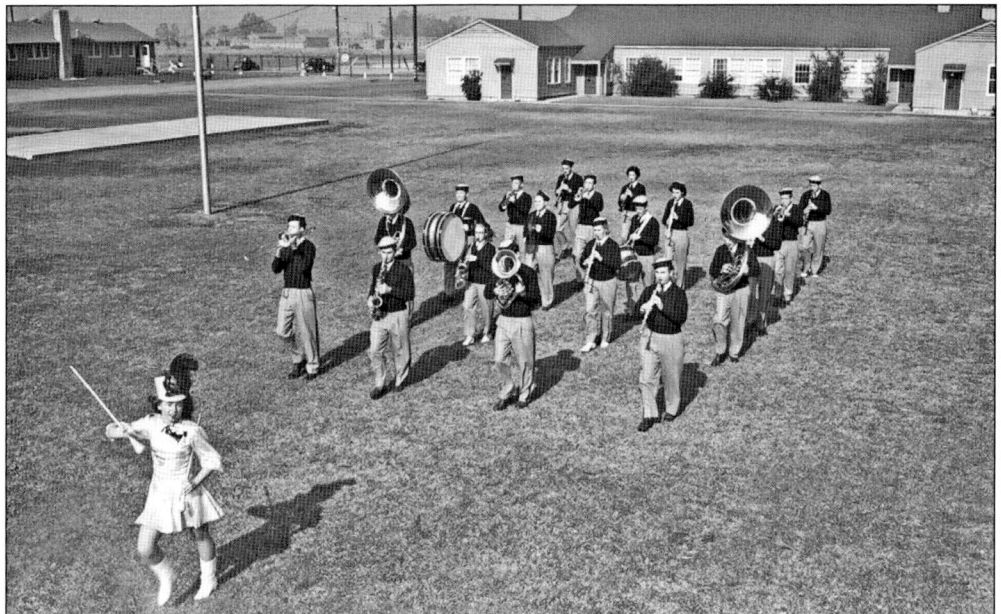

In August 1946, the War Department announced that the Santa Ana Army Air Base was for sale to any educational institution for $1. After hurried discussions and several trips to Washington, DC, 243 acres and 69 base buildings were transferred to the newly formed Orange Coast Junior College District. Orange Coast College opened on September 13, 1948, admitting about 500 students. Classes were held in former base buildings, such as those in the background of this photograph of the college's marching band taken on November 24, 1948. (Courtesy of Old Orange County Courthouse, Orange County Parks.)

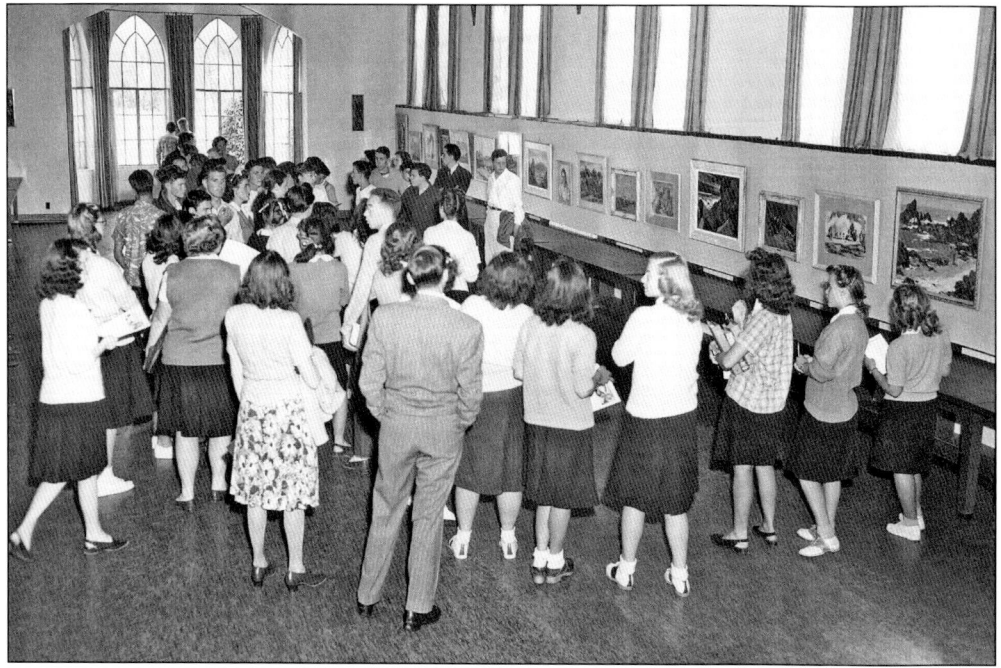

Throughout the war years, most of Costa Mesa's high school students attended Newport Harbor Union High School. By 1947, attention had turned from the war to more traditional interests. The 1947 yearbook, the *Galleon*, highlighted the second annual art exhibit sponsored by the Newport Harbor Ebell Club. Here, a group of students listens to school librarian Ruth Stover describe the paintings on display. (Courtesy of Orange County Archives.)

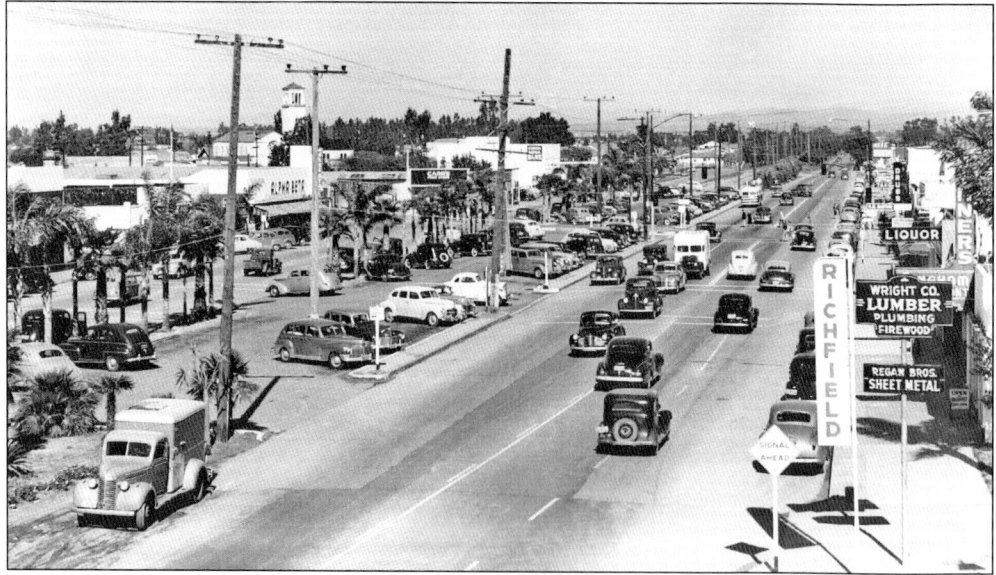

By the end of 1948, downtown Costa Mesa was bustling with postwar energy. An August 6, 1948, article in Costa Mesa's local newspaper, the *Globe-Herald*, summarized the moment eloquently: "Our Home Town has come a long way [since 1923]. From a scattered area of 400 homes to a closely knit community of more than 3,700 families. There's been a change in our thinking, too. Today we think of our Home Town with pride, as a mighty good place to live—and an entity in itself."

Two
INCORPORATION

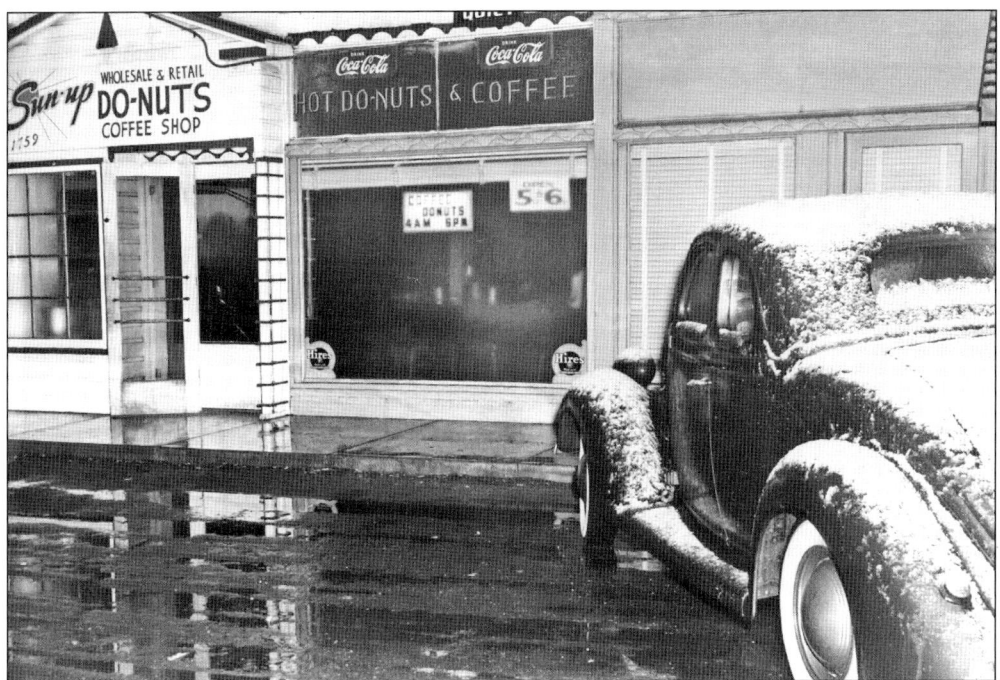

Mother Nature provided a rare event to usher in 1949: snowfall. In Costa Mesa's Mediterranean climate, snow is indeed rare. This photograph, reminiscent of the film noir era, was taken at Sun-Up Do-Nuts and Coffee Shop, 1759 Newport Boulevard, on January 11, 1949. The hot donuts and coffee were welcome, but sunshine would have to wait a day or two.

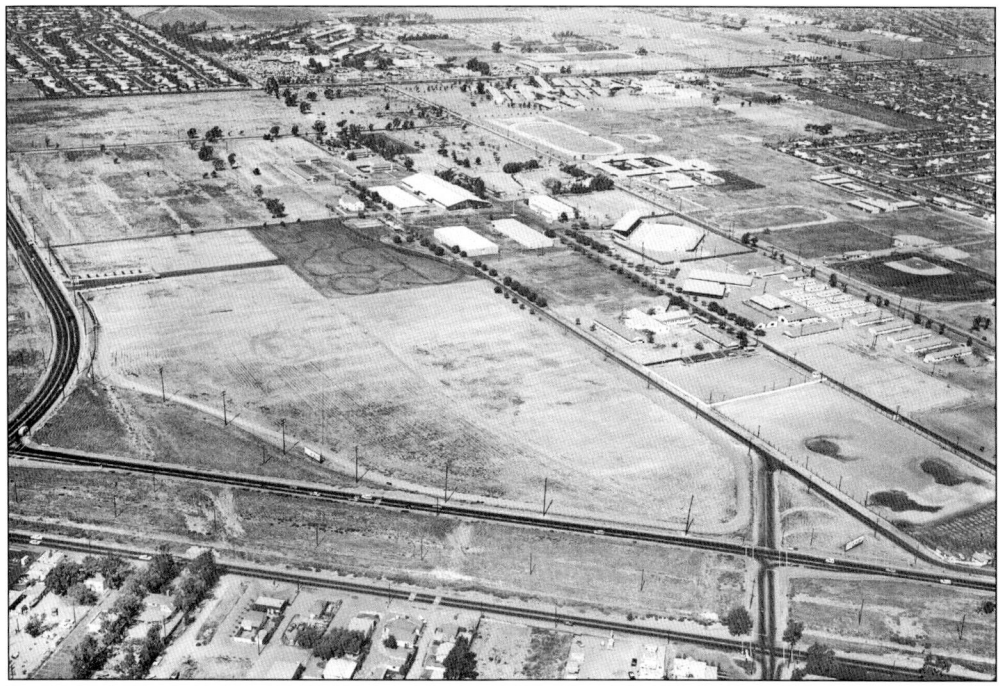

In 1890, the Orange County Fair Corp. put on its first fair. After changing locations and sponsors over 50 years, the State of California purchased 125 acres of Santa Ana Army Air Base land in 1949 to be used as a permanent home for the Orange County Fair, under control of the state's 32nd District Agricultural Association. In this 1966 photograph, Newport Boulevard runs diagonally across the bottom, while Fair Drive appears at far left.

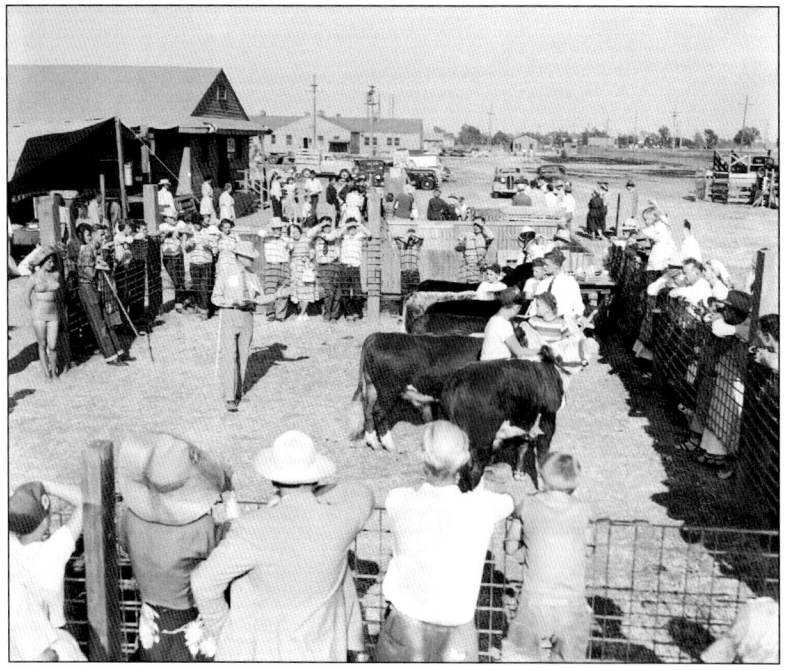

In 1949, 4-H Clubs were big in Orange County, with an emphasis on agricultural activities as well as personal growth and lifelong learning. In this August 1949 photograph, 4-H Club members show their livestock to fairgoers and to a judge standing behind them. (Courtesy of Orange County Archives.)

In 1949, the US patent on drive-in theaters was overturned, and drive-ins really caught on. The July 8, 1949, issue of the *Santa Ana Register* advertised the opening of the Paulo Drive-In Theater, promising Hollywood stars and fireworks. The opening films were *Streets of Laredo* and *City Across the River*. Pictured here in February 1976, the Paulo is being demolished to make way for residential development. The intersection of Newport Boulevard and Paularino Avenue appears at bottom.

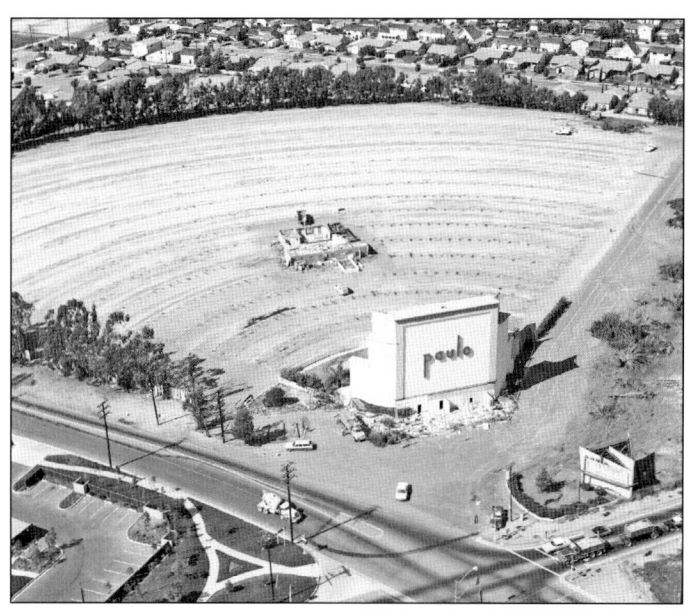

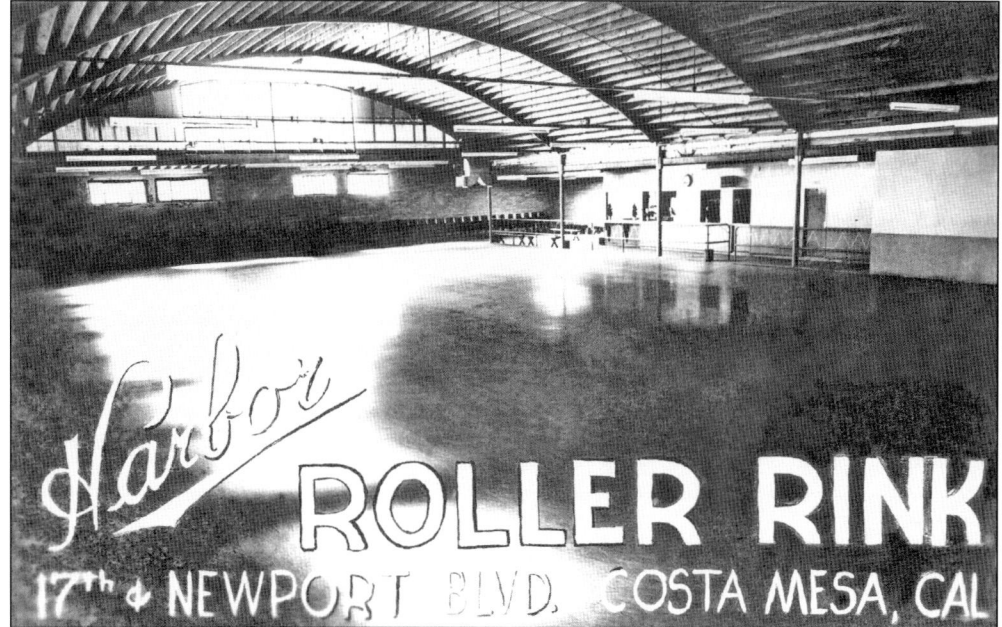

The Harbor Roller Rink opened on March 30, 1950. An advertisement for the rink's opening in the *Costa Mesa Globe-Herald* boasted modern amenities such as air-conditioning, a dust-free plastic floor, and music styled for skating pleasure. Longtime resident Doreen Healey remembered, "That's where the boys chased the girls—at the skating rink." By 1982, the building housed a Liquor Barn store, followed by a Tower Records store, before being demolished in 2013. (Courtesy of Orange County Archives.)

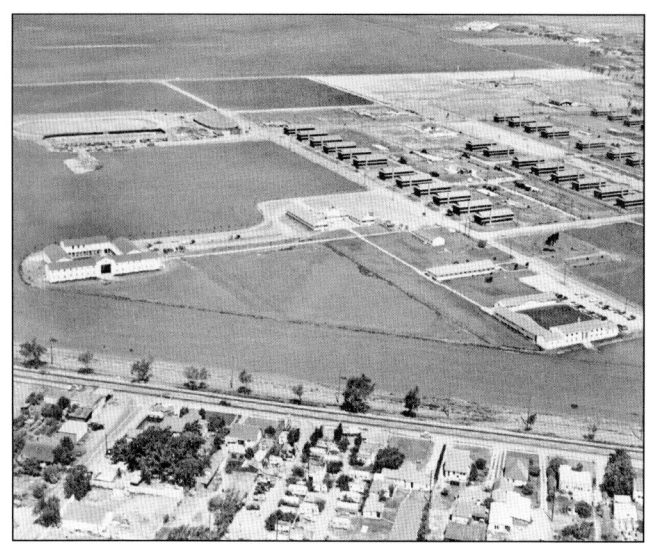
The Southern California Bible College acquired 129 acres of base land in September 1948 and admitted its first students two years later. In this c. 1950 photograph, Newport Boulevard runs across the bottom and intersects with Monte Vista Avenue at bottom left. The building at center left served as student dormitories, while the other buildings served as classrooms and offices. The college was renamed Vanguard University in 1999.

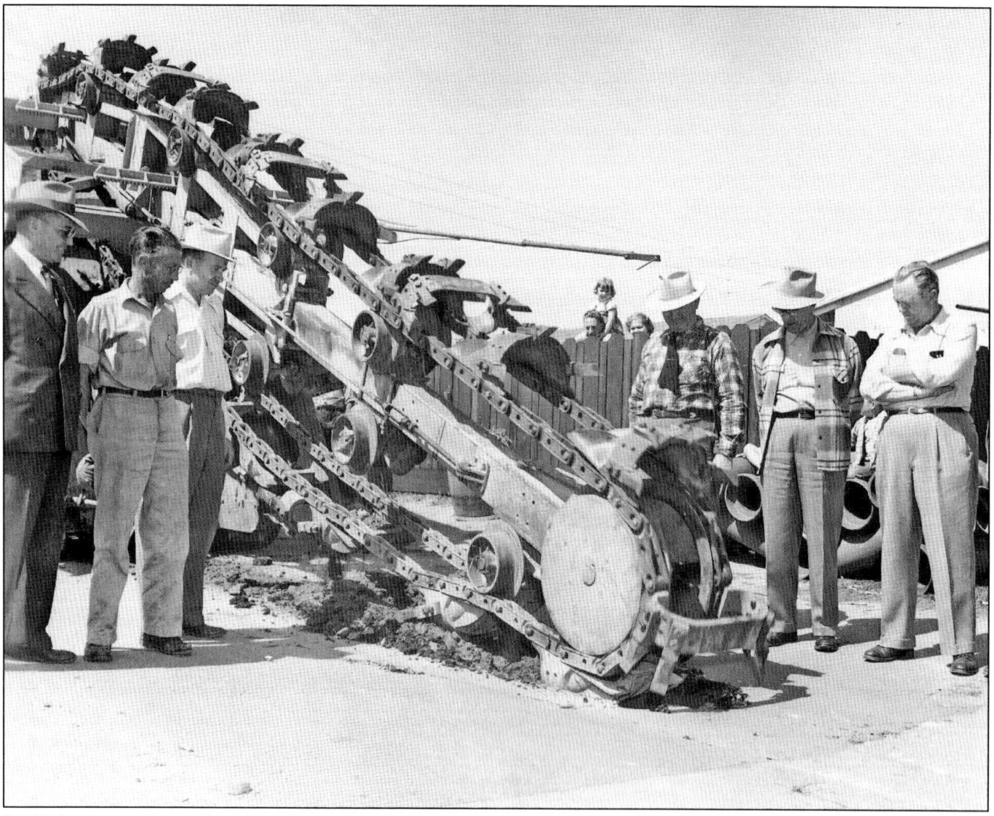

In February 1944, the Costa Mesa Sanitary District was formed, but only to collect trash. By 1951, population had grown to approximately 13,000, and the district added sanitary sewers to its services. Here, district officials observe the first ditch-digging operation on April 2, 1951. District officials are, from left to right, Pres. Charles TeWinkle, directors Paul Norman, Claire Nelson, Arthur Meyers, and William Lord, and county supervisor Heinz Kaiser.

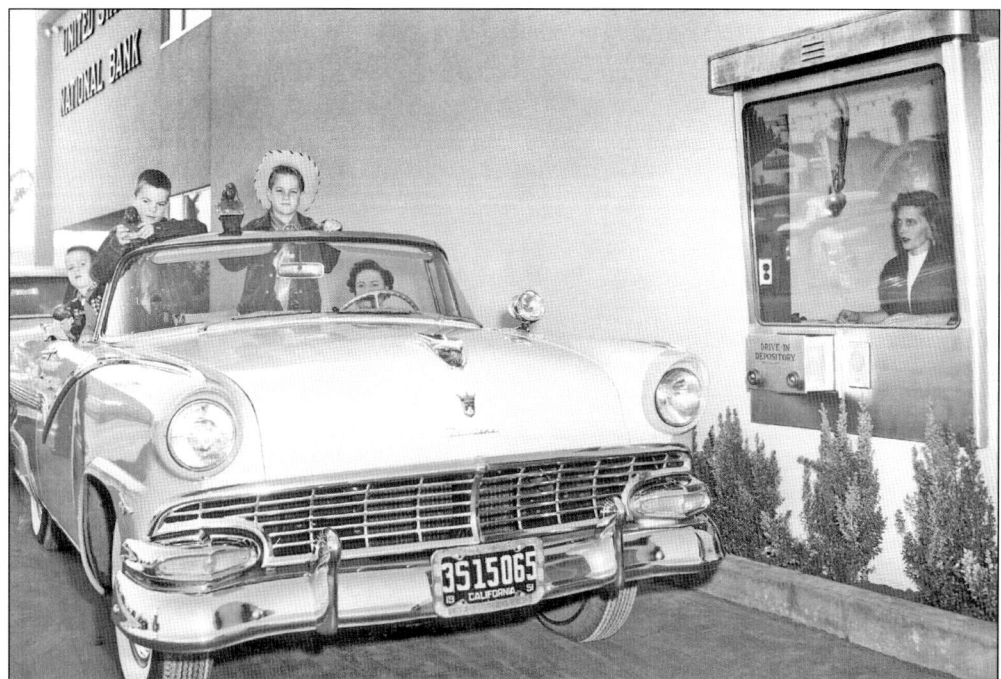

New businesses were opening in Costa Mesa to serve its growing population. The venerable Costa Mesa Bank at 1849 Newport Boulevard was superseded by the US National Bank at 1845 Newport Boulevard. The new bank featured the area's first drive-up teller window. In this January 1956 photograph, three boys show their Ben Franklin piggy banks while their mom does her banking. The Ford Fairlane carries license plate frames from local Ford dealer Theodore Robbins.

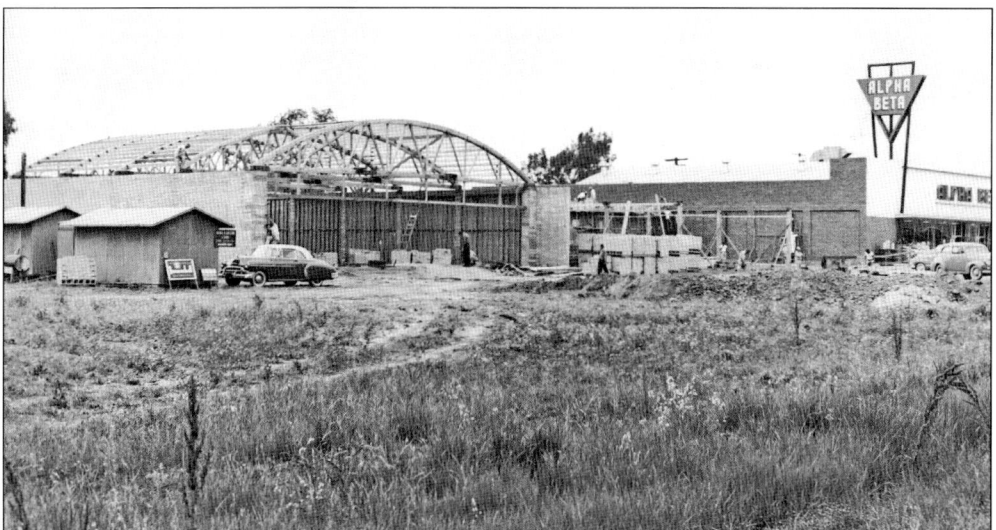

Costa Mesa's business districts were expanding beyond Newport and Harbor Boulevards. The January 25, 1953, edition of the *Los Angeles Times* carried an article about Jefferson Properties' plan to develop a large shopping center on East Seventeenth Street. The new center would extend from the existing Alpha Beta market at Orange Avenue towards Westminster Avenue. Taken on February 13, 1953, this photograph shows the ground-breaking for a Thrifty store on a section of East Seventeenth Street that was hyped as Costa Mesa's version of Los Angeles's Miracle Mile.

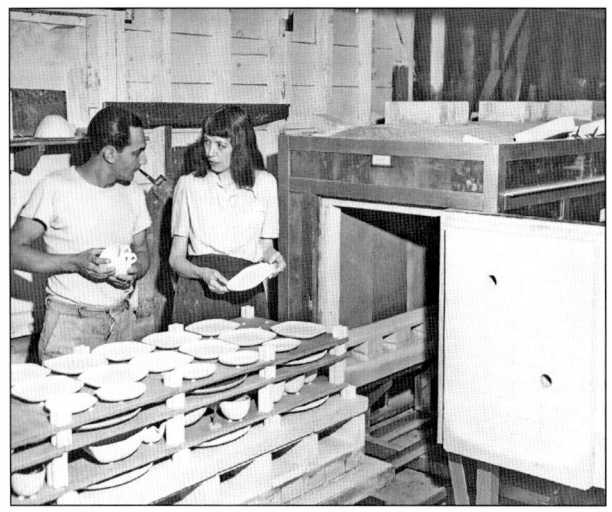

In addition to retail businesses, Costa Mesa also attracted small to medium-scale manufacturing, such as Denwar Ceramics, located at 236 East Sixteenth Street. Here, Gerald "Jo" Dendel (left) and Esther Warner Dendel are shown around 1952 inspecting a run of their Bantu line of dinnerware just before firing in the kiln. After low-cost dinnerware from Japan flooded the US market, the Dendels turned to decorative ceramic tiles, then ultimately to fiber arts, such as weaving, to maintain the viability of their craft-based family business.

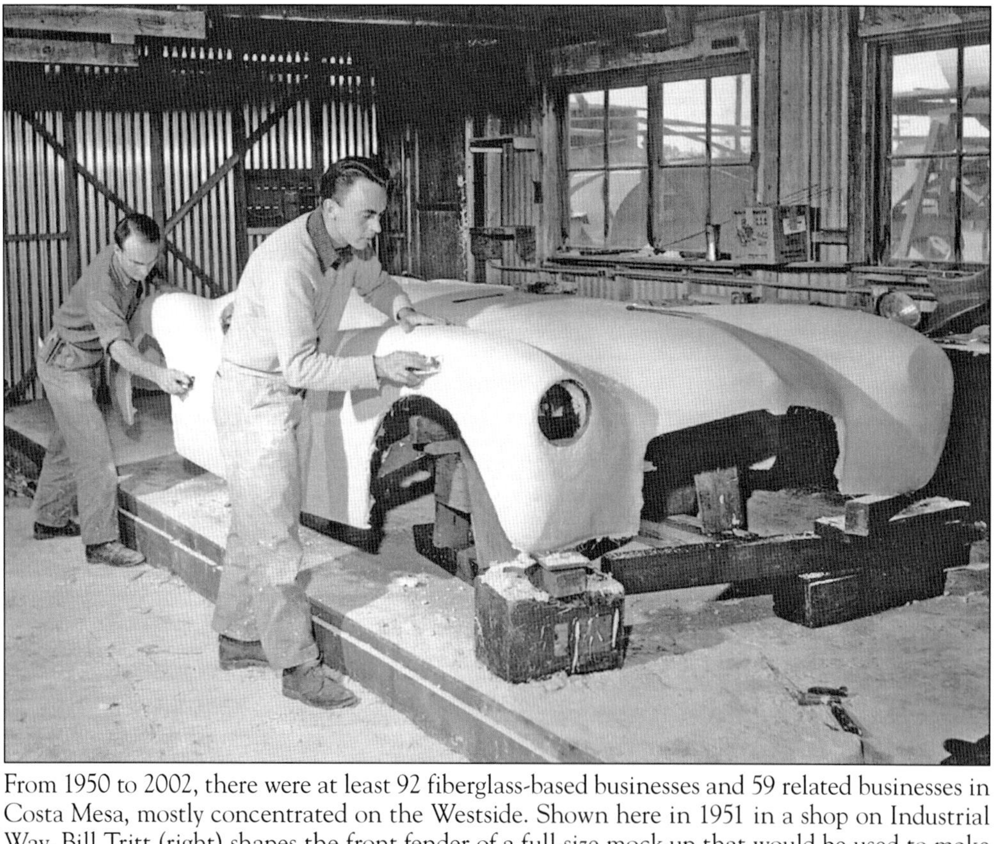

From 1950 to 2002, there were at least 92 fiberglass-based businesses and 59 related businesses in Costa Mesa, mostly concentrated on the Westside. Shown here in 1951 in a shop on Industrial Way, Bill Tritt (right) shapes the front fender of a full-size mock-up that would be used to make a mold for Glasspar's G-2 fiberglass sports car body. Soon, Glasspar would drop the auto business to concentrate on fiberglass boats. (Courtesy of Geoff Hacker, Forgotten Fiberglass.)

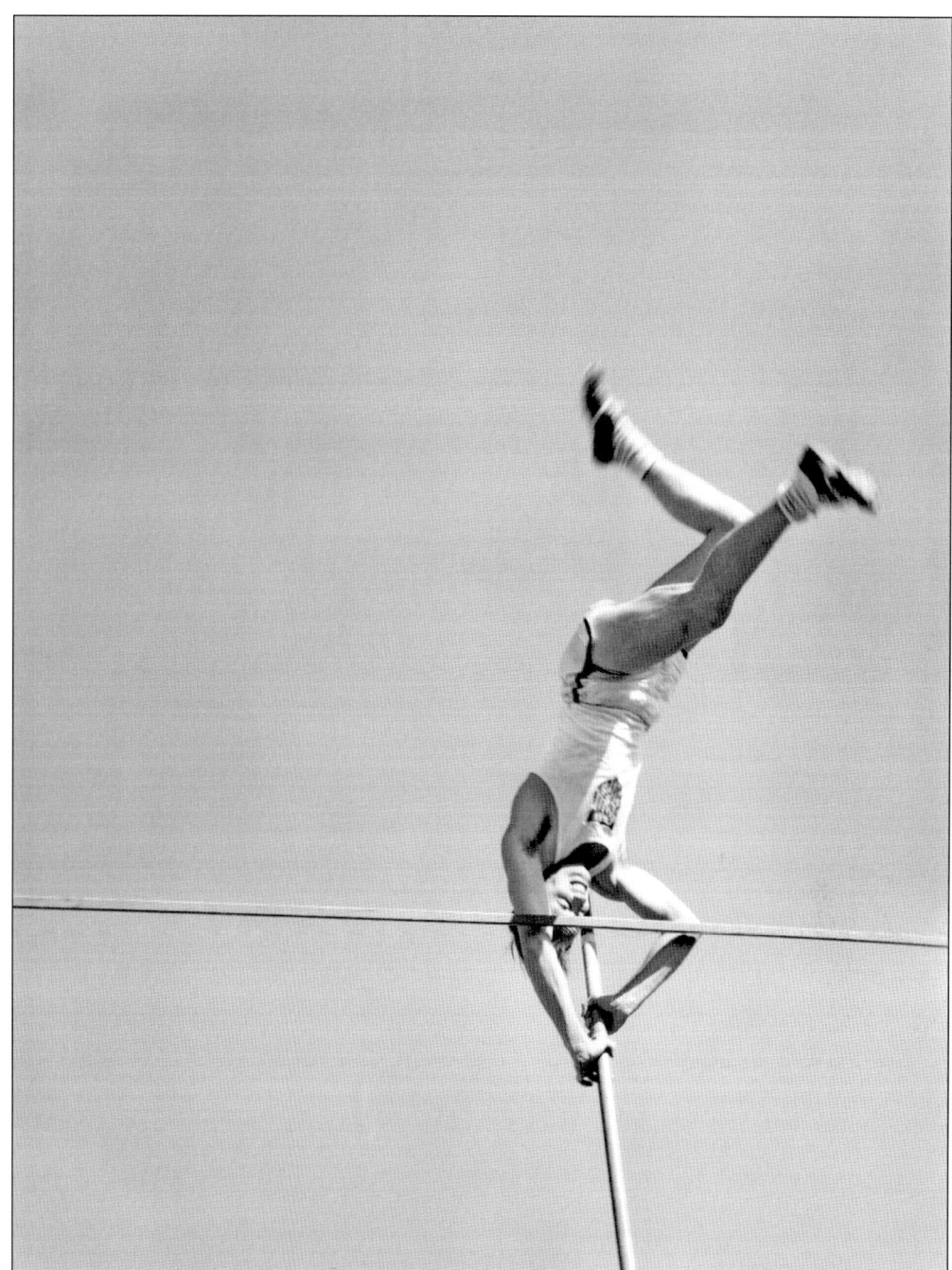

Fiberglass, a composite material consisting of glass fibers and polyester resin, was used successfully during World War II as an alternative to metals. After the war, fiberglass grew in popularity for aerospace, aviation, automotive, marine, electronics, medical, residential, leisure, and sports uses. Costa Mesa was home to many leading fiberglass-based companies, including Pacific Laminates at 1550 Superior Avenue. Shown here in 1951, Olympic decathlon gold medal winner Bob Mathias tests a Skypole fiberglass vaulting pole manufactured by Pacific Laminates. The fiberglass pole was a big improvement over conventional aluminum poles.

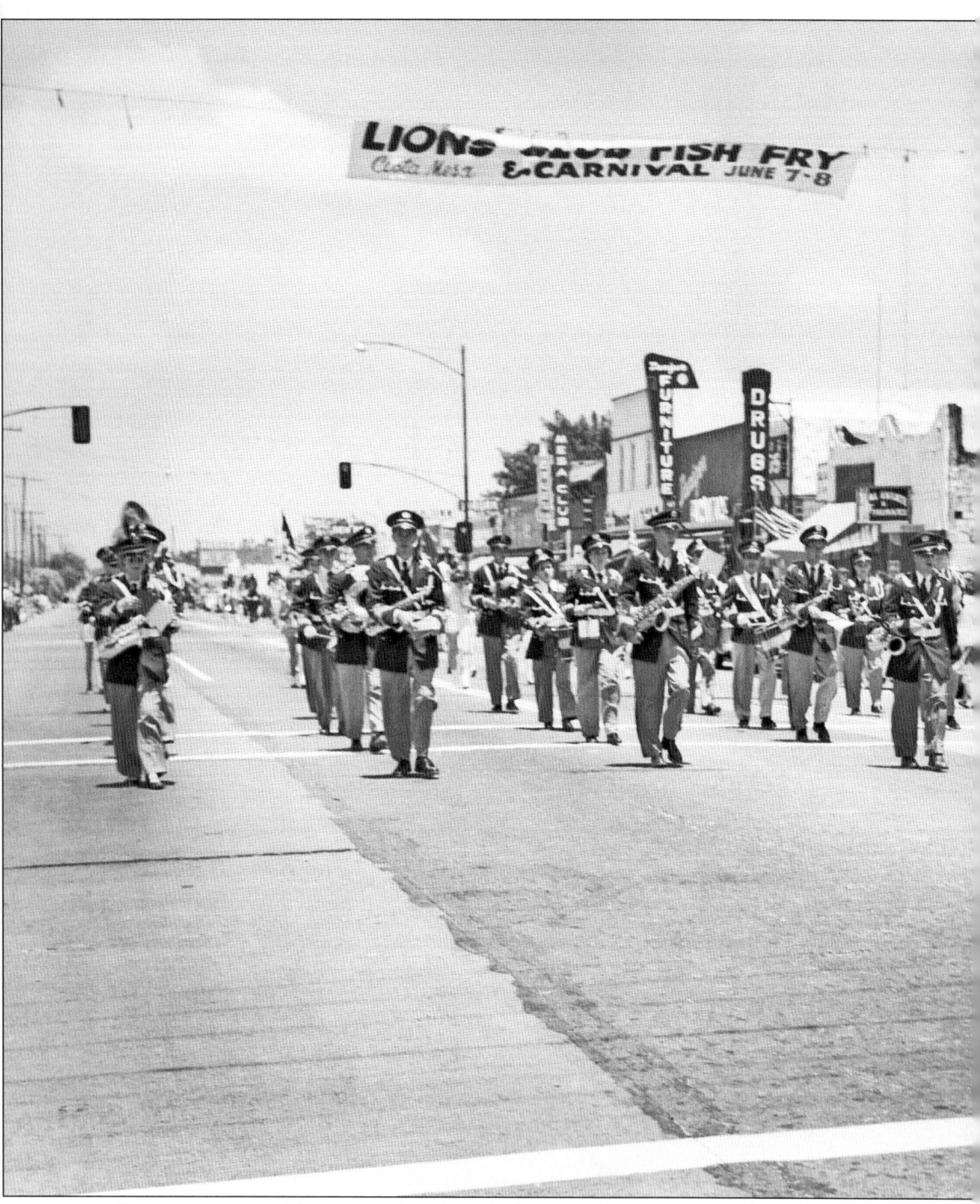

Strike up the band! Here comes Costa Mesa! The seventh annual Lions Club Fish Fry Parade and Carnival was held on June 7–8, 1952. Here, a spirited drum majorette exudes community pride as she leads her marching band down the middle of Newport Boulevard at Eighteenth Street. Visible in this iconic photograph are TeWinkle Hardware, Gerrish Insurance, Crawford's Drugs, Daniger Furniture, and Mesa Recreation Center. The parade ended at the carnival midway in

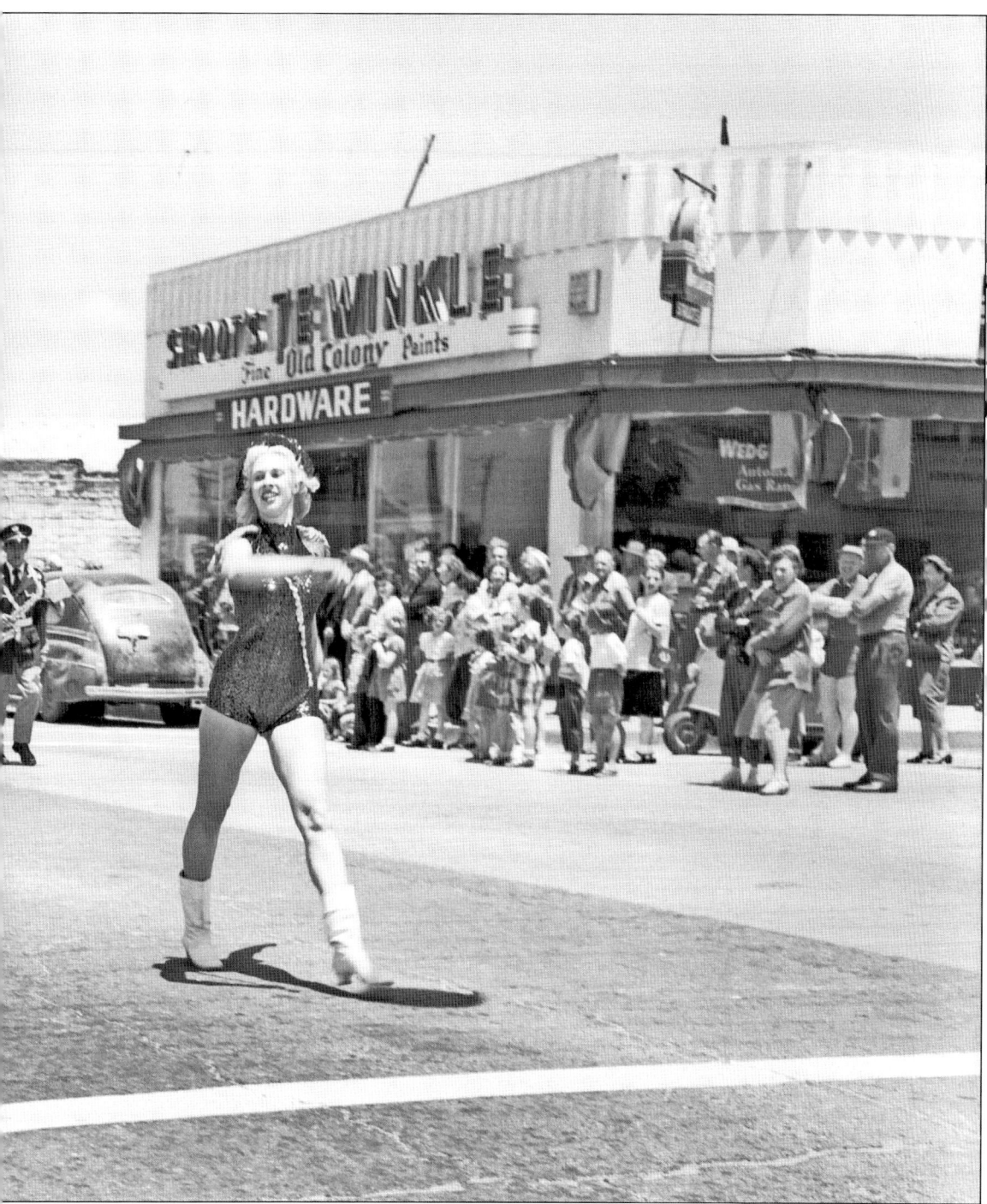

streets surrounding Costa Mesa Park (renamed Lions Park in 1978) where rides, games of chance, a beauty contest, raffle drawings, and of course, deep-fried fish dinners awaited the public. Not to be forgotten, though, was that time was running out for Costa Mesa either to incorporate or be annexed—to fish or cut bait.

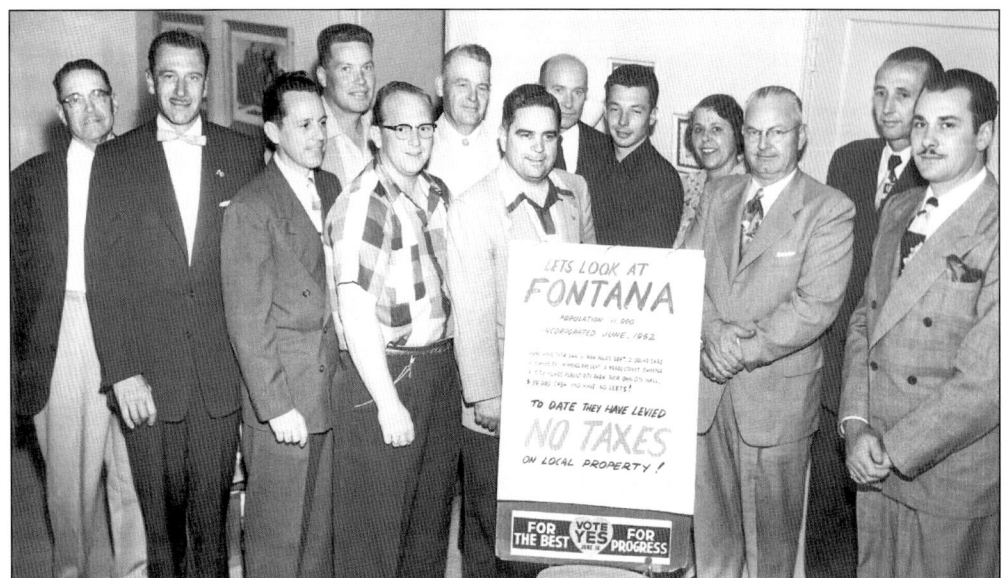

The clock was ticking for Costa Mesa. An earlier attempt to incorporate had failed in 1947. A Home Rule Group was formed in 1952 to try again. In this 1953 photograph, proponents of incorporation are using the recently incorporated city of Fontana as a success story to garner votes for Costa Mesa's incorporation. Future city leaders appearing here are Charles TeWinkle (far left), Walter Miller (fourth from left), Bruce Martin (seventh from left), Arthur Meyers (third from right), and Bertren "Bert" Smith (second from right).

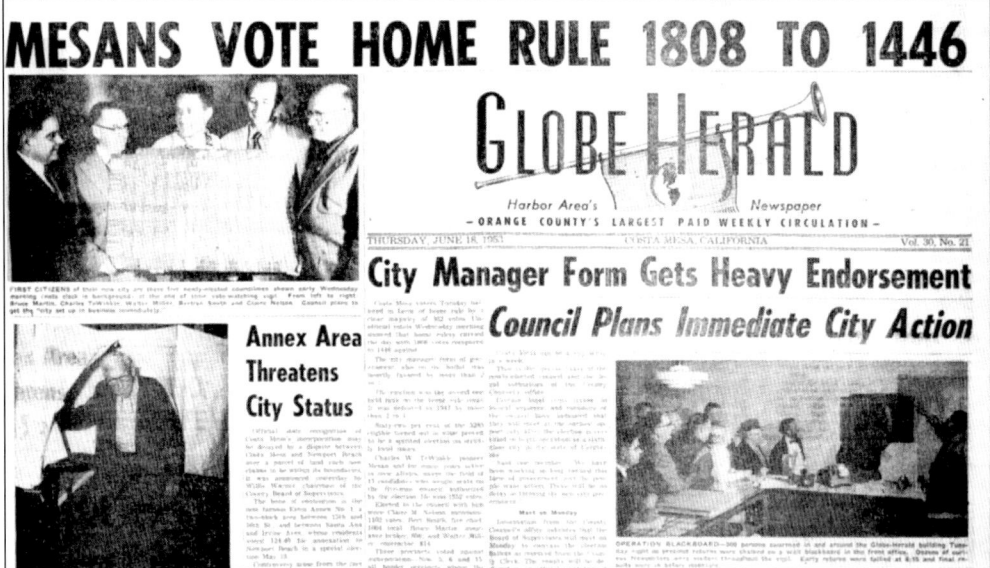

The headline says it all. At a special election on Tuesday, June 16, 1953, Costa Mesans voted to incorporate as a general law city under the city manager form of government. The city council planned immediate action, with one caveat. The property owners in the Estus Parcel No. 1 at East Fifteenth Street and Santa Ana Avenue had voted to be annexed by Newport Beach in a hurry-up election just one month earlier than Costa Mesa's election. An agreement between the two cities smoothed the way for Costa Mesa to get down to business. The first city council members were sworn in and held their first meeting on Monday, June 29, 1953.

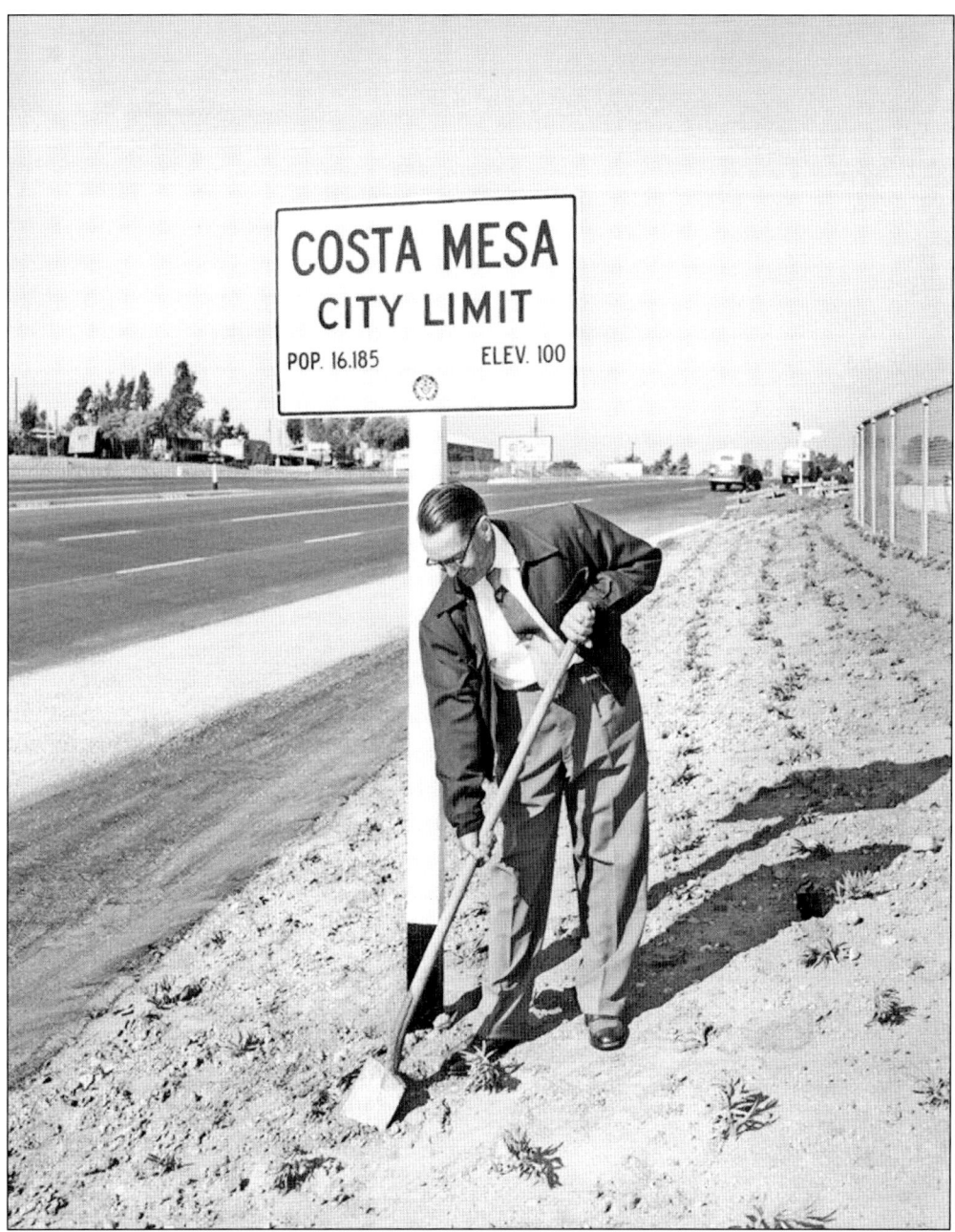

Newport Boulevard, otherwise known as State Route 55, was widened and received other improvements that were completed in the fall of 1953. By that time, the city of Costa Mesa was three months old. Here, in the midst of Eastside annexation skirmishes with Newport Beach, Mayor Charles TeWinkle puts the finishing touches on Costa Mesa's city limits sign along Newport Boulevard just south of Industrial Way. Motorists heading north out of Newport Beach were reminded there was a new kid in town. (Courtesy of Old Orange County Courthouse, Orange County Parks.)

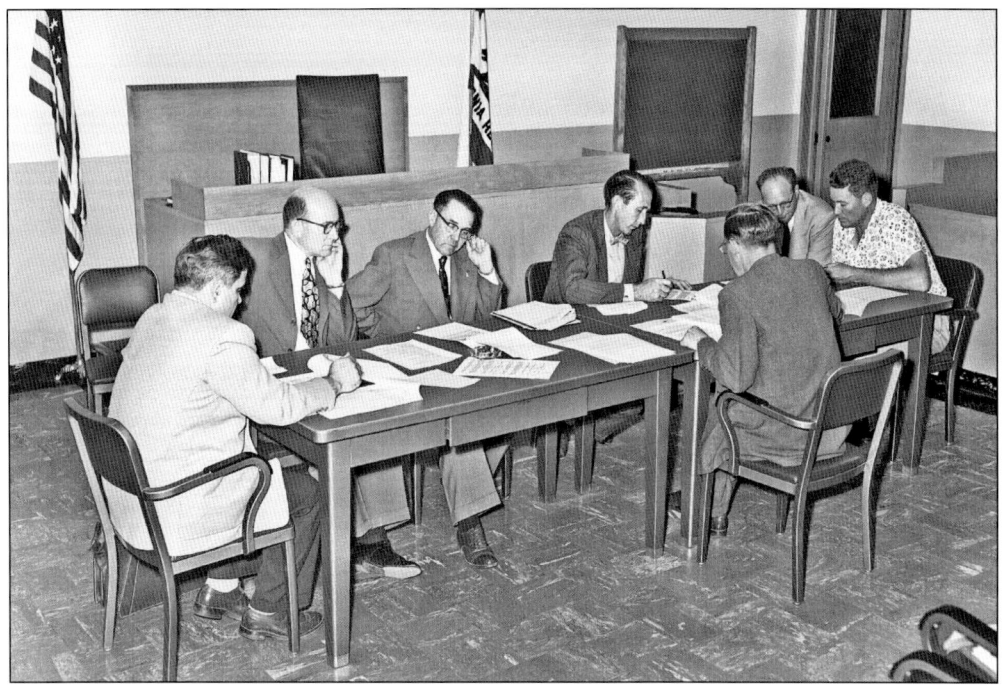

The newly elected city council met in the township courthouse on West Eighteenth Street in Costa Mesa. Each of the council members donated $20 to create a city treasury. An early act of the council was to pass a one-percent sales tax that would become effective on October 1, 1953. Appearing in the photograph, from left to right, are councilmembers Bruce Martin and Claire Nelson, Mayor Charles TeWinkle, councilmember Bert Smith, city clerk Arlington "Arlie" Swartz, city attorney Donald Dungan, and councilmember Walter Miller. (Courtesy of Special Collections and Archives, University of California, Irvine Libraries, Hugh R. McMillan Collection.)

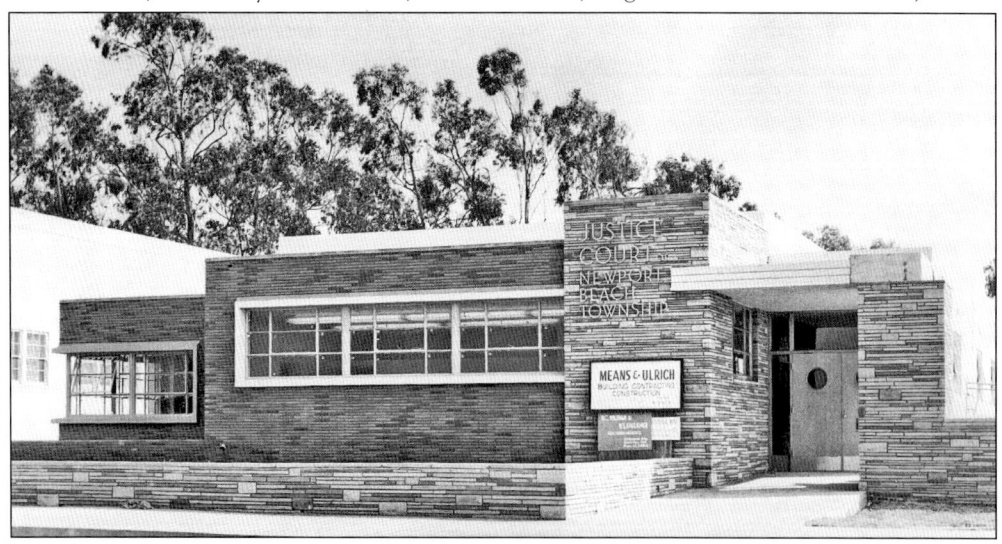

Completed in 1950, the Justice Court of the Newport Beach Judicial District was located in the new city of Costa Mesa upon the latter's incorporation. The new courthouse replaced the "shack" that had served Judge Donald Dodge for decades. Built in a distinctive modern architectural style, the courthouse at 567 West Eighteenth Street later served as a veterans' hall and a police substation.

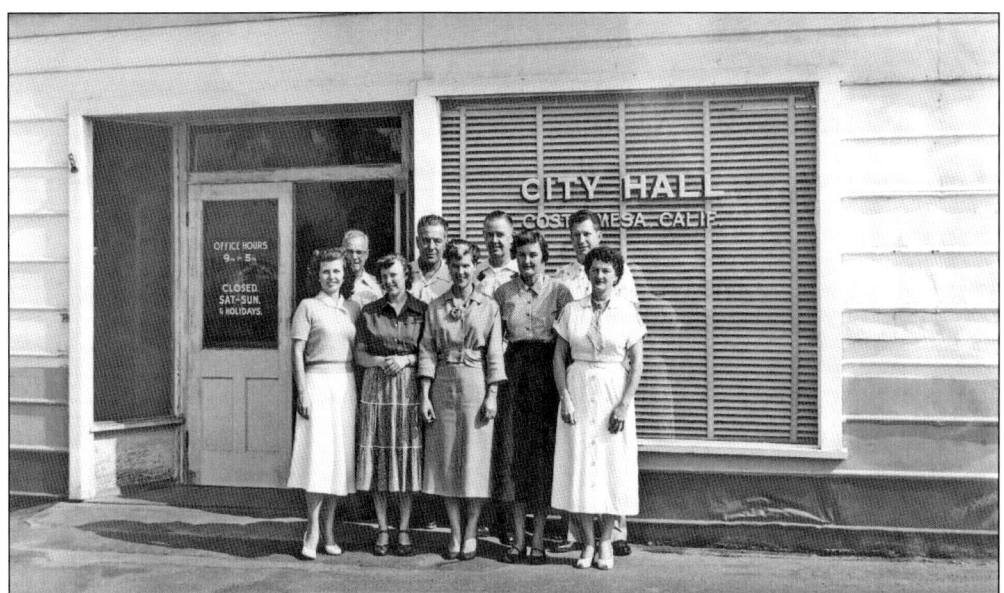

Costa Mesa's first city hall was located in a former auto parts store at 1998 1/2 Newport Boulevard. City officials soon changed the address to the more respectable 111 East Twentieth Street. Shown here in 1953 from left to right are (first row) Margaret Murray, Margaret Peterman, Tommie Flanagan, Ethel Nuzum, and Dorothy Ellis; (second row) Ray Hartzler (finance), A.J. Volz (building), George Coffey (city manager), and Arthur McKenzie (police chief).

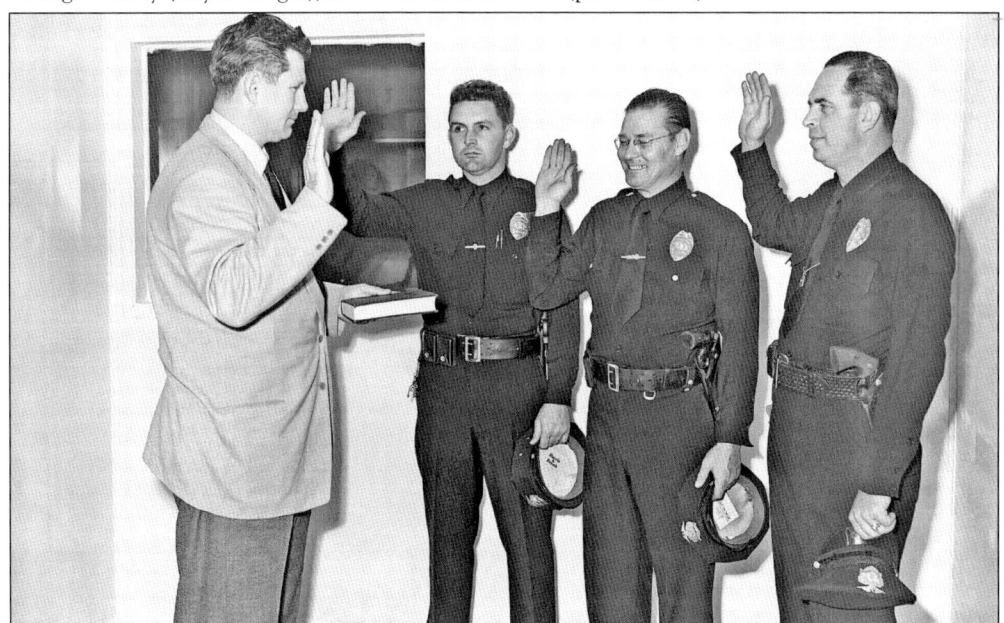

The city's first police department hit the streets in December 1953. Shown here at the swearing in ceremony on December 15 are, from left to right, Chief Arthur McKenzie and officers Roger Neth, David Gregg, and Lee Lester. Costa Mesa operated with two patrol cars and a four-man department until the following fiscal year. Officer Neth wrote the department's first traffic citation on December 28, 1953. (Courtesy of Special Collections and Archives, University of California, Irvine Libraries, Hugh R. McMillan Collection.)

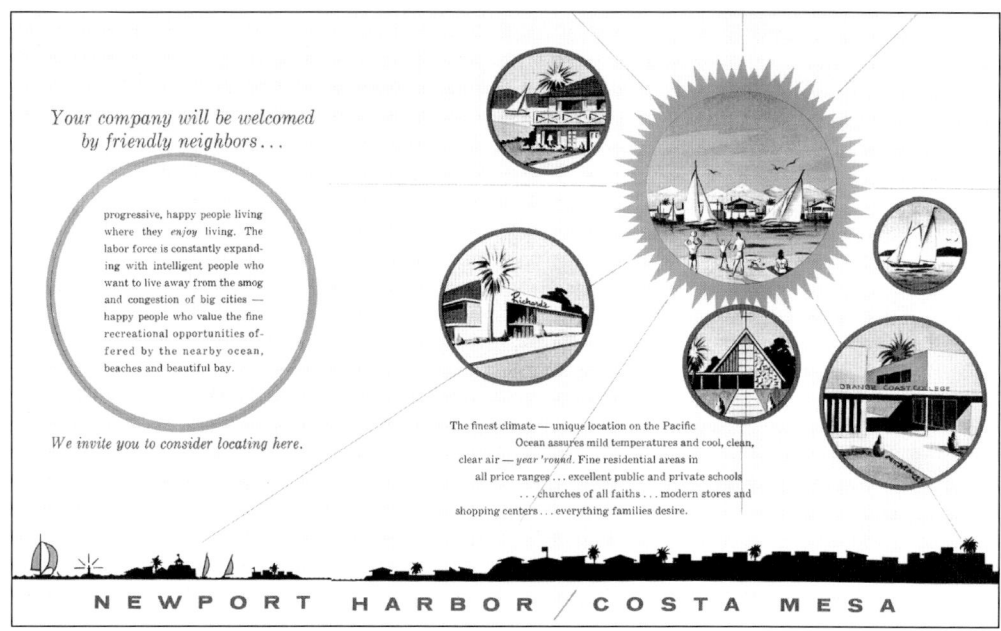

Costa Mesa worked hard to attract businesses to the new city. This 1957 brochure stated, "Ample level land zoned for manufacturing and commercial" and "Prominent firms now located here." The brochure referred to the area as "Newport Harbor/Costa Mesa," showing the city was still trying to hitch its star to the harbor area.

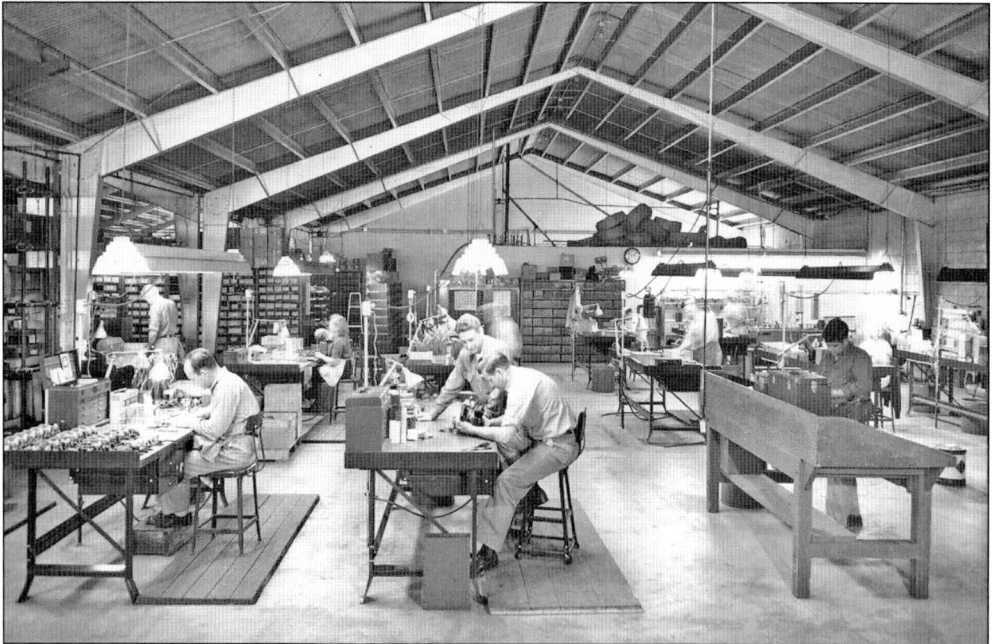

One company that moved to the area was Cla-Val. Founded in South Pasadena in 1936, the company moved to a 20-acre property at 1701 Placentia Avenue in 1954. The Costa Mesa facility, which served as the worldwide headquarters, featured two in-house foundries as well as manufacturing operations with more than four acres under roof. Shown here in the 1950s is an assembly area for pilot valves. (Courtesy of Cla-Val.)

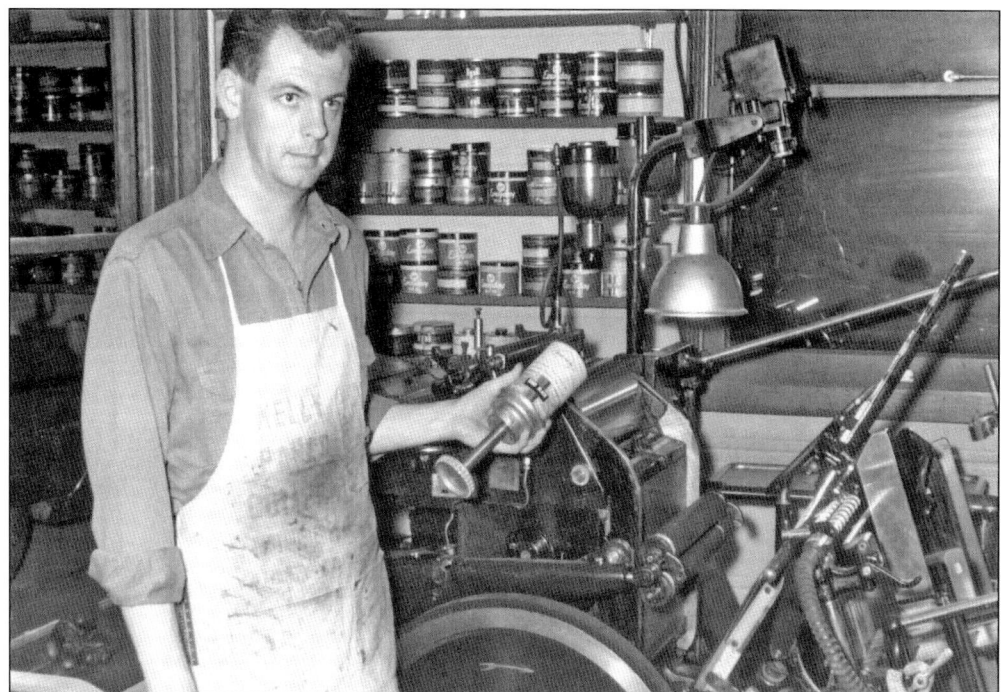

Family-owned businesses also prospered in Costa Mesa. Gardner Press at 2028 Newport Boulevard was one example. In this 1955 photograph, Dave Gardner tends a Heidelberg 10-by-15-inch letterpress. The family moved to Costa Mesa in 1937, settling on a two-acre plot that they operated as a chicken ranch before going into the printing business in 1947. Soon after city incorporation, Gardner formed the Costa Mesa Police Reserves at the request of Chief Arthur McKenzie.

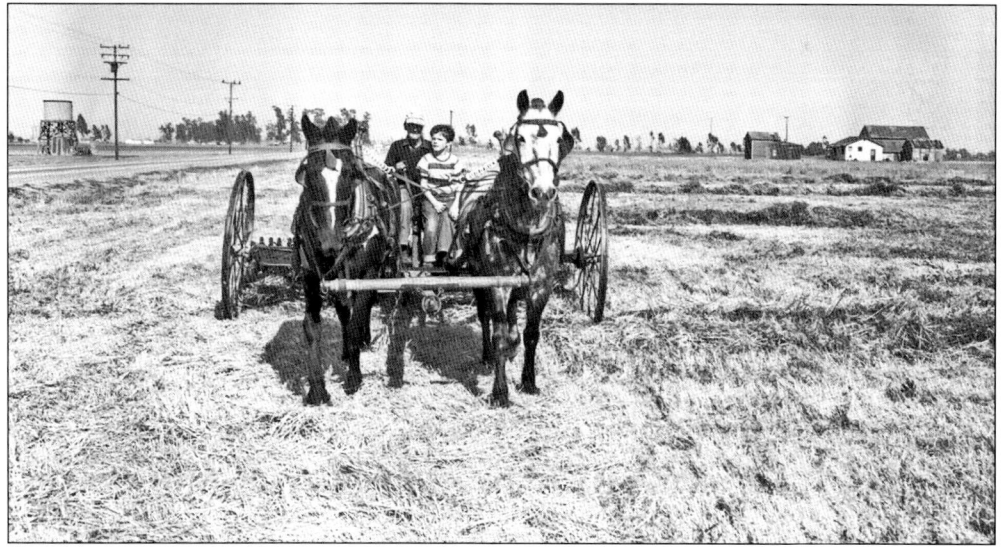

In the mid-1950s, the 200-year agricultural tradition on the mesa was still going in spite of incorporation and suburban growth. In addition to medium-scale farming, family farms operated on the Westside and in the area that would become North Costa Mesa. Shown here in April 1953 are Roscoe Jones (left) and a young helper making hay on his farm at 2373 Harbor Boulevard. (Courtesy of Old Orange County Courthouse, Orange County Parks.)

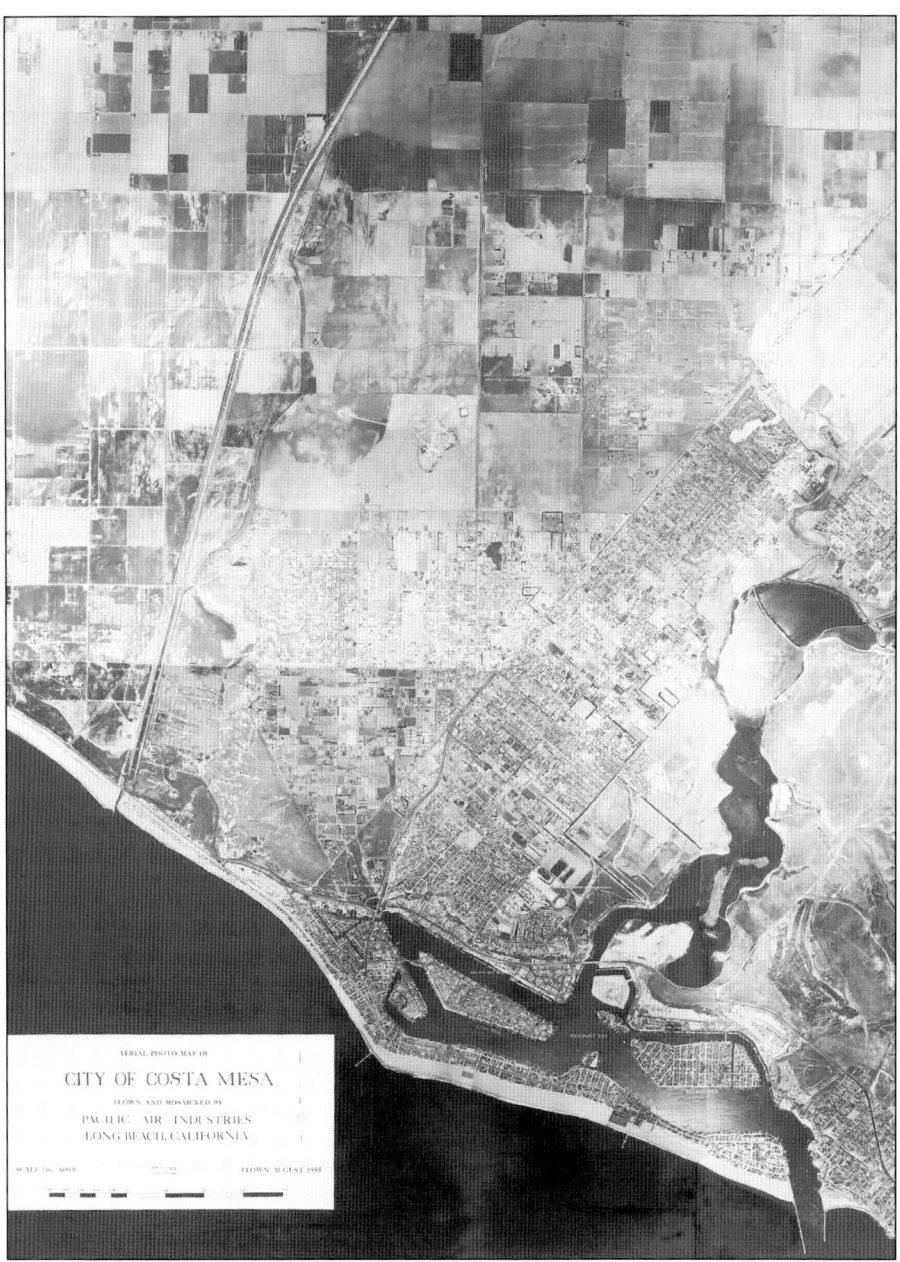

The period from 1949 to 1955 was decisive for Costa Mesa. After earlier failed attempts, the community voted for home rule in 1953. Born out of humble beginnings, the city was up and running and taking steps to achieve critical mass. A revenue stream had been developed, and a professional police department had been formed. Costa Mesa was far ahead of any other city in Orange County in terms of new building permit valuations, amounting to more than $10 million in 1955. But that was only the beginning; much more was about to happen. In this aerial photograph dated August 1955, Wilson Street runs east-west and Harbor Boulevard runs north-south from the center. Concentrations of commercial and housing areas appear in the Eastside and Westside areas of Costa Mesa, while open fields appear north of Wilson Street. Also visible north of Wilson Street are the Fairview State Hospital and the remnants of the Santa Ana Army Air Base.

Three

ANNEXATION AND GROWTH

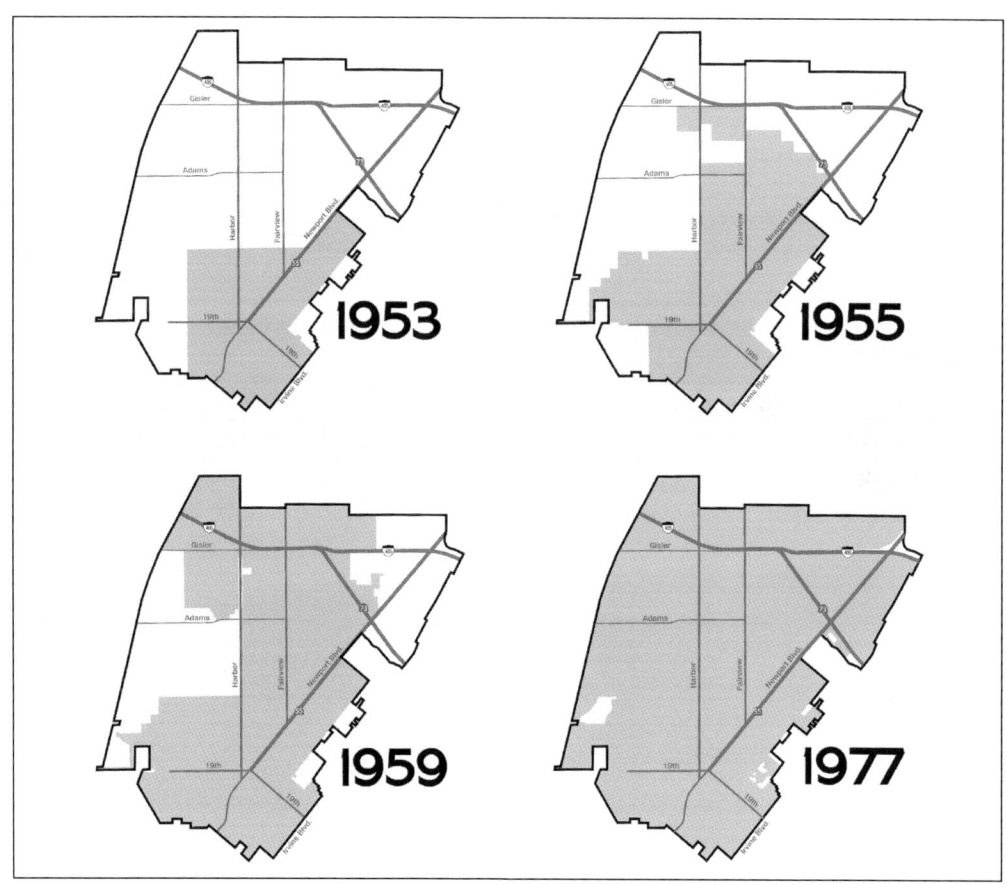

For Costa Mesa, there was only one game in town: growth via annexation. The first annexation in 1954 brought the Freedom Homes tract into the city. Annexations in 1955 included a 200-foot-wide strip running across the Santa Ana River to stop end-run moves by Newport Beach on the Westside. By 1959, Costa Mesa's northern boundary was established via annexations that included what would become South Coast Plaza. Subsequent annexations up to 1977 added more meat to the bones, while annexations after 1977 filled in remaining gaps. (Courtesy of Keith Hall.)

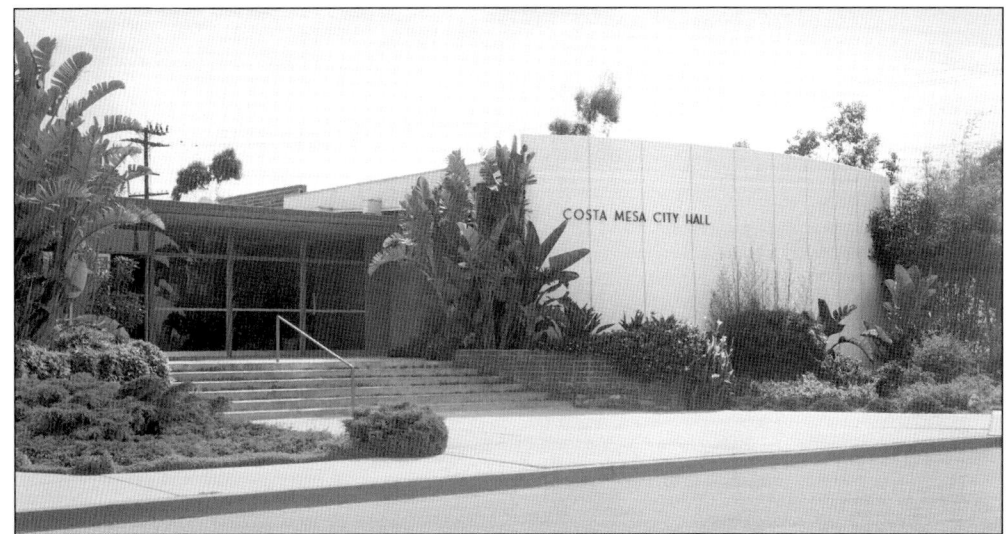

By 1957, the city needed a larger city hall. City leaders were averse to bond financing, so they entered into a lease-purchase agreement whereby the city sold the building site to a leaseholder and then leased back the site—with the new building in place—for the next 25 years. The completed building shown here housed city staff except for the engineering, police, and fire departments from late 1957 to 1967.

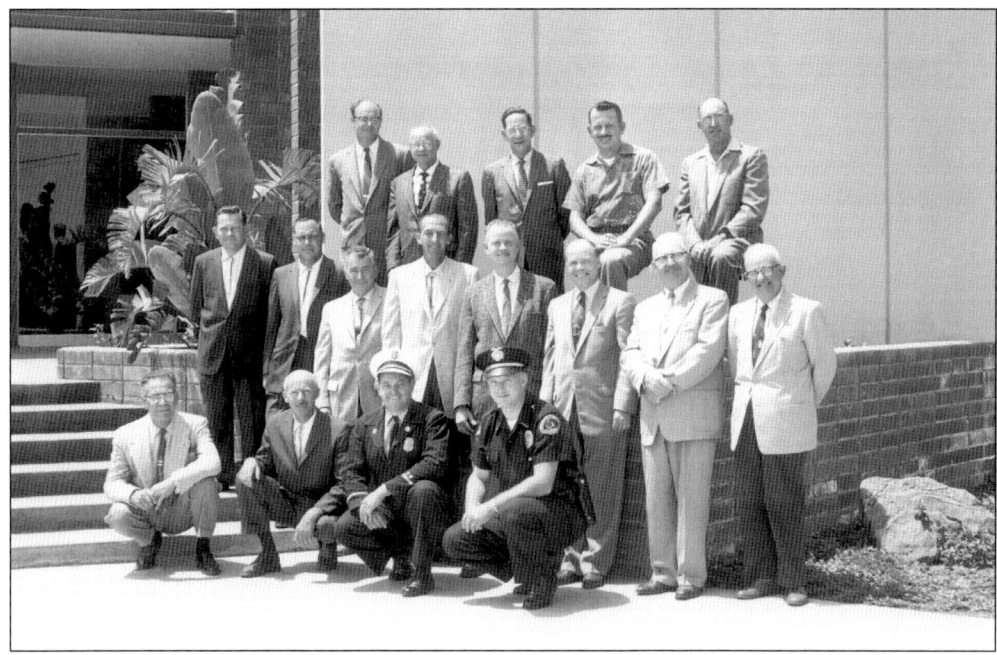

City leaders posed for a group photograph in front of city hall after the council election of April 1958. Shown here from left to right are (first row) Harlan Wood (planning commission), unidentified, Ralph Lee (fire chief), and Arthur McKenzie (police chief); (second row) two unidentified, Donovan Southworth (city engineer), Bertren Smith (councilmember), Alvin Pinkley (councilmember), John Smith (mayor), Arthur Meyers (councilmember), and Everett Rea (councilmember); (third row) Donald Dungan (city attorney), William Dunn (planning director), Arlington Swartz (city clerk), Robert Unger (city manager), and unidentified.

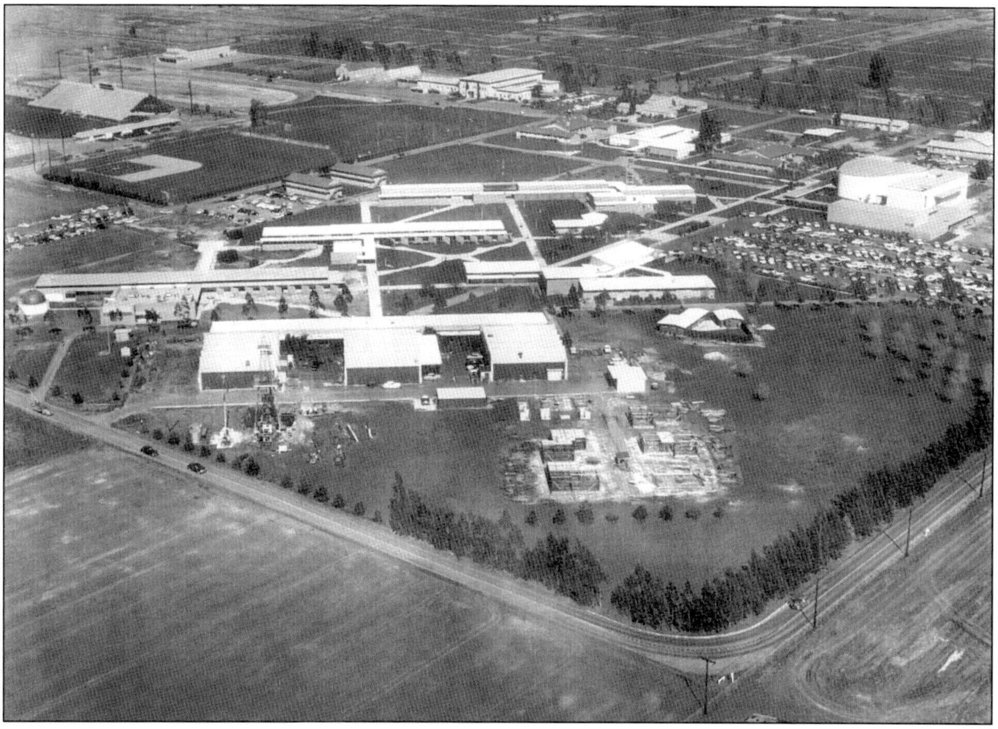

In less than nine years since opening, Orange Coast College had come a long way. Shown here are the results of a seven-year building program led by noted architects Robert Alexander and Richard Neutra. Across the center are, from left to right, the planetarium, math wing, technology building, business education building, art center, library, main quad, student center, and theater arts building. Also visible at left center are two barracks buildings that served as men's dormitories. The street running diagonally from right center to bottom would become today's Merrimac Way.

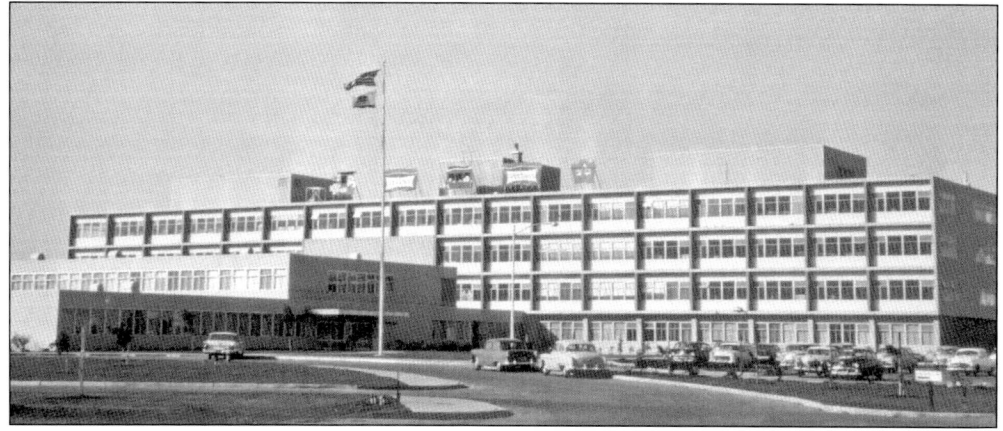

In early 1950, the State of California condemned 750 acres adjoining Harbor Boulevard as the site of a new hospital for mentally disabled patients. Three years later, funds were appropriated for construction. Finally, in January 1959, Fairview State Hospital admitted its first patients. The hospital was sized to handle 4,000 patients and was expected to create 1,500 jobs with a monthly payroll of $500,000 by 1963.

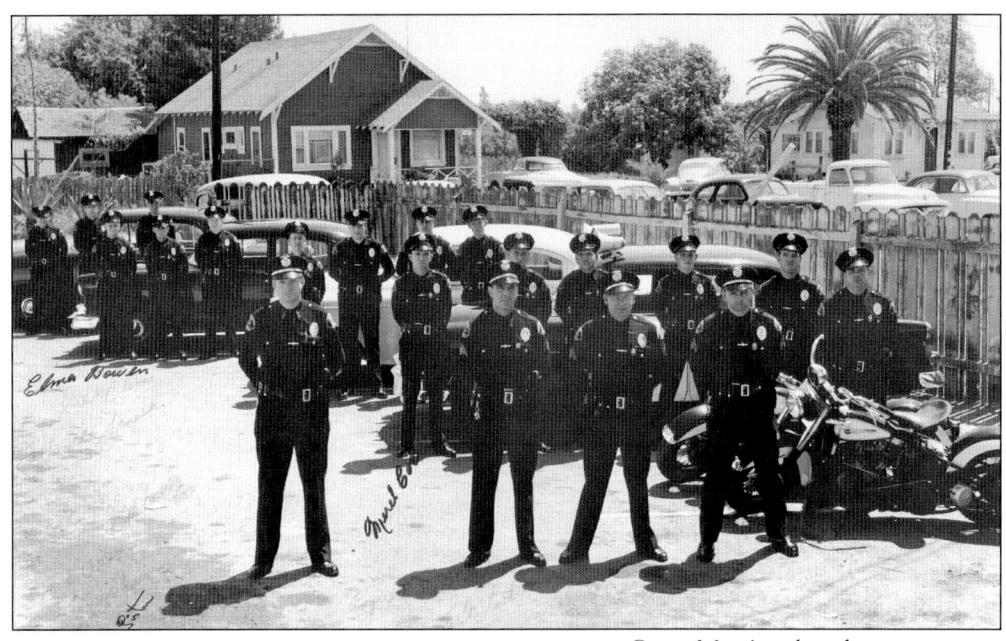

Costa Mesa's police department had grown to more than 20 officers by the late 1950s. After city staff moved to the new city hall on West Nineteenth Street in the fall of 1957, the police department expanded into the vacated space at the old city hall at 111 East Twentieth Street. Appearing in the first row of this group photograph are Chief Arthur McKenzie (far left) and Sgt. Roger Neth (far right).

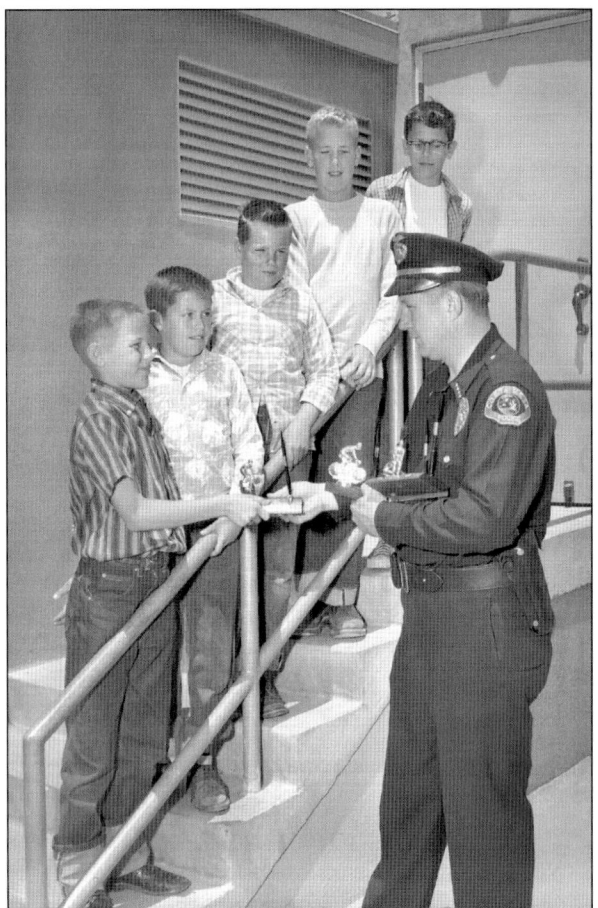

Community policing became an early objective for Costa Mesa police. Here, Chief McKenzie is awarding desk pen sets to recognize local boys who won competitive events at a bicycle rodeo sponsored by the police department. Bicycle safety had become a priority for the city.

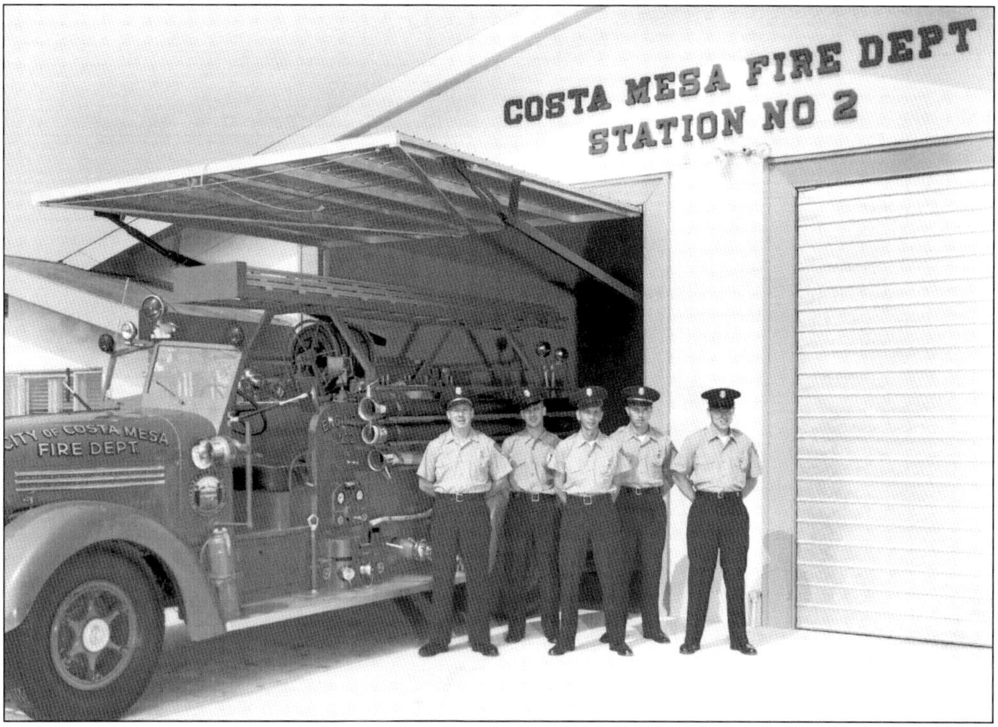

After incorporation, Costa Mesa continued with a volunteer fire department under county control. In 1954, the city hired Ralph Lee as a fire prevention officer, and in March 1956, Lee became the city's first fire chief. On July 1, 1956, control of the fire department passed to the city, and six city firemen reported for duty. In the spring of 1958, Station No. 2 opened on the northwest corner of Fairview Road and Adams Avenue to provide fire protection to the new housing tracts in North Costa Mesa. A new Station No. 2 was opened on Baker Street in 1967.

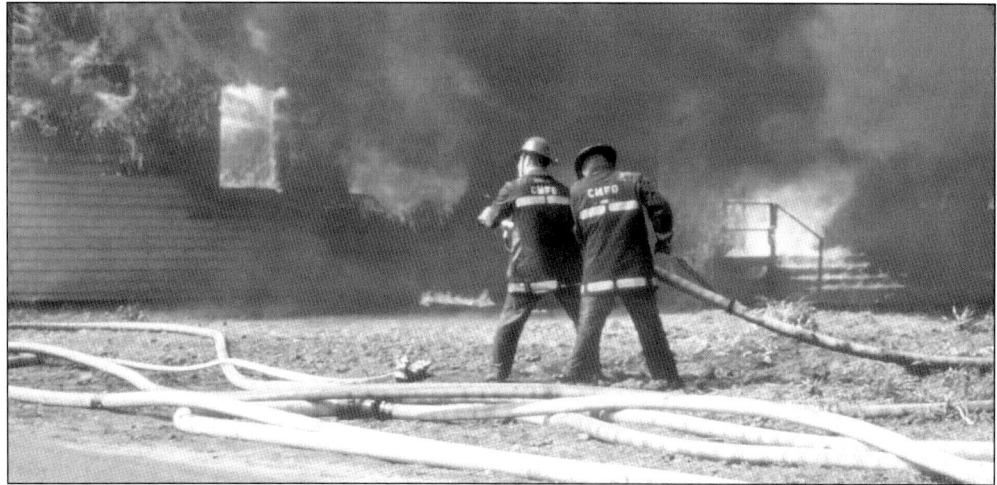

Since its formation in 1956, the Costa Mesa Fire Department (CMFD) has strived to optimize its Community Fire Protection classification through equipment upgrades, additional staff, education, and training. In the mid-to-late-1960s, surplus buildings at the deactivated Santa Ana Army Air Base provided an opportunity for live-fire training. Shown here in March 1967, CMFD firefighters tackle a blaze at one of the abandoned barracks buildings.

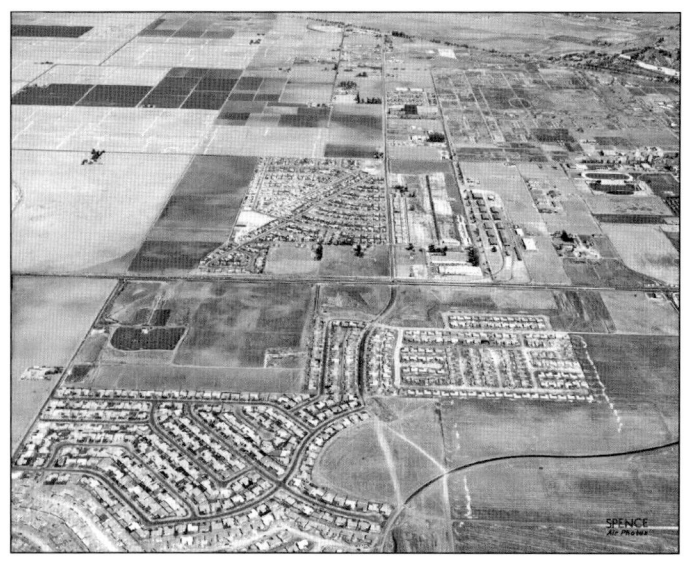

The Halecrest and Mesa Verde housing tracts were two North Costa Mesa areas developed in the late 1950s. In this 1959 aerial view looking east, Harbor Boulevard runs horizontally and Baker Street runs vertically, intersecting at the center. The Halecrest tract appears just above center, while the Mesa Verde tract appears across the bottom half. Segerstrom Home Ranch appears at left, just above the center, along Fairview Road.

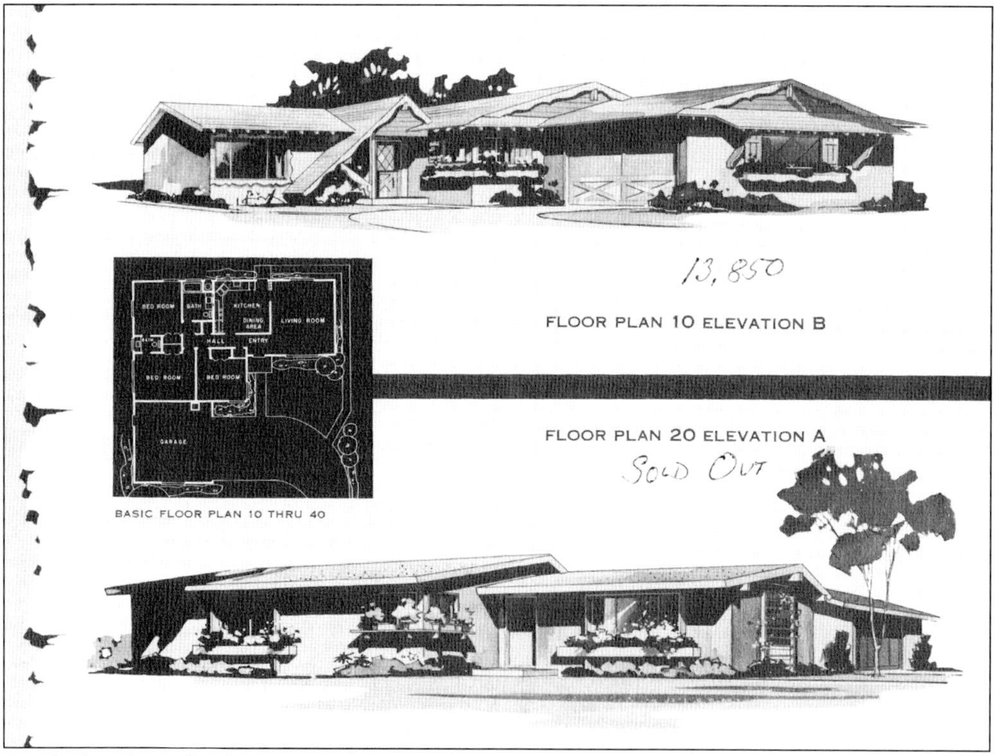

A sales brochure for the Mesa Verde tract promised a planned community close to the freeway and "330 days [per year] of ocean freshened, smog-free, air-conditioned sunshine with average temperatures ranging between 52 and 69 degrees." The brochure went on to explain that one should live in Mesa Verde because it was the place where one could live, work, shop, learn, worship, and play. The tract offered 12 floor plans at prices ranging from $13,850 to $14,800.

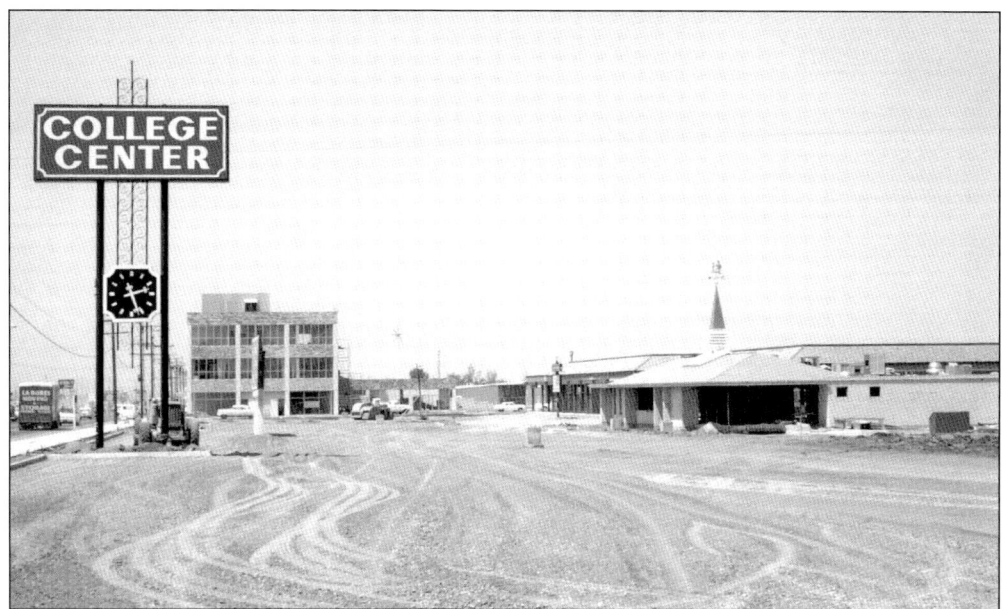

Commercial development kept pace with new housing in North Costa Mesa. College Center was located on the southeast corner of Harbor Boulevard and Adams Avenue to serve the Mesa Verde, College Park, and Orange Coast College communities. The three-story building and strip mall shown here in 1965 still stand. The Howard Johnson's restaurant at 2750 Harbor Boulevard lasted until 1974, when it became the Ground Round restaurant.

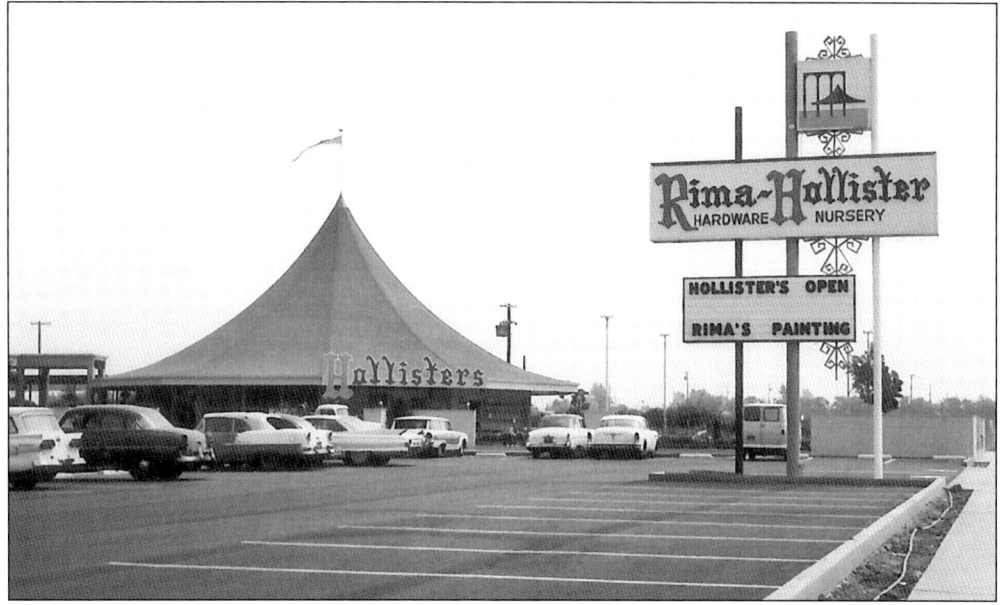

Albert Hollister was one of hundreds of World War II servicemen who settled in Costa Mesa after the war. He started in the nursery business as an adjunct to the family feed store business at Harbor and Newport Boulevards. Hollister's nursery business migrated north, first to the 1900 block of Harbor Boulevard, then to the pavilion-shaped building pictured here at 2640 Harbor Boulevard. Kerm Rima Hardware moved about the same time to 2666 Harbor Boulevard. Both buildings still stand today.

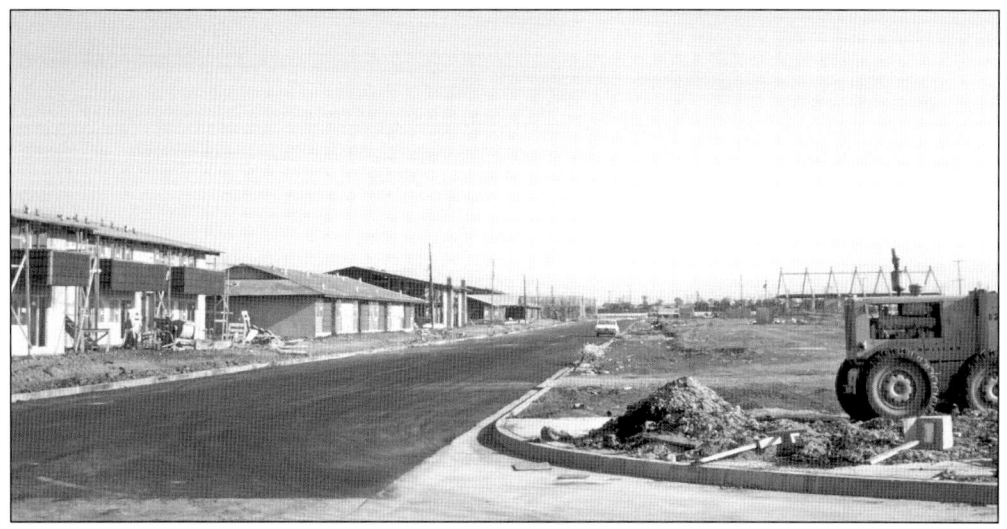

The area immediately east of College Center was under construction in this May 1964 photograph. The photographer stood at the curb of Adams Avenue, looking south along Peterson Place. At left is Harbor Greens Village, while to the right, behind the construction equipment, stands the framework for California Federal Savings and Loan at 2700 Harbor Boulevard.

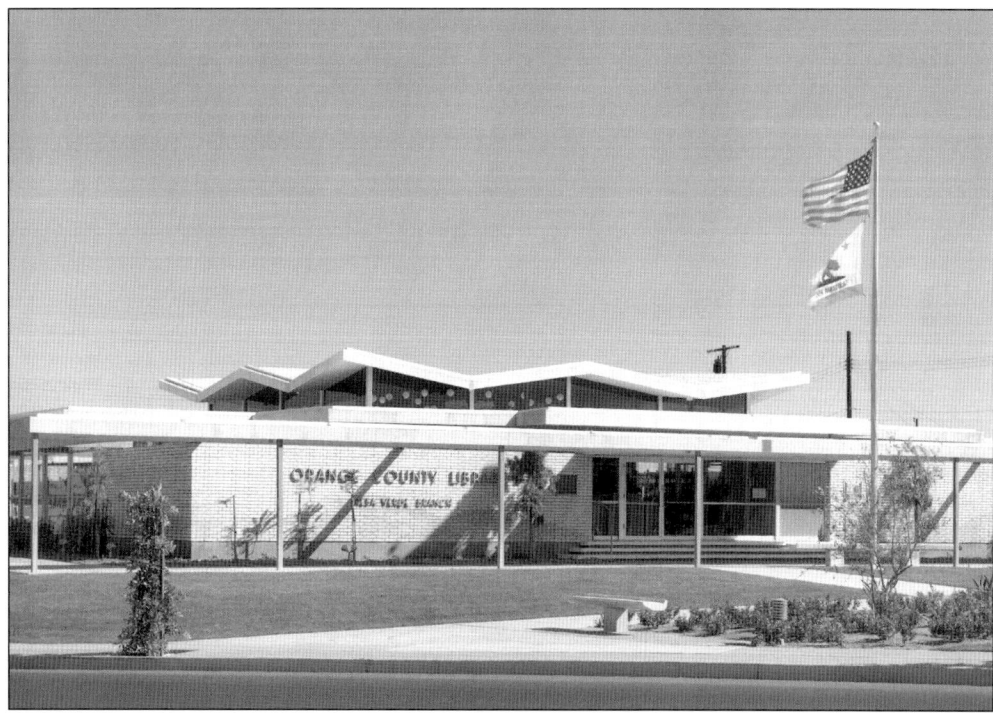

Costa Mesa was an early adopter of the Orange County Public Library system, opening its first one-room branch library in 1923. The Mesa Verde Branch Library, shown here, opened in 1965 to serve North Costa Mesa. Together with the Costa Mesa Branch Library at 566 Center Street, the city had 11,900 square feet of library space to serve a population of 65,300 people, a ratio of 0.18 square feet per capita, well below the Orange County benchmark of 0.3 square feet per capita. By 2003, the library space ratio would drop even further, to 0.15 square feet per capita.

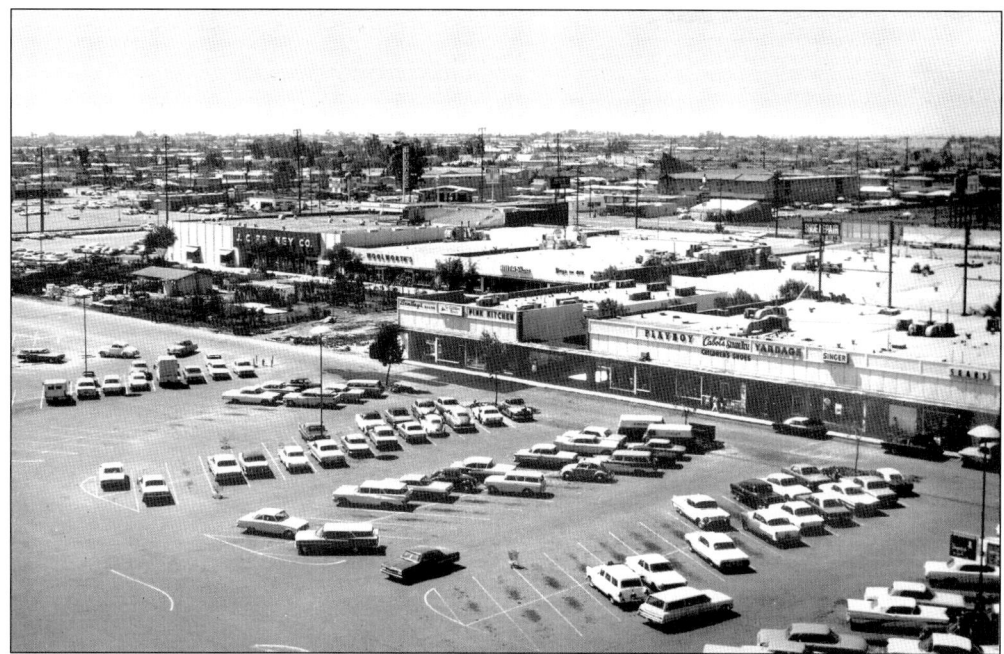

By the mid-1960s, Harbor Center was in full swing, as shown in this view looking southwest from the back parking lot towards the intersection of Harbor Boulevard and Wilson Street. Costa Mesa was elated whenever a major corporation or chain, such as JC Penney, established a store in town. Also seen here are Woolworth's, Singer Sewing Machines, and Sears, along with several regional and local retail businesses.

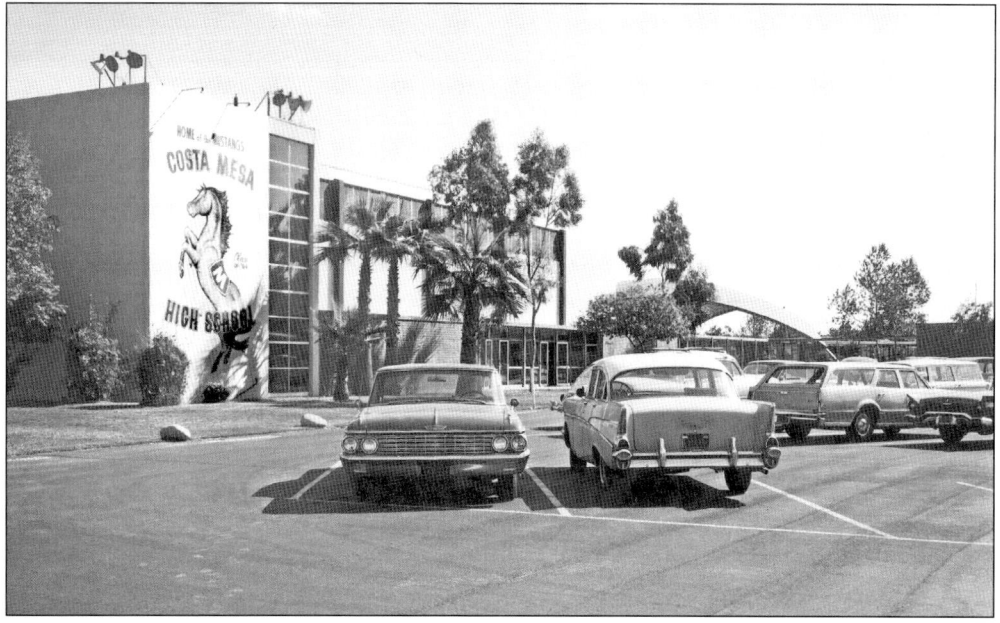

Costa Mesa High School opened in 1958 to accommodate increasing numbers of students. Leslie "Les" Miller not only served as the school's first principal but also helped to secure financing and land as well. In this late 1960s view, the class of 1964 had left its imprint on the school: a supersized "Home of the Mustangs" logo.

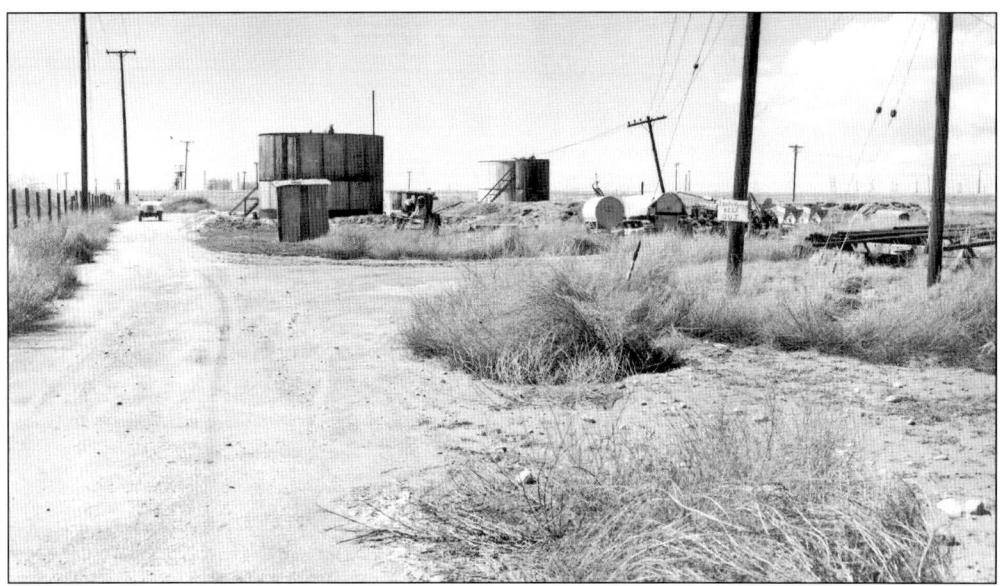

Not every proposed building development went on to fruition. Keys Marina was a bold project with a vision to establish 953 homes, each with Pacific Ocean access via the Santa Ana River. The marina would be located on former oil land shown here along the Santa Ana River at Victoria Street. Hopes were high in 1962, but by 1985, after two trips to Washington by Mayor Donn Hall, the project sank when the city council balked at paying part of the $250,000 cost of a federal feasibility study.

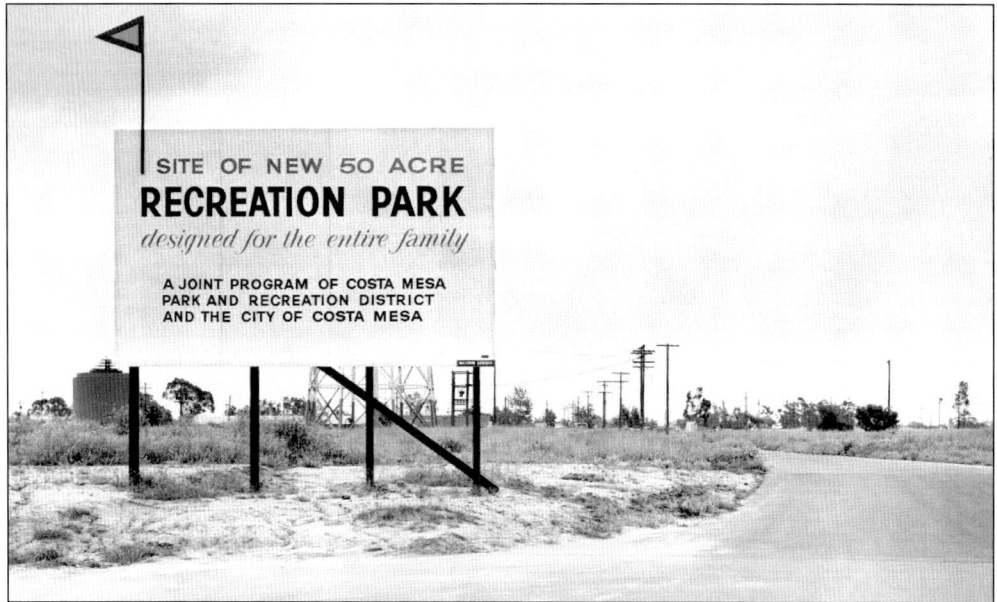

Parks and recreation evolved to a high priority on Costa Mesa's to-do list. In early 1962, the city gained control of the Costa Mesa Park and Recreation District, which had been administered by the Orange County Board of Supervisors. The city planned to establish a new 50-acre park that would serve all Costa Mesa residents, especially those in the Mesa Del Mar tract. The park was later named TeWinkle Park. In this view looking west from Newport Boulevard, the steel latticework of the old Santa Ana Army Air Base water tower appears behind the sign's legs.

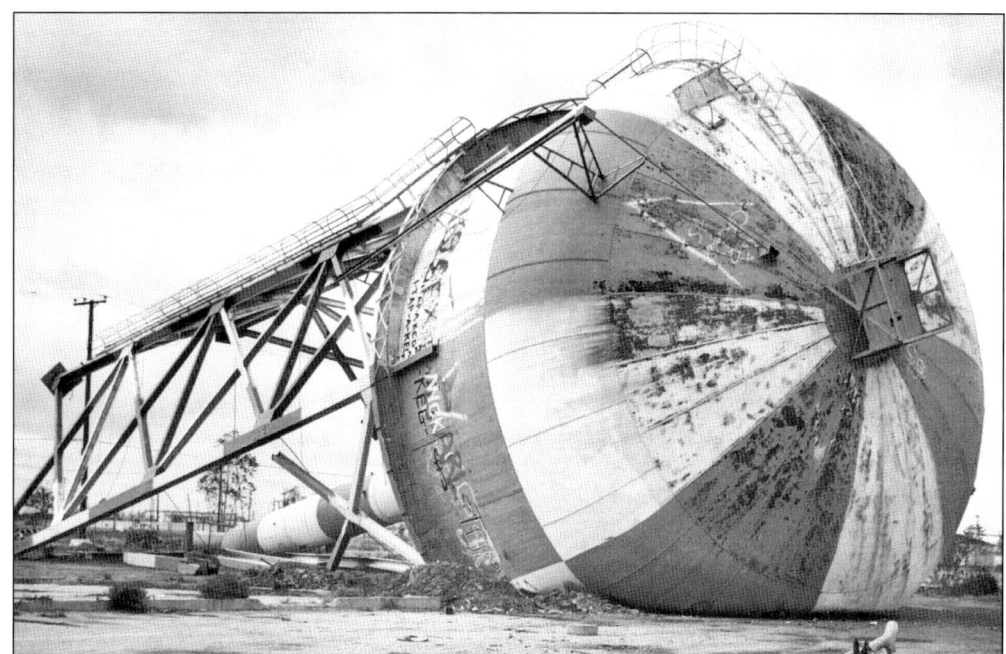

Unless the old Santa Ana Army Air Base (SAAAB) water tower was to be used as an observation platform or jungle gym, it had to be demolished to make way for TeWinkle Park. Accordingly, on April 18, 1964, a few well-placed explosive charges brought the tower down. After SAAAB was deactivated in 1946, the water tower had served as a graffiti platform for such phrases as "I-TAP-A-KEG" and other inscriptions.

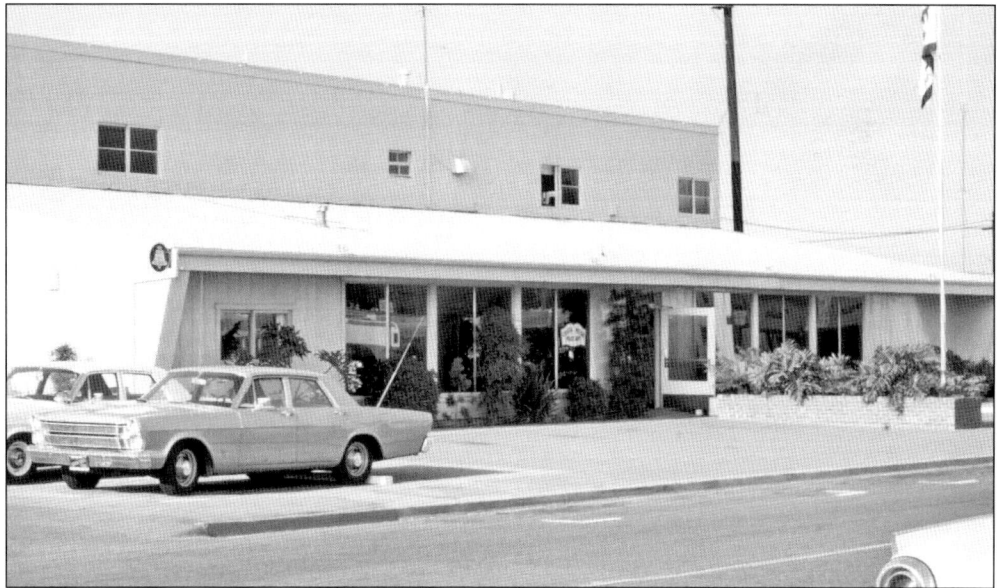

By 1961, the Costa Mesa Police Department had outgrown its digs at the old city hall at 111 East Twentieth Street. In that year, the department moved across the street to the former Barr Lumber site, shown here, at 1957 Newport Boulevard. The department operated from this location until the new civic center was completed in 1967. The building shown here eventually housed Antiques of the World.

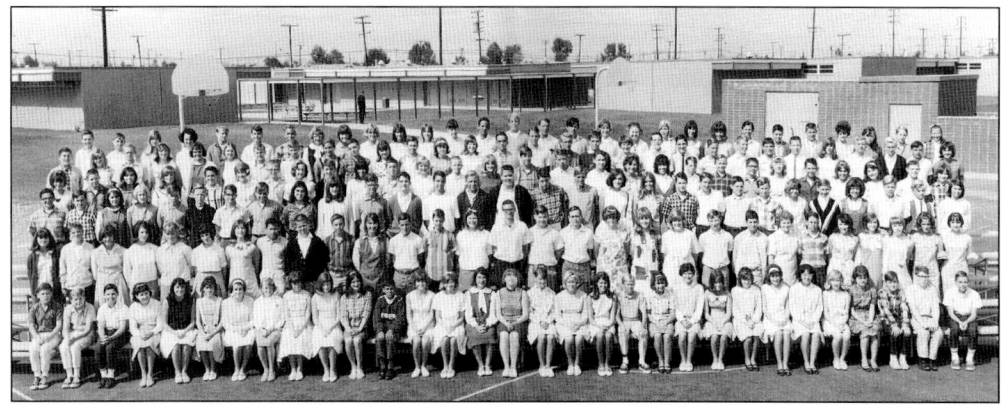

Ever since the formation of Costa Mesa's early communities of Fairview, Paularino, and Harper around the beginning of the 20th century, citizens were proactive about schooling for their children. That tradition endured over the decades and resulted in neighborhood schools being built to keep pace with the growing population. Shown here is the first graduating class at TeWinkle Middle School in June 1965. Go Trojans!

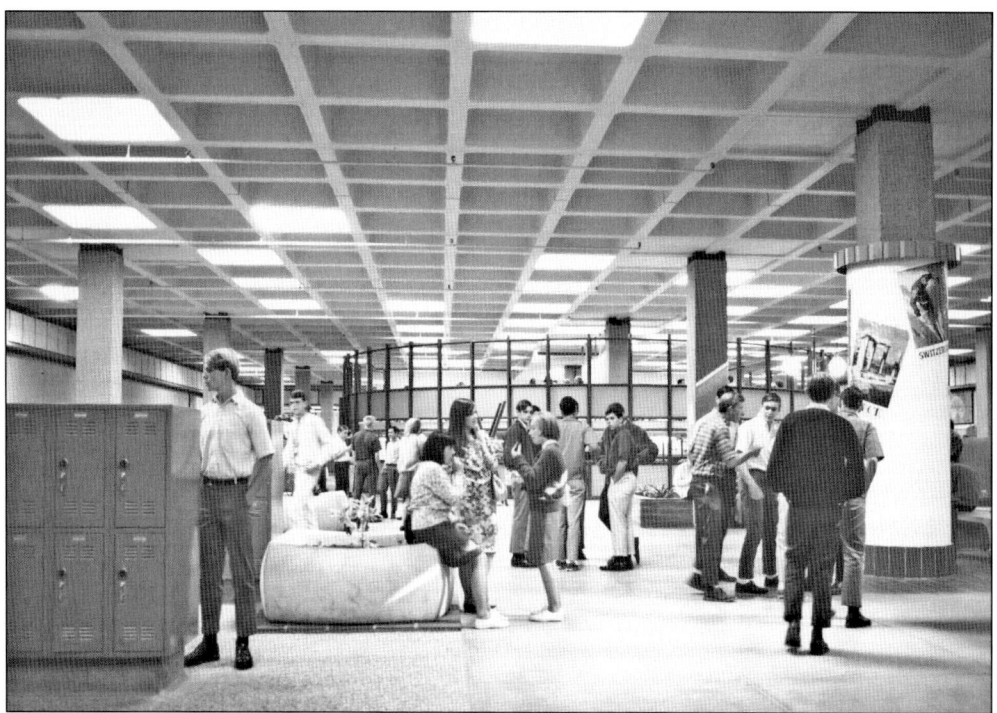

By the mid-1960s, Costa Mesa needed another high school to serve Mesa Verde and the Westside. In September 1965, Estancia High School opened its doors. The Eagles' first yearbook, *El Vuelo* (The Flight), published in 1966, was dedicated to Principal Floyd Harryman. Estancia's first year was administratively challenging, as the issue of unified school districts came to a head. On Tuesday, June 22, 1965, an election was held to decide the issue. Costa Mesa favored unification, while Newport Beach opposed it. But the ayes carried the day, and the Newport-Mesa Unified School District was formed on July 1, 1966. Dr. Norman Loats was credited with guiding the school district through the transitional period. (Courtesy of Getty Research Institute, Los Angeles [2004.R.10], © J. Paul Getty Trust.)

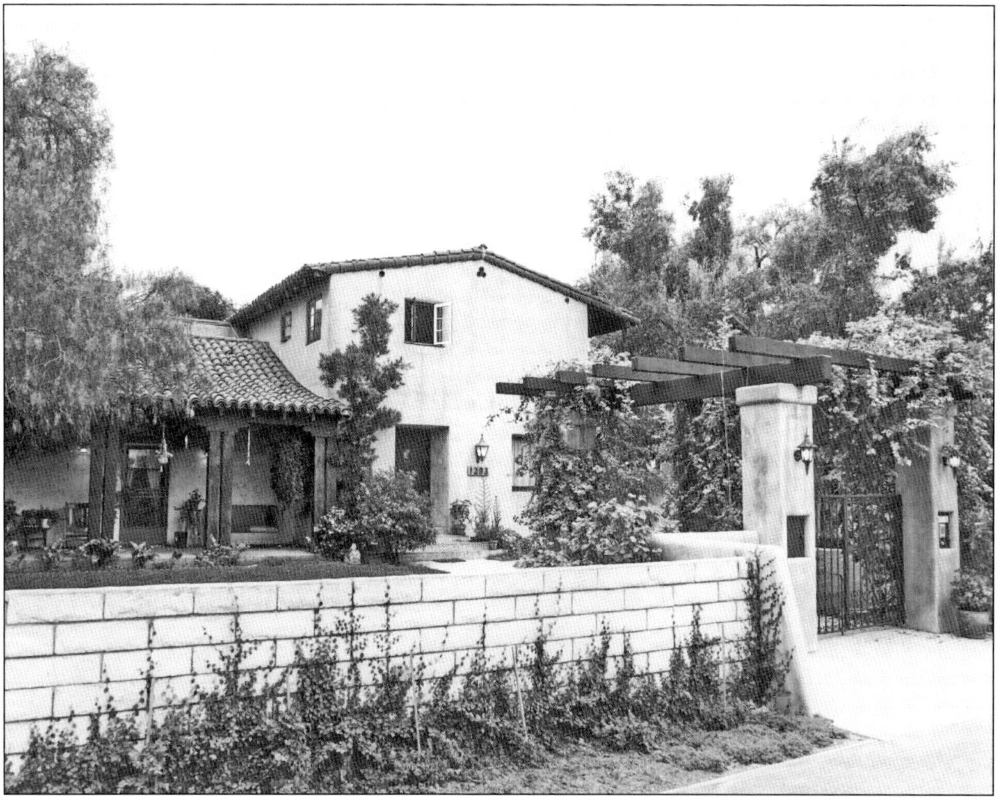

Cornelius McClintock was an early settler in the Fairview area along Baker Street west of Fairview Road. In the early 1930s, the family built this home in the Spanish Colonial Revival style. The home still stands at 1293 Baker Street, albeit behind a much higher front wall. The McClintock house is one of 29 sites included in a historic resources listing in Costa Mesa's 2000 General Plan.

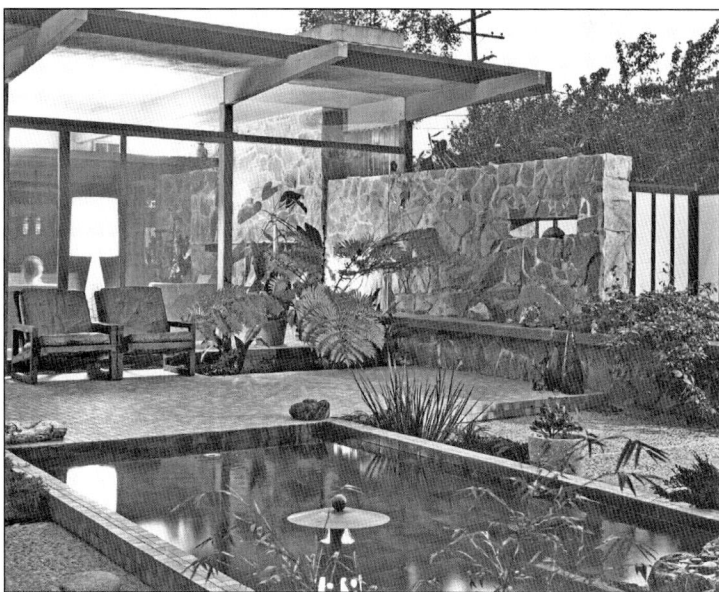

Jo and Esther Dendel built their Midcentury Modern home at 240 East Sixteenth Street in the 1950s. In designing their home, the Dendels applied what they had learned about African arts while working on a rubber plantation in Liberia—namely that art should be integrated into everyday life. The Dendels' business, Denwar Ceramics, was next door to the home. (Courtesy of Lee Payne.)

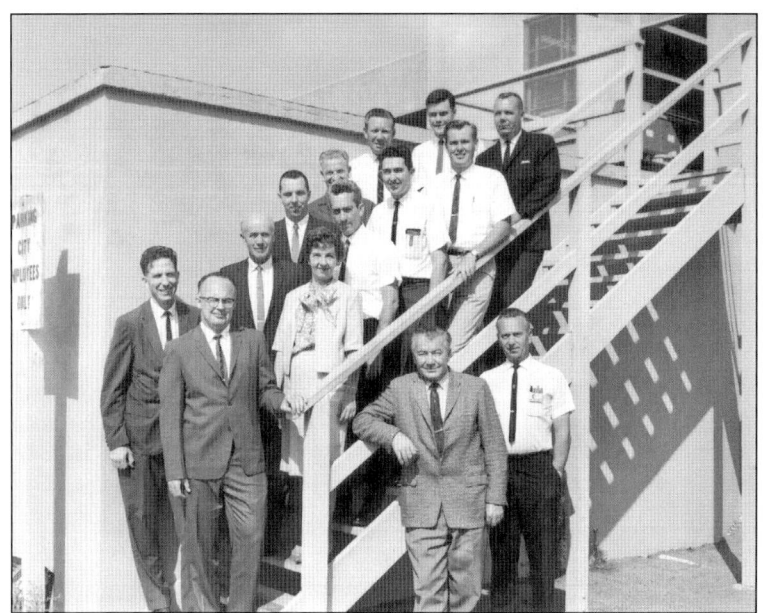

Even though the city had built a new city hall on West Nineteenth Street, several departments were still scattered around the downtown area, including the police and fire departments and the engineering department, shown here in the mid-1960s. City engineer Donovan "Don" Southworth appears in the first row, second from right.

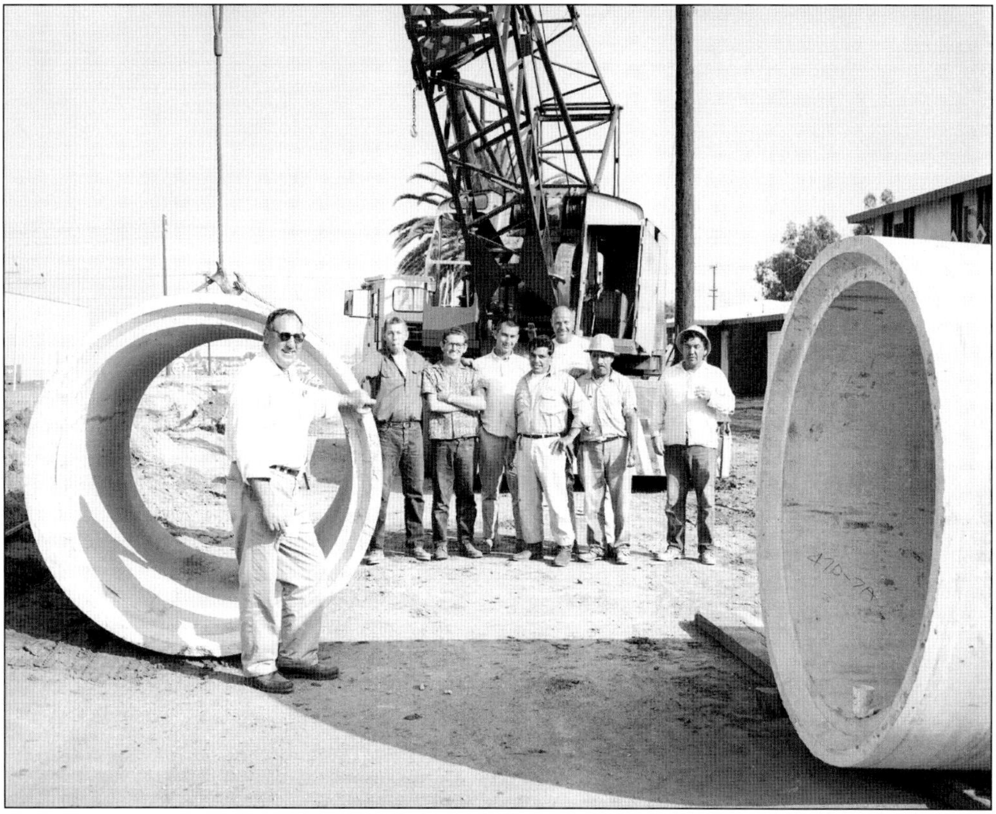

One major city project was the installation of storm drains. Shown here in 1963, a work crew is installing precast concrete pipe along College Avenue between Wilson and Victoria Streets. This storm sewer line still serves as part of the town's master drainage plan as depicted in Costa Mesa's 2000 General Plan.

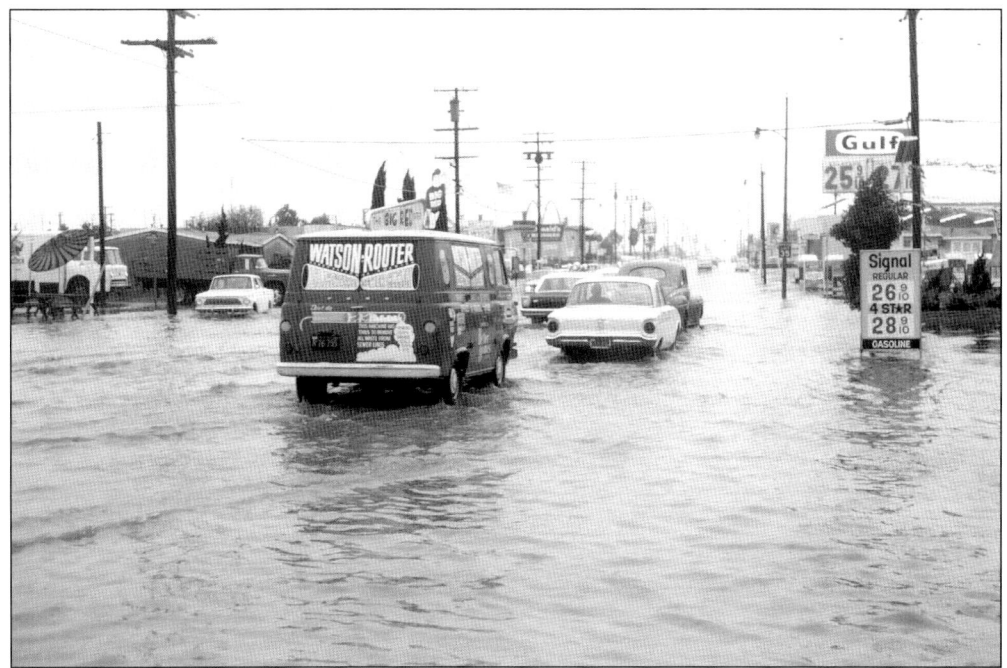

Despite the city's public works efforts, drainage problems persisted on West Nineteenth Street and surrounding areas, as shown in this November 1965 photograph. The view is looking west along West Nineteenth Street, with the Anaheim Avenue intersection just past the two utility poles on the left. Flooding after heavy rain was experienced for decades until a catchment basin was completed along Anaheim Avenue in 2015.

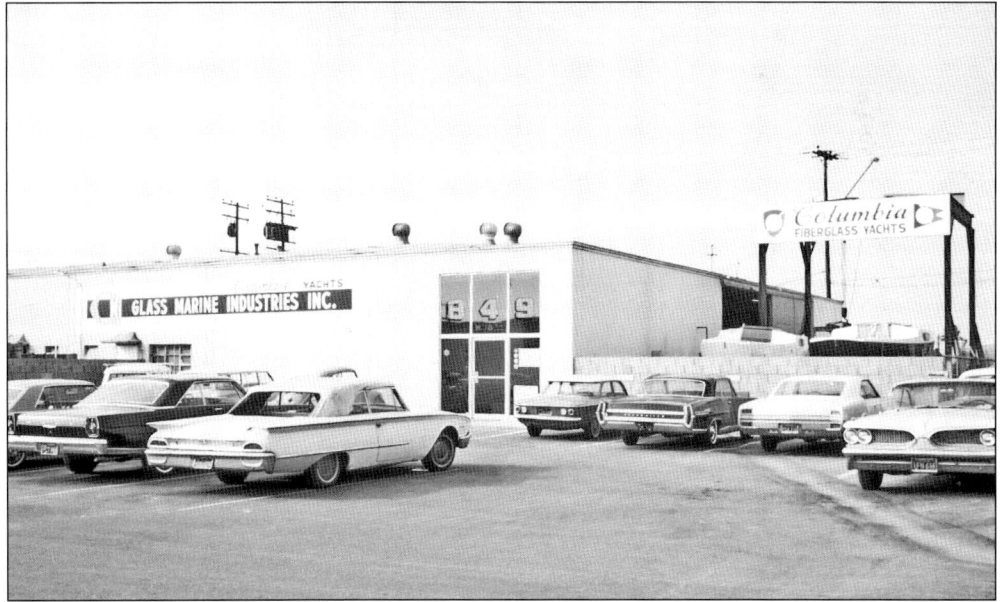

During the 1950s and 1960s, Costa Mesa was a major center of fiberglass boat building. Pictured here in January 1965 is Columbia Fiberglass Yachts, located at 849 West Eighteenth Street. By the time of this photograph, Columbia's annual sales had already surpassed $2.5 million. By the late 1960s, Columbia had become the world's largest manufacturer of fiberglass sailboats.

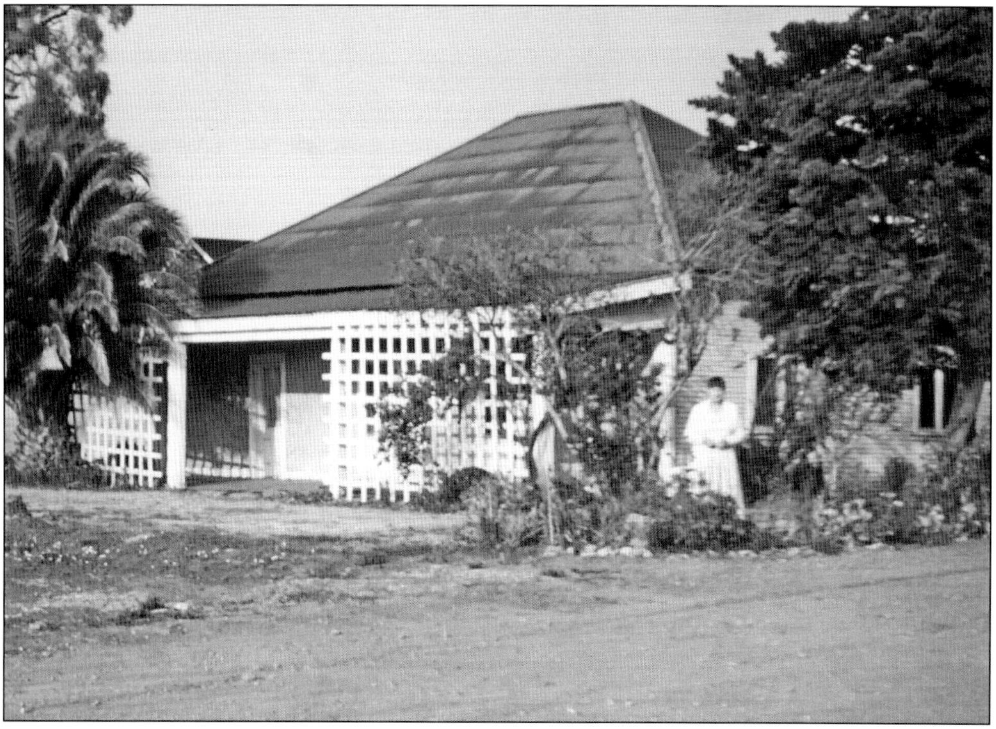

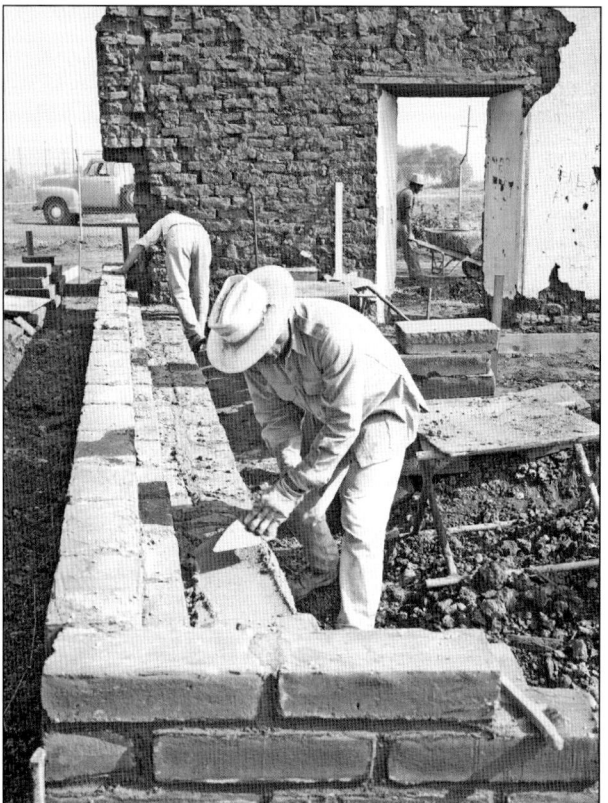

The Diego Sepulveda Adobe did not always look as historical as it does in the photograph on page 4. The fact that the adobe walls were covered by a wood frame for at least 80 years is widely believed to have preserved the adobe for future generations to enjoy. In August 1962, the house appeared as shown here. Later, the Segerstrom family donated the house and surrounding five acres to the city as a perpetual monument to preserve the heritage of the community.

The actual gift of the adobe to the city occurred on September 23, 1963. The first order of business was to demolish the wooden structure shown at the top of this page and assess the condition of the adobe walls. In this photograph, taken on November 5, 1965, the original east wall appears in the background, while the north wall is being reconstructed by workmen.

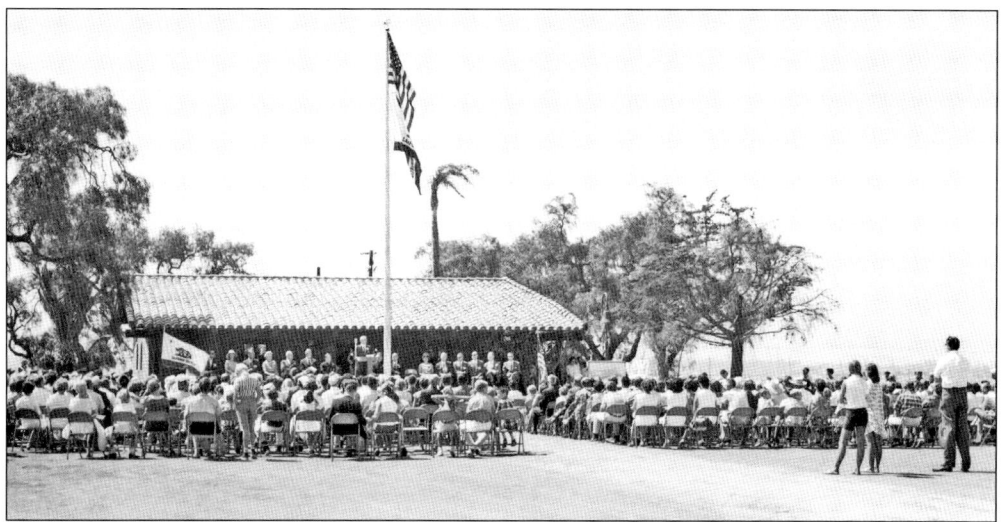

By the time of the dedication ceremony in Estancia Park on August 25, 1966, the Costa Mesa Historical Society had been formed and held its first board of directors meeting. The newly formed group transformed the adobe into a museum. The dedication was widely attended, and music was provided by the 3rd Marine Aircraft Wing Marching Band from El Toro Marine Corps Air Station.

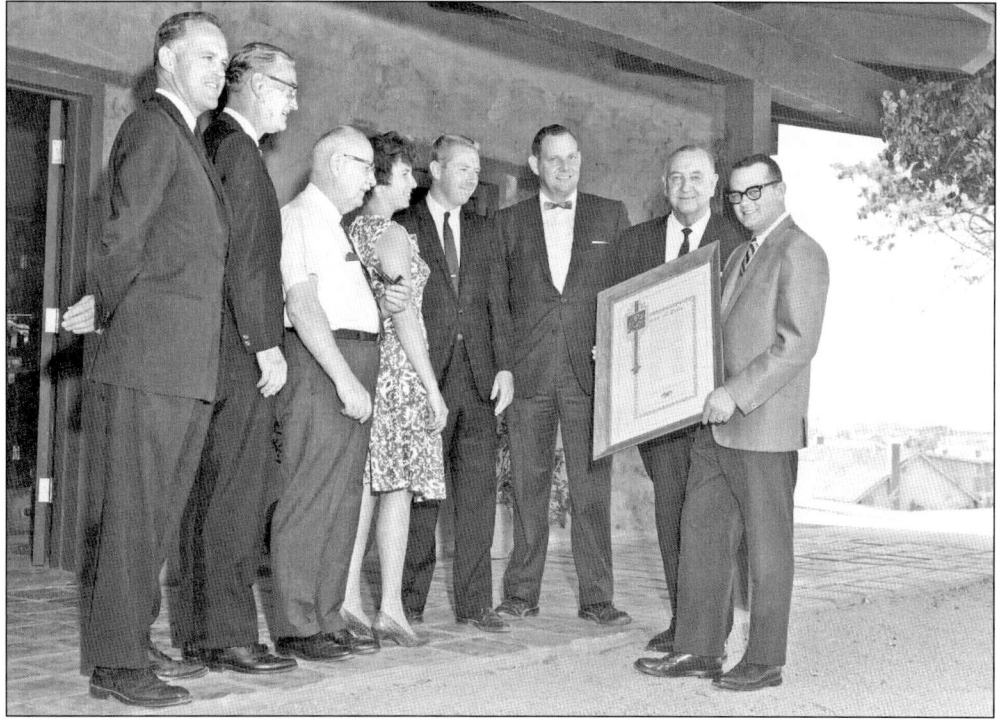

On the same day as the dedication ceremony pictured above, a representative of the First American Title Insurance Co. presented a chain of title for the adobe that began with the King of Spain and ended with the City of Costa Mesa. Pictured here are, from left to right, Henry Segerstrom, Willard Jordan (mayor), Charles Priest (city clerk), Beverley Barck (Costa Mesa Historical Society president), Calvin Barck (city councilman), Harold Segerstrom Jr., Harold Segerstrom Sr., and an unidentified representative of American Title Insurance Co.

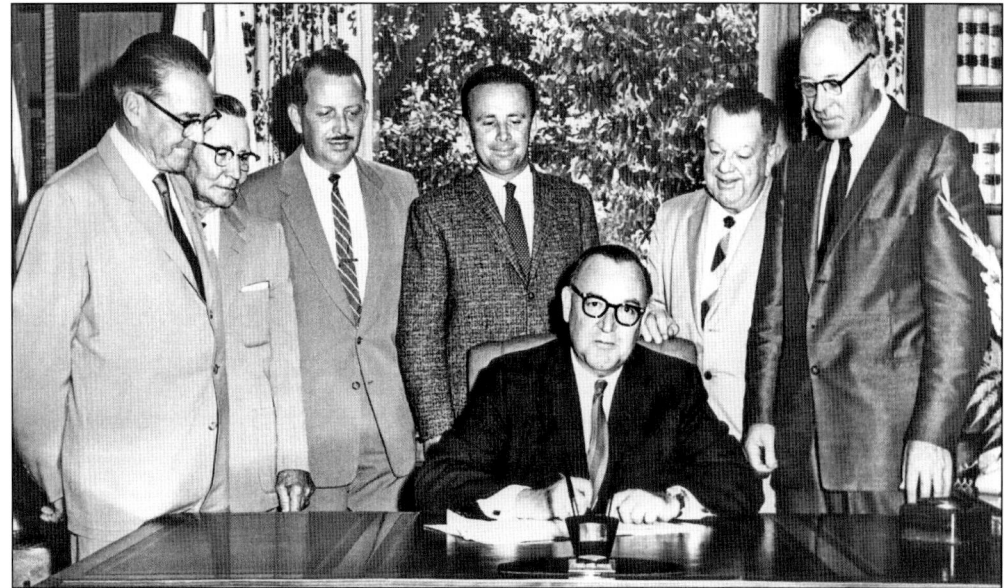

Although dry farming was the norm for early 20th century grain farmers, Costa Mesa was quick to learn that centralized, reliable sources of water were essential to the growth of the area. In 1955, the city formed its own water district in addition to four existing water districts. The four existing districts were in favor of consolidation but not under city control. In June 1959, Gov. Edmund "Pat" Brown signed Senate Bill 1375, which created the Costa Mesa County Water District, with the Santa Ana Heights Water District opting out. Shown standing behind Governor Brown are, from left to right, Charles TeWinkle, Prentice Thompson, Robert Unger, Mario Durante, Fred Wilson, and state senator John Murdy.

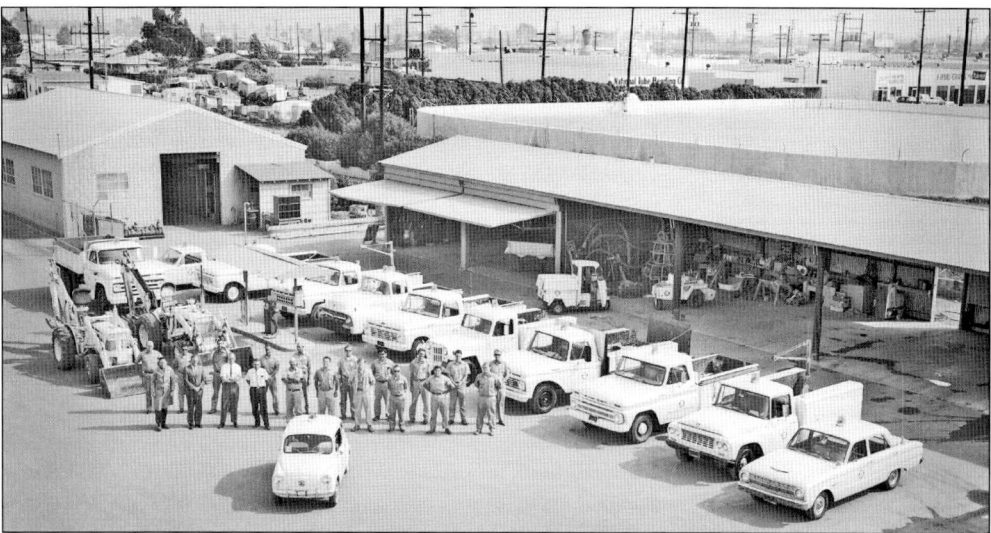

Staff and equipment of the Costa Mesa County Water District are assembled in the district yard at 1971 Placentia Avenue for this group photograph on October 21, 1966. During the 1960s, the district pumped some water from the Orange County groundwater basin, but imported water purchased from the Metropolitan Water District was plentiful and cheaper than well water. The Placentia Reservoir, inherited from the predecessor Fairview County Water District, can be seen behind the equipment shed at right.

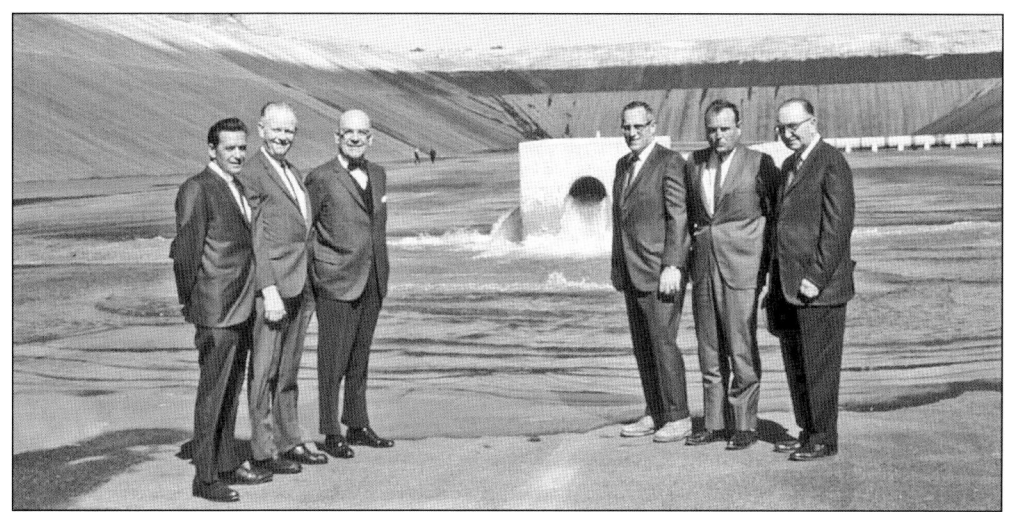

By 1970, the Costa Mesa County Water District had more than doubled its service connections and had begun servicing new areas such as South Coast Plaza and the Orange County Airport industrial area. To address this demand, the district leased 600 acre-feet of storage capacity in the San Joaquin Reservoir. Shown here in March 1966, the new reservoir is filling with water for the first time. Pictured from left to right are Carl Stevens (director), Alvin Pinkley (director), Nicholas Ziener (executive manager, Costa Mesa Chamber of Commerce), DuWayne Lidke (engineer), Ray Wallace (manager), and Edward Bennett (director). After the enactment of more stringent water-quality regulations, the reservoir was emptied in 1994.

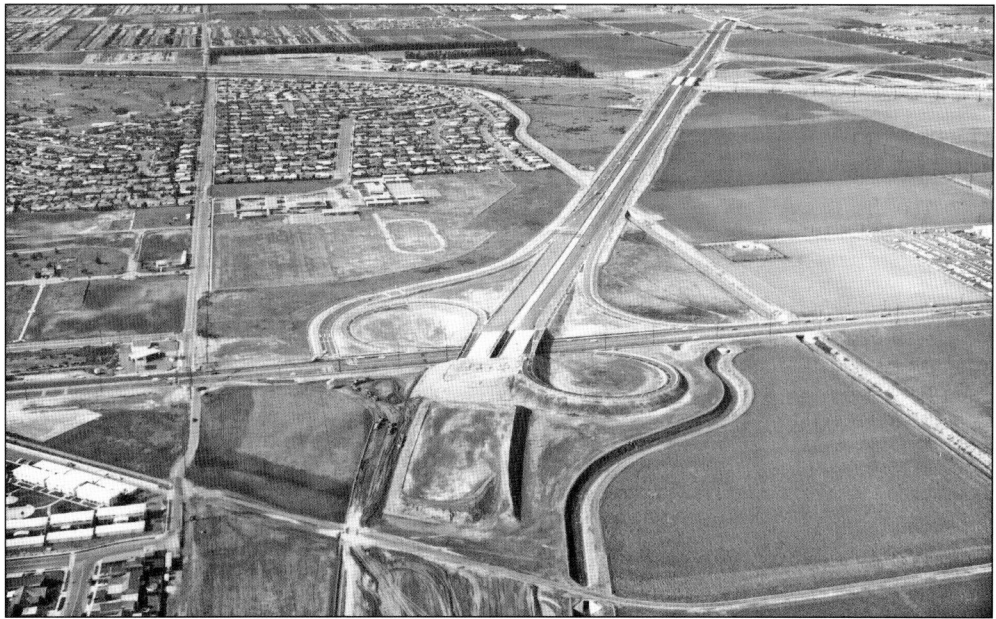

When this aerial photograph looking west was taken on December 12, 1966, the San Diego Freeway had been open to Harbor Boulevard for just a few days. In this view, Gisler Avenue runs vertically left of center, while Harbor Boulevard runs horizontally at center. Orange County Flood Control Channel No. D03 runs diagonally from lower right to upper center, where it curves to the left and drains into the Santa Ana River. The final link of the San Diego Freeway (I-405) opened to the Santa Ana Freeway (I-5) in 1968. The San Diego Freeway had taken 13 years to complete.

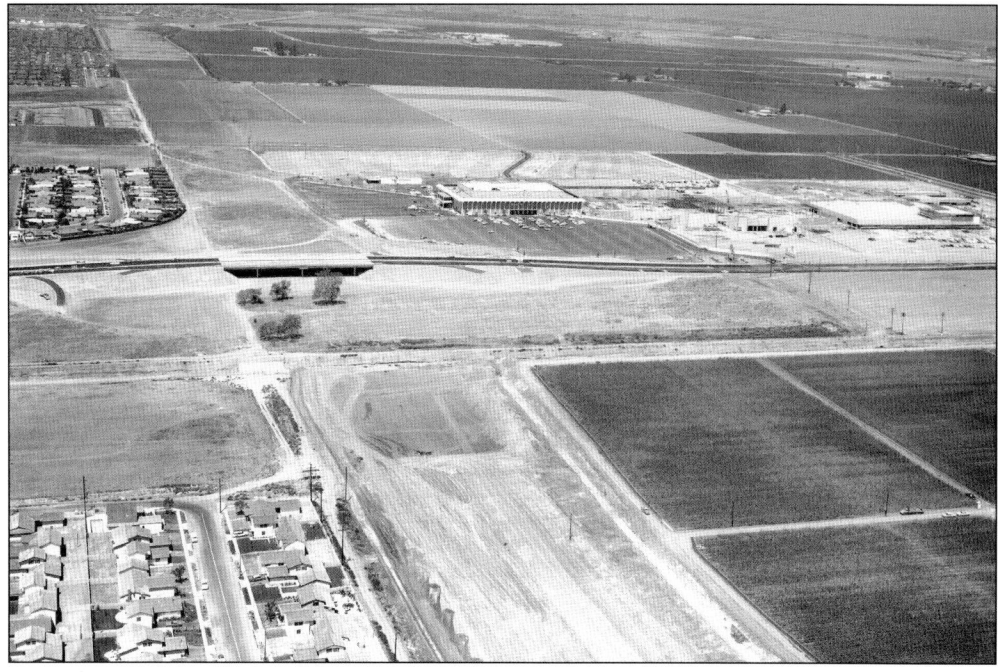

With the route of the San Diego Freeway decided, construction work began on a new, freeway-adjacent project, South Coast Plaza, that was destined to make Costa Mesa a world-renowned destination. Shown here in 1966, May Company, at center, had opened, while Sears Roebuck, at right, was still under construction. Also under construction were 86 mall shops located between the two anchor stores. South Coast Plaza represented a gamble by Harold and Henry Segerstrom to convert one of their lima bean fields to a more suburban purpose.

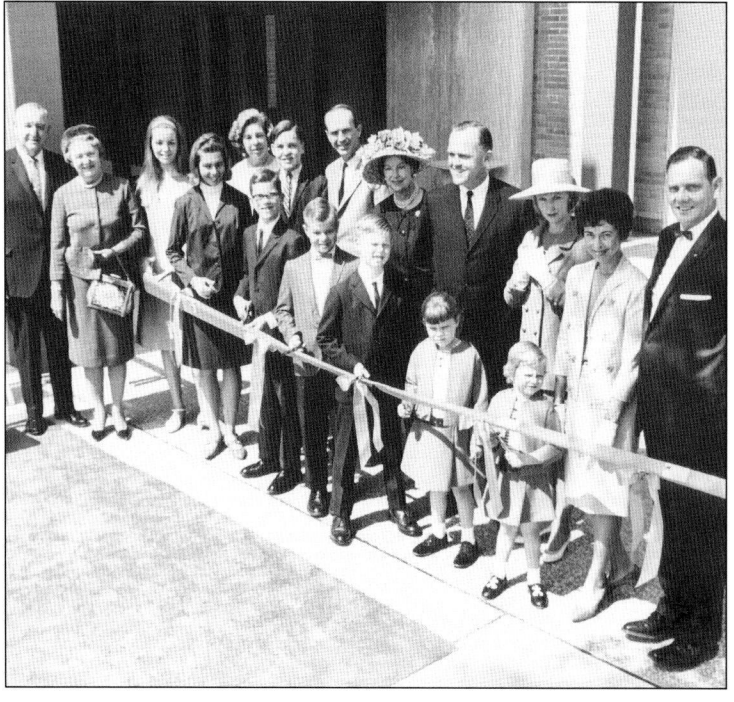

March 15, 1967, was the date of the official grand opening of South Coast Plaza. The ribbon-cutting was a Segerstrom family affair. Adults in the back row are, from left to right, Harold Segerstrom Sr., Veronica Segerstrom, Ruth Ann Moriarty, Eugene Moriarty, Ruth Segerstrom, Henry Segerstrom, Yvonne Segerstrom, Jeanette Segerstrom, and Harold Segerstrom Jr. Seven Segerstrom children stand at the ribbon with scissors at the ready.

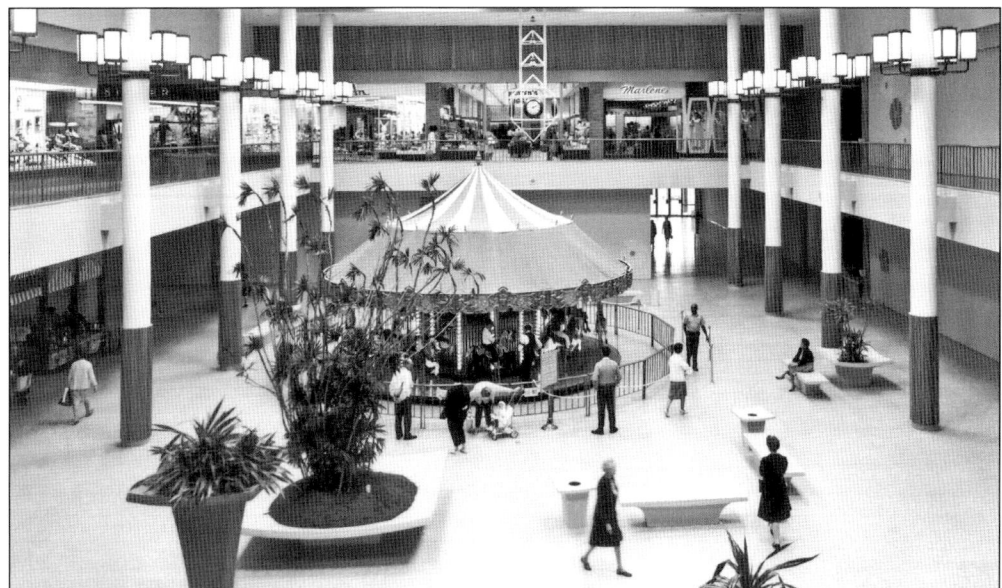

One of several foresights of Segerstrom and Sons was to enclose South Coast Plaza. Costa Mesa was known for enjoying a Mediterranean climate, so why go to the additional expense of building an enclosed, climate-controlled environment? The enclosure paid off handsomely, as South Coast Plaza became the largest mall on the West Coast, with the highest annual sales in the United States. Shown here in 1972 is Carousel Court, featuring an old-fashioned carousel that gave rides to more than 300,000 children annually.

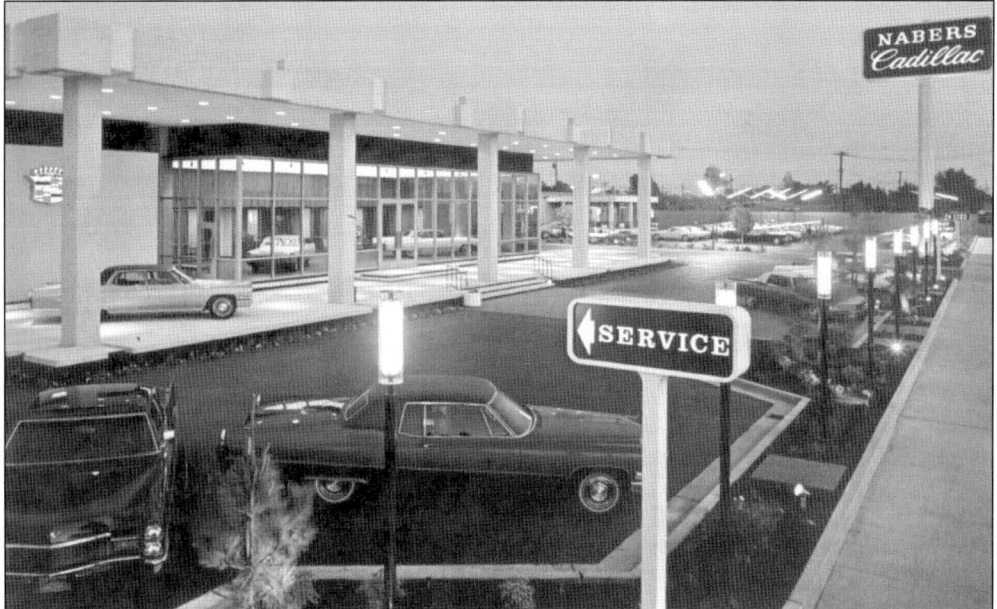

Although South Coast Plaza generated a major portion of Costa Mesa's sales tax revenues, the Harbor Boulevard of Cars was also a major source. The Boulevard Car Dealers Association was made up of 12 main dealerships representing the largest American and foreign automobile brands. Shown here in late 1968 is the recently opened Nabers Cadillac, at 2600 Harbor Boulevard. Theodore Robbins Ford had moved from Coast Highway to 2060 Harbor Boulevard in August 1966.

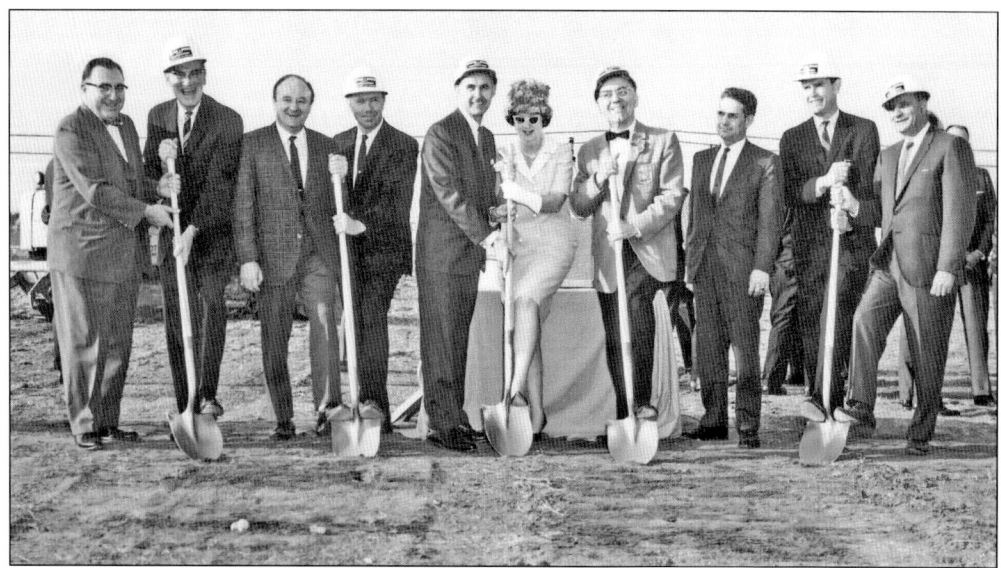

By the mid-1960s, Costa Mesa had grown to a population of more than 65,000 people. Some city departments such as police, fire, engineering, and parks still were not located at the city hall at 695 West Nineteenth Street. After spirited debate, the city council decided to build a new civic center on Fair Drive across from the Orange County Fairgrounds. Groundbreaking took place on March 17, 1966. Pictured here are, from left to right, Carl Boswell, Willard Jordan (councilmember), Lou Benny, Calvin Barck (councilmember), Robert Wilson (mayor), Peggy Reinert, Nicholas Ziener, unidentified, Thomas Thompson (councilmember), and Phillip Sullivan.

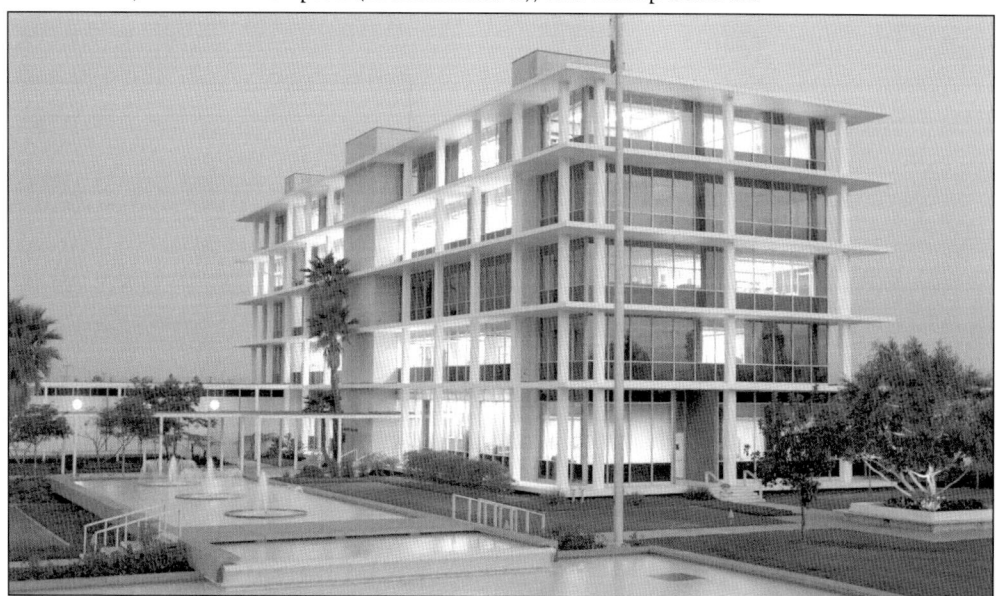

Costa Mesa's new civic center was dedicated on June 29, 1967, the date of the city's 14th anniversary. The $4-million civic center, including the adjacent police headquarters, gained recognition as the most complete and modern in Orange County. Finally, all city departments could be located on one campus. By 1969, the former city hall on West Nineteenth Street was leased to the Mardan School of Educational Therapy. In 1991, the old building was demolished to make way for the Costa Mesa Senior Center.

Four

COMING OF AGE

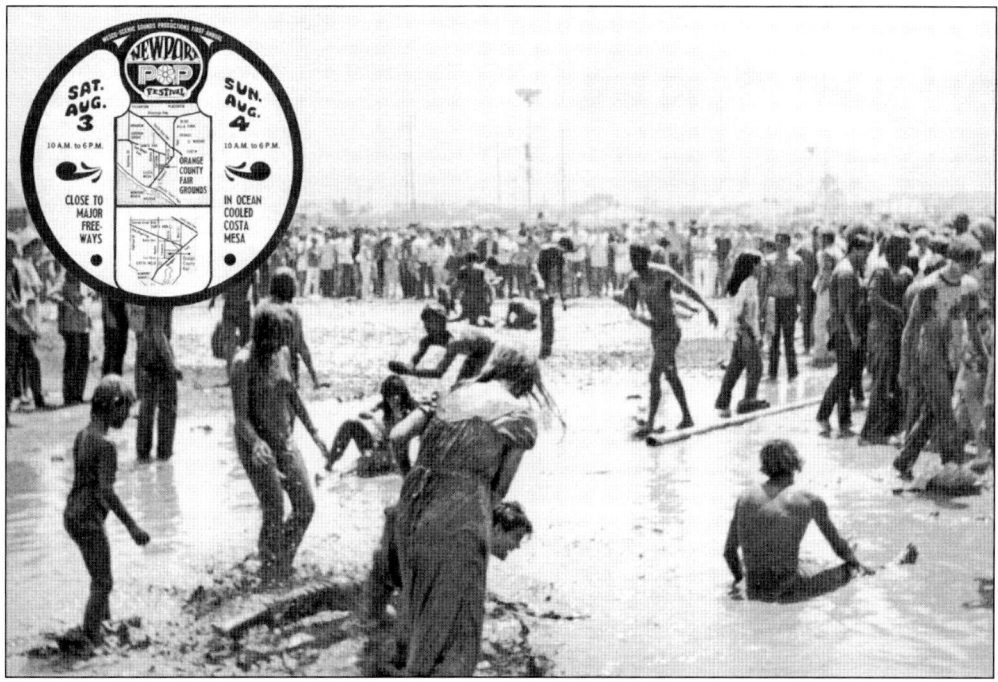

On the weekend of August 3–4, 1968, the view of the Orange County Fairgrounds from Costa Mesa's new civic center could not have been more displeasing to city officials. While the Vietnam War raged, the Newport Pop Festival was being held on the fairgrounds. More than 100,000 young people showed up to enjoy headliners such as Jefferson Airplane, Tiny Tim, Eric Burdon and the Animals, the Grateful Dead, and Steppenwolf. The weather was hot, so the festival area was hosed down and attendees took advantage of free mud baths. City officials vowed "never again." One year later, the first Woodstock Festival was held in New York State, featuring many of the same headliners listed here.

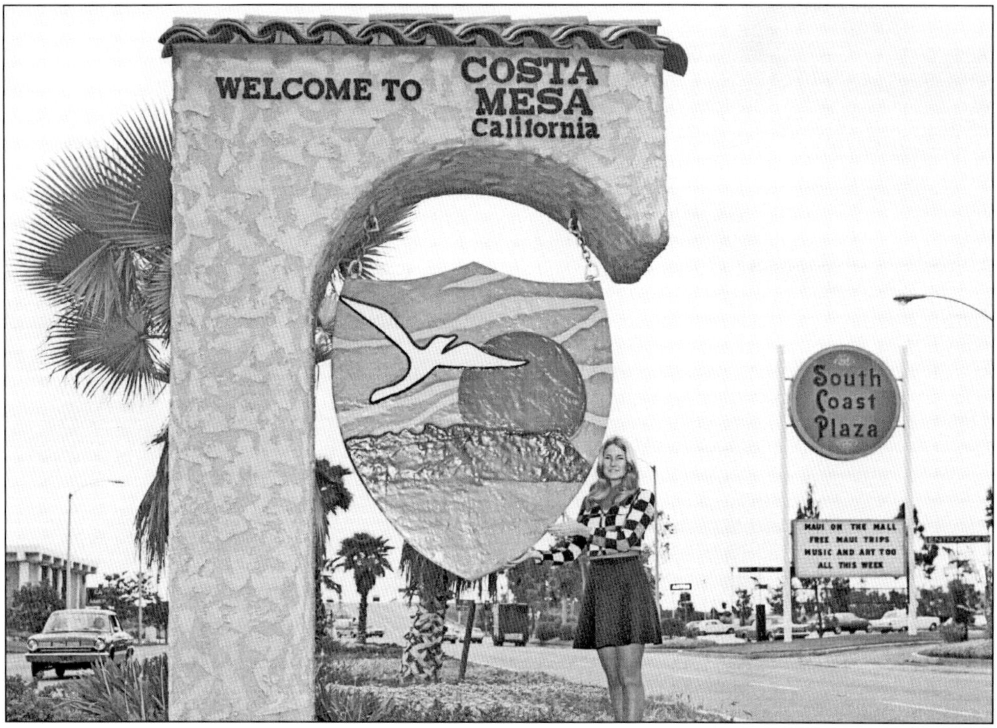

In the 1970s, Costa Mesa's branding effort included "Welcome to Costa Mesa" signs in place of conventional city limits signs. In 1972, Miss Costa Mesa Kiki Bowring added a bit of glamor to the welcome sign on Bristol Street at South Coast Plaza. The city's branding effort included a sun and sea emblem suspended from an arch built in the Spanish Colonial Revival style. When this picture was taken, South Coast Plaza was featuring a week of "Maui on the Mall," featuring music performances, art exhibits, and free trips to Maui.

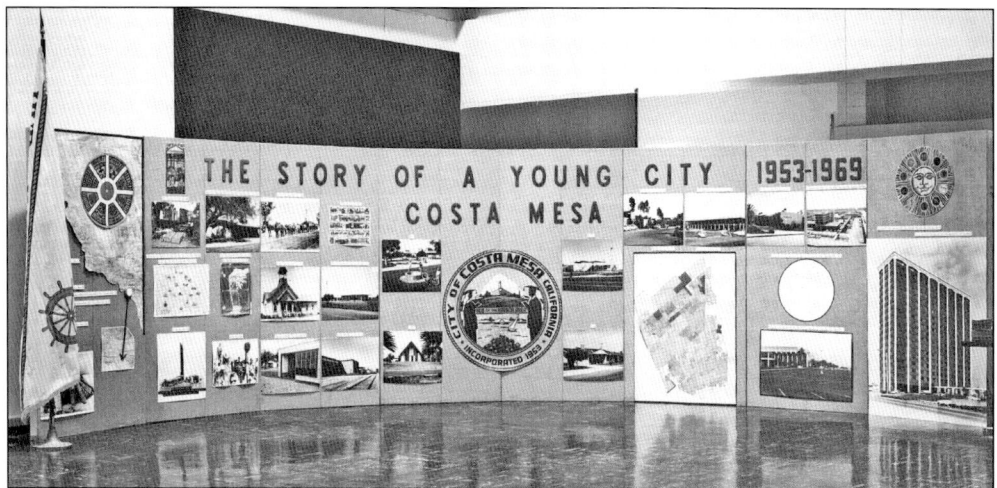

By 1969, Costa Mesa felt it had much to celebrate. Most of the strategic annexations had been completed. The city had built a state-of-the-art civic center. Orange County's tallest building, Bethel Towers, had been built. The 405 Freeway had been completed. Hyland Laboratories had opened a 162,000-square-foot facility in northwest Costa Mesa. Population had grown to 72,950. Costa Mesa had spread its wings during the "Soaring Sixties."

Bethel Towers, at 666 West Nineteenth Street, was built and operated by the Assemblies of God to provide reasonable-cost housing to senior citizens. The building, designed in the midcentury New Formalism style, was funded by a 50-year low-interest loan from the US Department of Housing and Urban Development. Construction was completed in the summer of 1968. Nearly 300 seniors moved into the 18-story high-rise apartment building. The building was later renamed the Tower on Nineteenth, and the address would be renumbered from 666 to 678 West Nineteenth Street to eliminate any reference to the Biblical "mark of the beast."

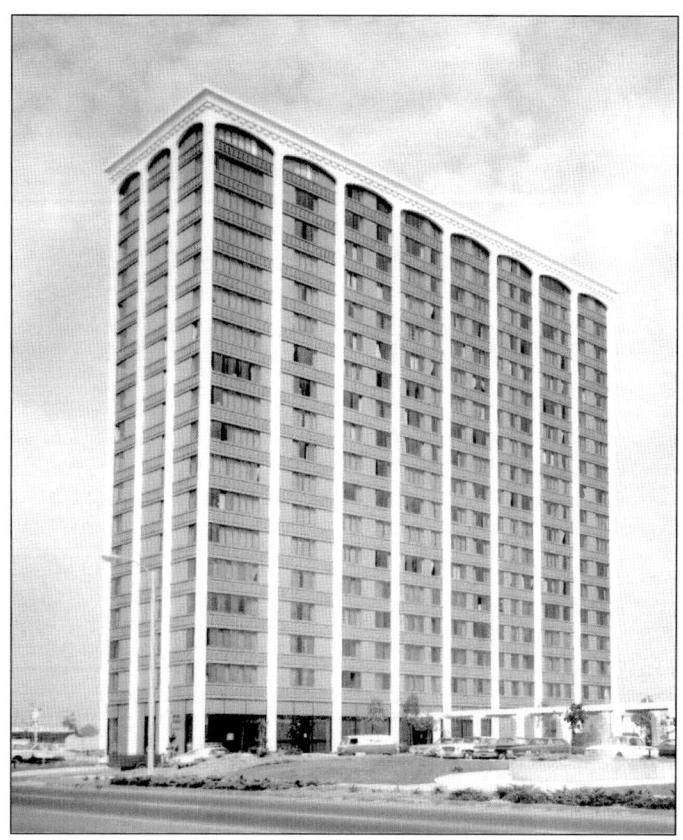

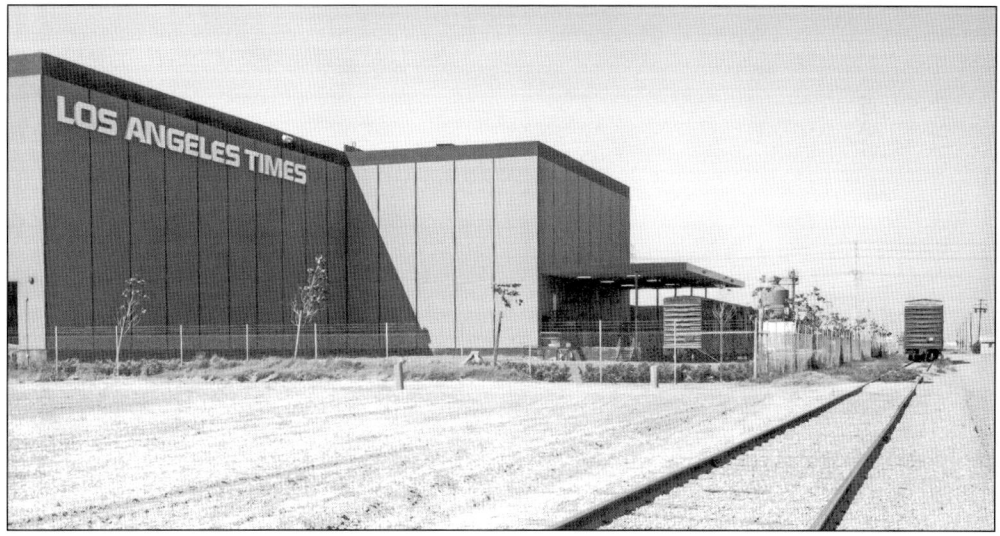

In 1968, the *Los Angeles Times* opened a printing plant on a 26-acre site in Costa Mesa to help produce the paper's Orange County edition. The new facility at 1375 Sunflower Avenue was adjacent to a rail spur that had previously run down to the warehouse area of the Santa Ana Army Air Base. The rail access was important for delivery of large rolls of newsprint to the printing plant. The *Times* shut down the Costa Mesa printing operation in 2010 and relocated all remaining staff by October 2014.

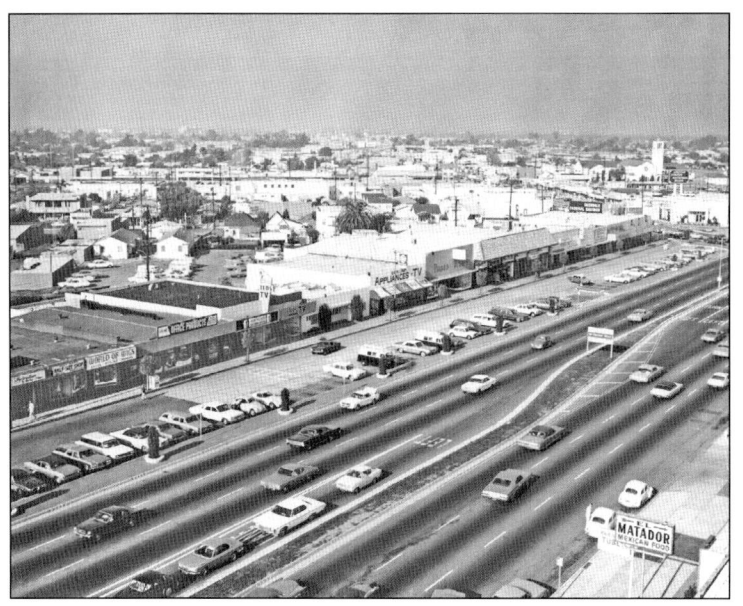

In the early 1970s, the Costa Mesa Fire Department undertook a project to photograph the downtown commercial district block-by-block in order to enhance fire protection. The photographs were taken from the top of a fully extended aerial ladder truck. This view, looking north, shows the 1801–1845 block of Newport Boulevard, with the intersection with Harbor Boulevard at upper right.

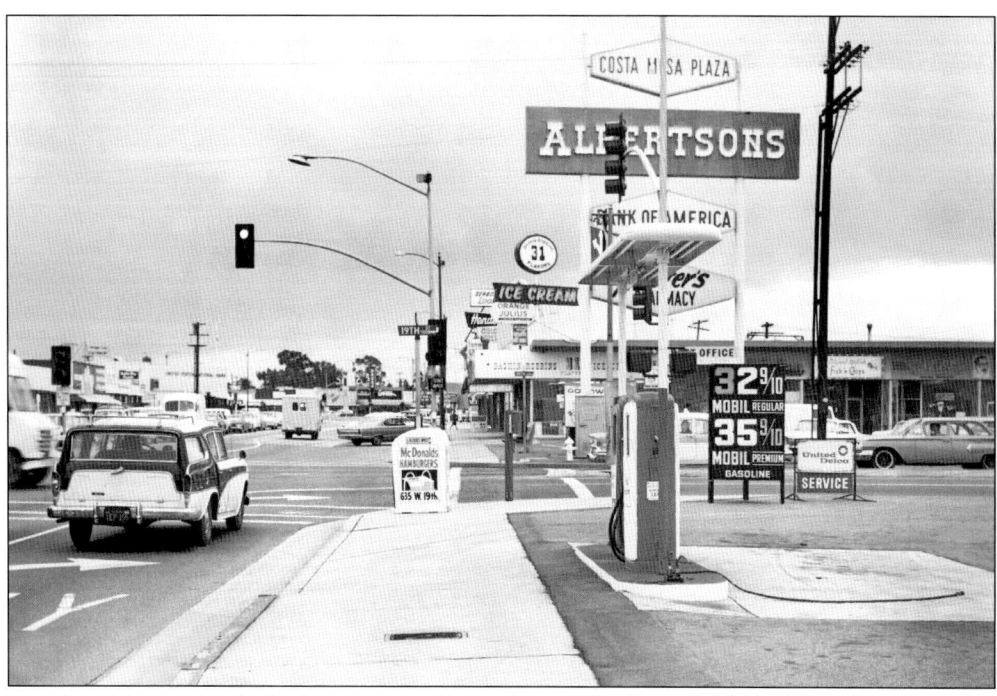

Gasoline prices seemed a bit more reasonable back in 1967, when oil sold for $3 per barrel. In this view south at the busy intersection of Harbor Boulevard and West Nineteenth Street, signage promoted businesses located farther west on Nineteenth Street, such as Albertsons, Bank of America, and McDonalds. The latter two still have branches on West Nineteenth Street, while Albertsons and Baskin-Robbins have moved farther north along Harbor Boulevard.

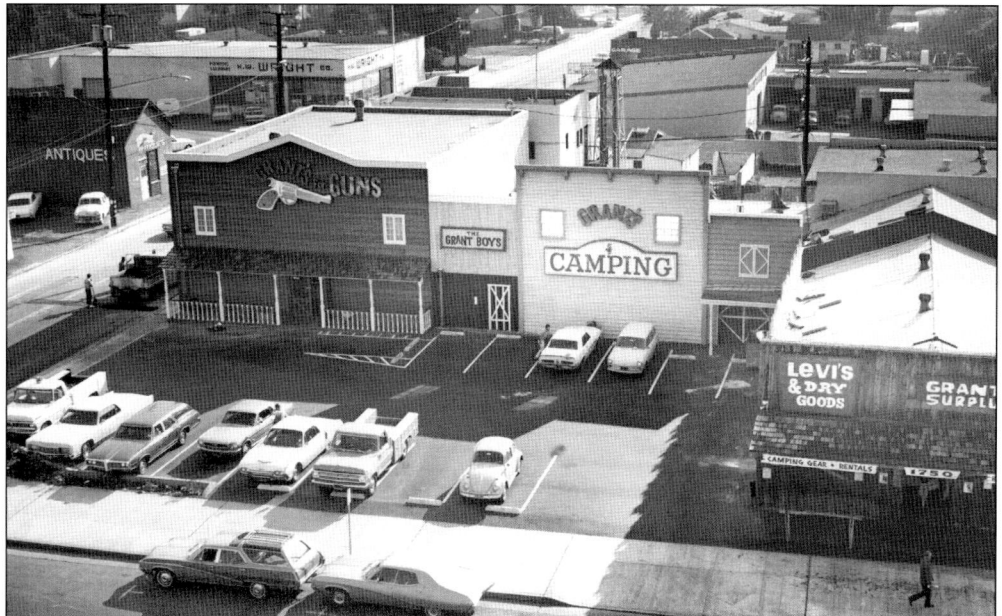

Grant Boys has run its family-owned sporting goods business at 1750 Newport Boulevard since 1949. This c. 1970 aerial ladder view shows the sprawling false-front store, with a portion of Costa Mesa Fire Station No. 3 at 111 East Rochester Street appearing behind the left-hand Grant Boys building. Farther along East Rochester Street is H.W. Wright Co., a family-owned business founded in 1932.

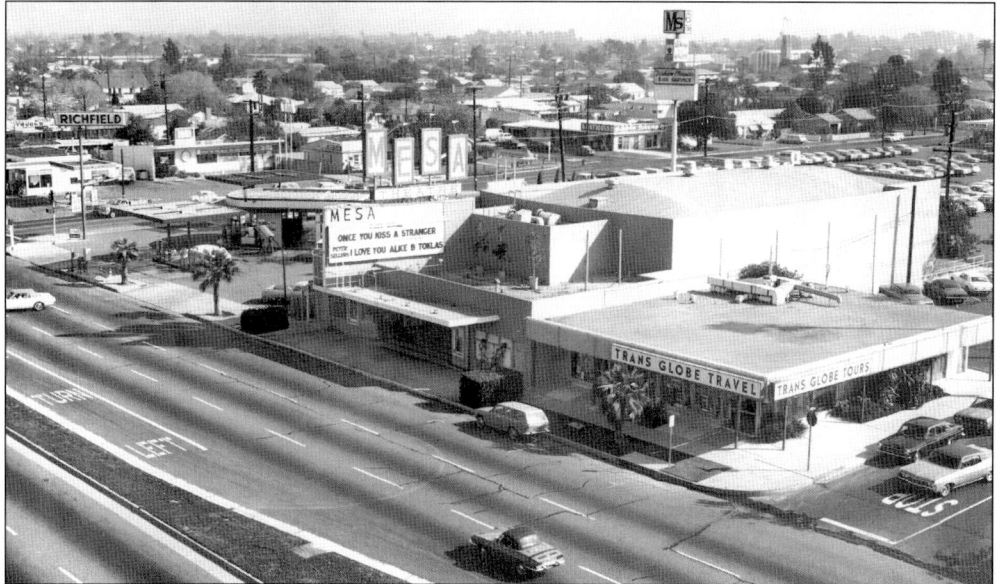

Although there had been talk of building a moving picture house in Costa Mesa as early as 1924, the city did not have its own movie theater until November 1948, when the Mesa Theater had its gala opening. Located at 1884 Newport Boulevard, the theater turned to screening second-run movies at bargain prices. In this c. 1970 aerial ladder view, the double feature included *Once You Kiss a Stranger* (1969) and *I Love You Alice B. Toklas* (1968). The theater was demolished in 1998 to make way for a Borders bookstore.

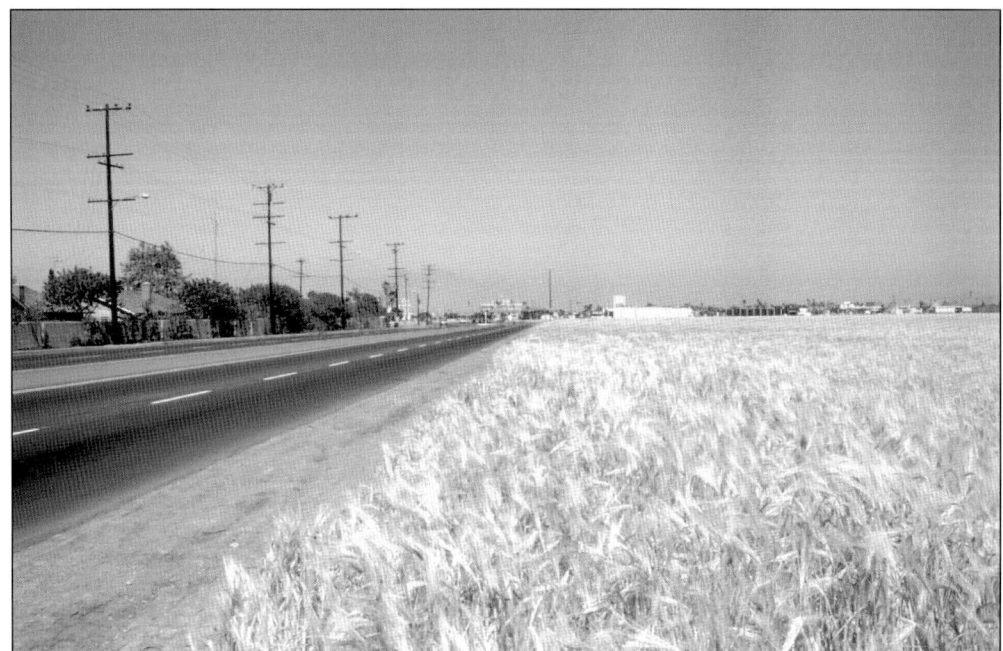

Shown here is a view looking east along Adams Avenue in June 1970. On the horizon at center appears the Thriftimart store at 2701 Harbor Boulevard. The lower property tax rates on agricultural land incentivized ongoing farming of undeveloped parcels in North Costa Mesa. The field shown here became a housing tract known as the Upper Bird Streets, comprising 304 upscale homes.

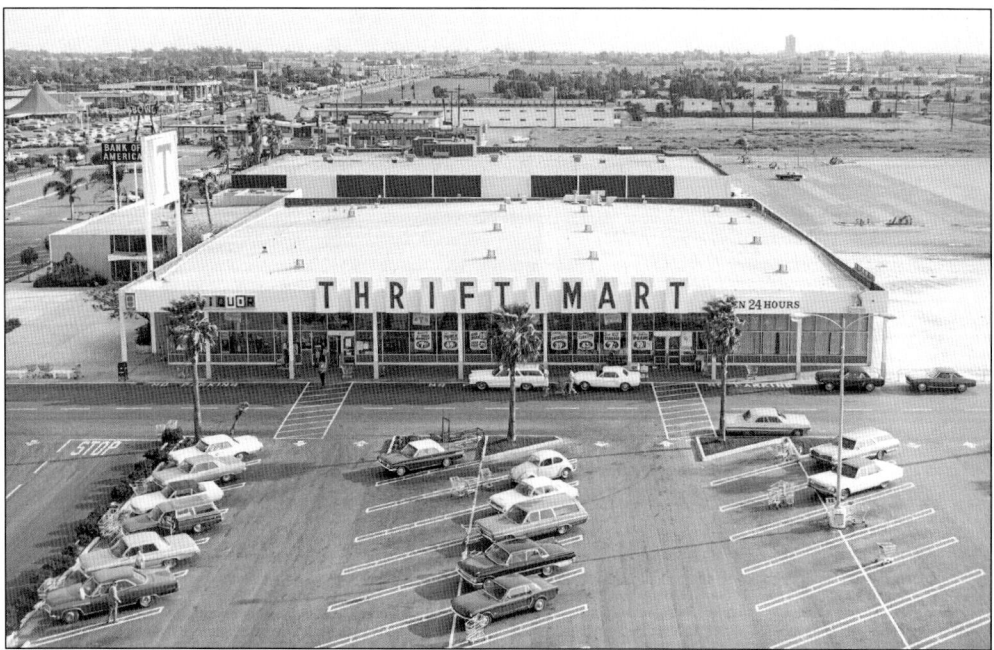

Thriftimart, "The Tall T," had its roots in the Fitzsimmons Stores, Roberts Markets, and Smart & Final Iris Co. By 1961, there were more than 60 stores in the chain. This 1968 view shows Mesa Verde Center, anchored by a Thriftimart branch store that was open 24 hours. Appearing in the background at upper left are Kona Lanes, Bel Congo Motel, and Hollister's Nursery.

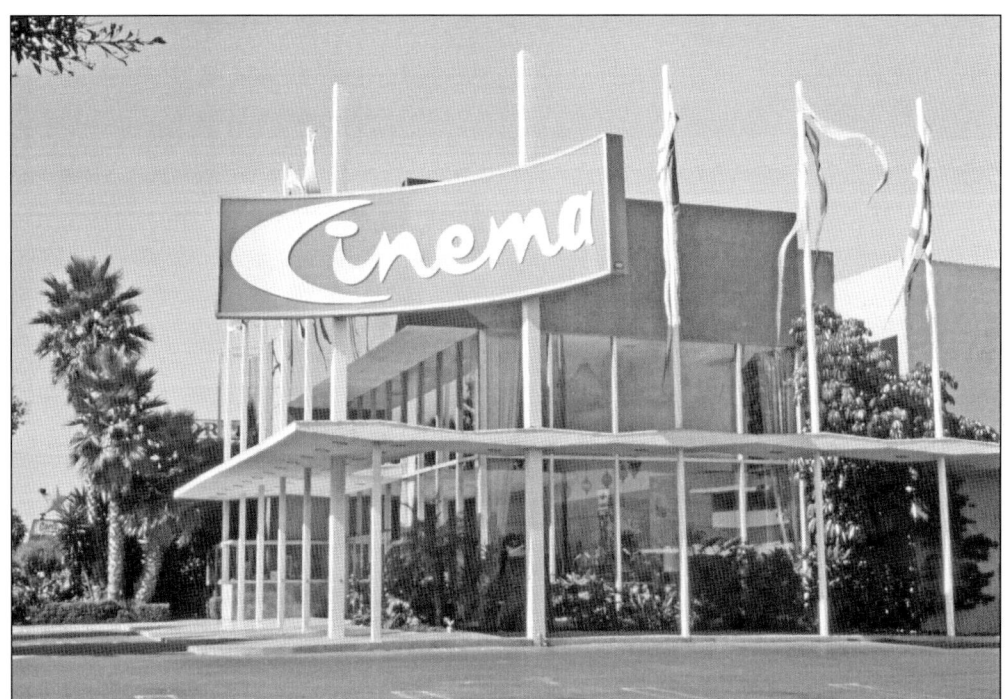

Edwards Cinema Theater at 1534 Adams Avenue was opened in 1963 as James Edwards II came out of retirement and convinced film distributors that Orange County could compete with Los Angeles for first-run movies. The theater closed in 2000 because of Edwards's bankruptcy and the fact that single-screen theaters had become noncompetitive. The renovated theater building later housed a Paul Mitchell school and then multiple restaurants. (Courtesy of Orange County Archives.)

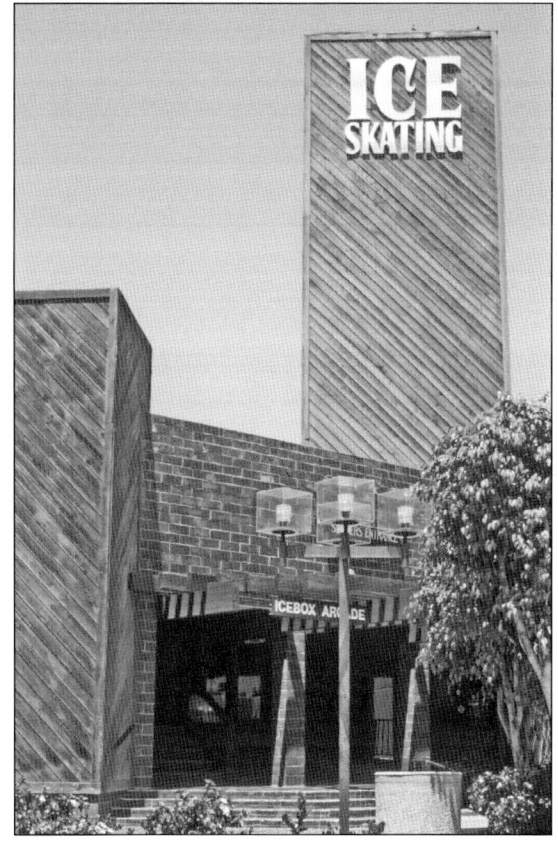

Across Adams Avenue from Edwards Cinema Theater was the Ice Capades Chalet, which opened in Mesa Verde Center in 1973. By 2000, business had declined, and despite the pleas and petitions of local parents, the Ice Chalet closed its doors on January 28, 2001. Olympic medalist Sasha Cohen had trained at the facility along with other skating hopefuls.

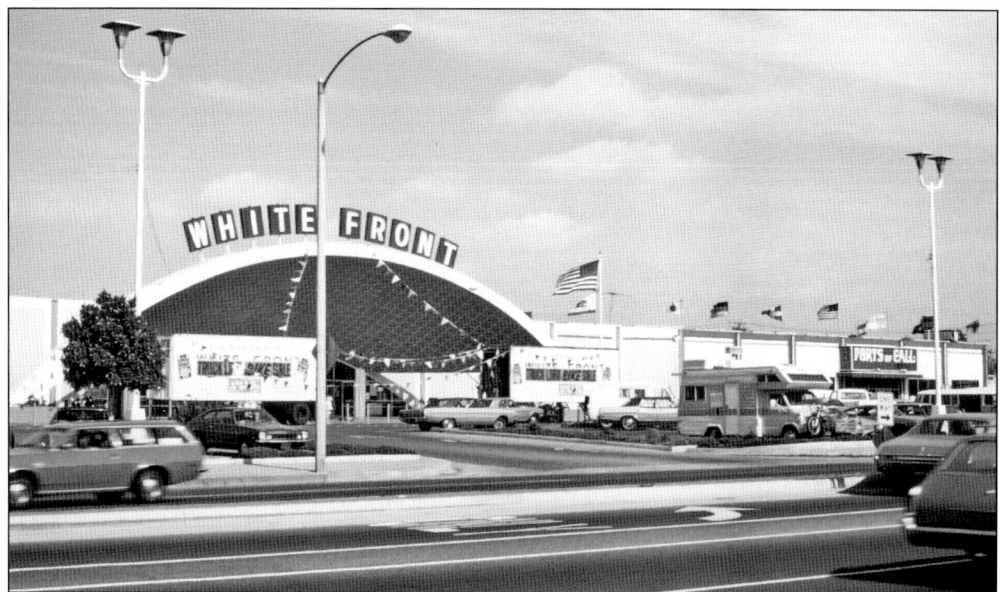

A White Front discount store opened in November 1966 at 3088 Bristol Street. Perhaps the store's location was intended to catch shoppers headed to or from upscale South Coast Plaza. On this afternoon in June 1973, store signs proclaimed "You can afford the things you want at White Front" and "Truck Load Bike Sale." The store closed after the parent company, Interstate Department Stores, filed for bankruptcy in 1974. White Front Pharmacy at 801 Baker Street inherited the name of its host store.

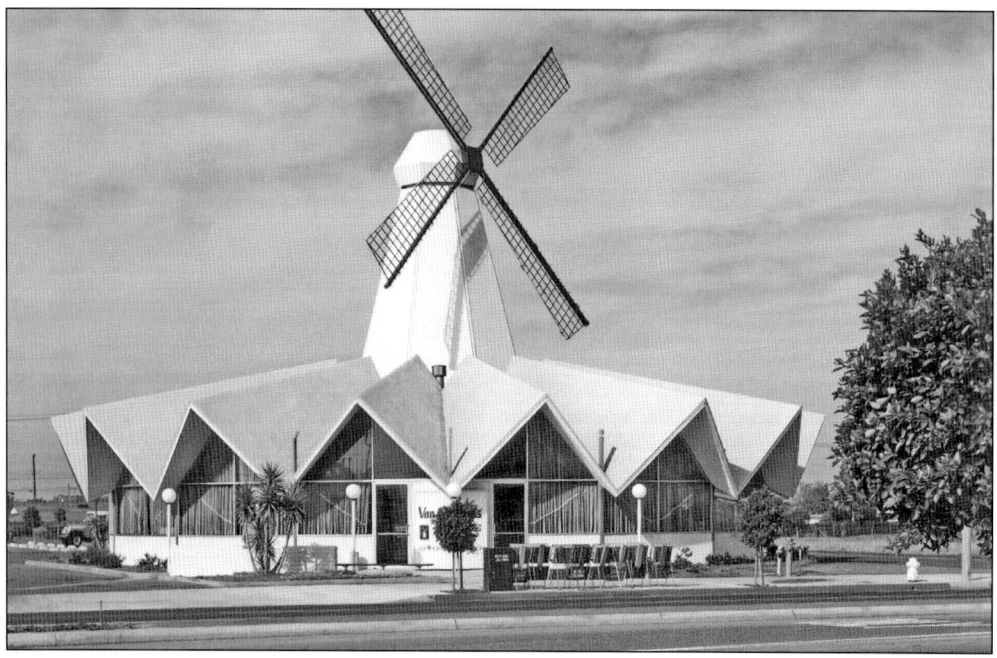

This Van de Kamp's coffee shop was relatively new when it was photographed in January 1971 at 3099 Bristol Street, across from the White Front discount store pictured above. By that time, Van de Kamp's had been acquired by General Host Corp. Faced with declining revenues, General Host sold the coffee shops to Tiny Naylors Restaurants in the mid-1970s.

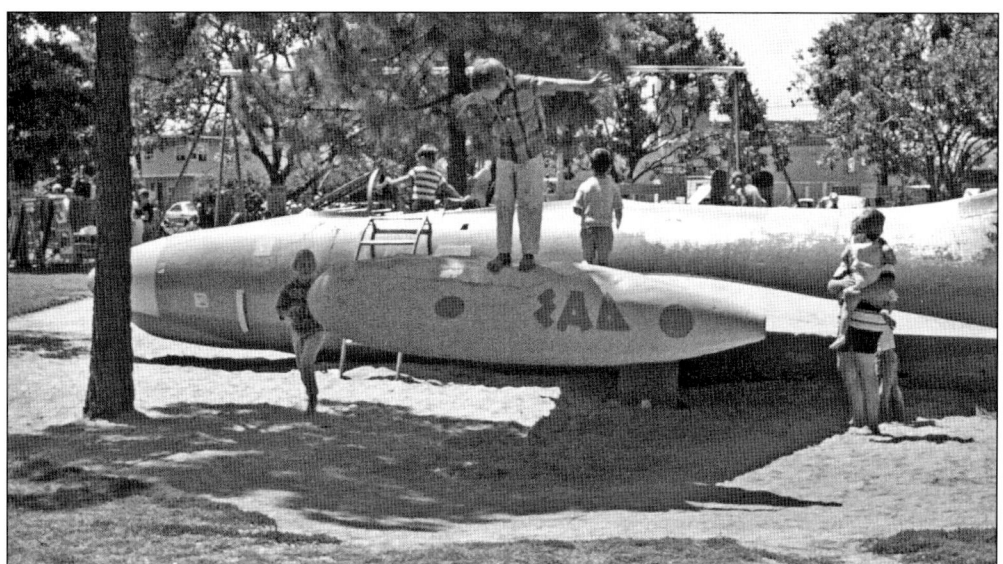

Airplane Park became the popular name for Costa Mesa Park (later Lions Park) after the Costa Mesa Exchange Club purchased a retired Korean War era F9F-4 Panther for $1 and installed the jet in the park in 1960. For more than 50 years, the airplane has been a source of enjoyment for local children. After years of wear and tear, the airplane was encased in a concrete skin. The photograph shown here was taken before the concrete in 1969. The most recent refurbishment was in 2013.

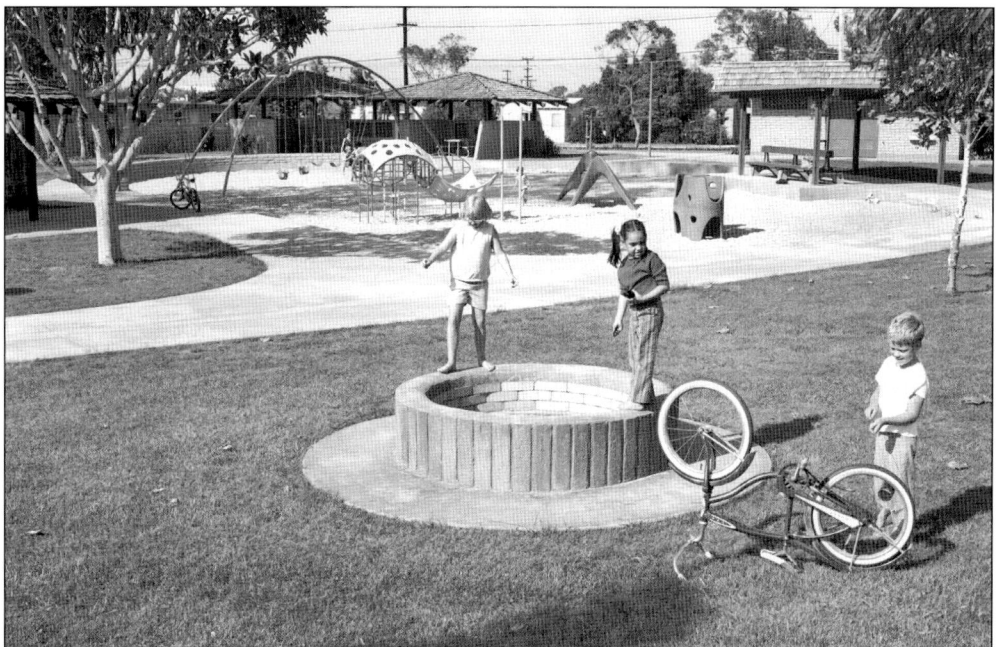

During its formative years, the City of Costa Mesa made a commitment to parks and recreation. By 1969, when this photograph of recently opened Heller Park was taken, the city had won an honorary award for excellence from the National Sports Foundation. A 1969 summer program brochure listed 11 neighborhood parks, 13 staffed playgrounds, and programs in aquatics, athletics, physical fitness, and social-cultural activities.

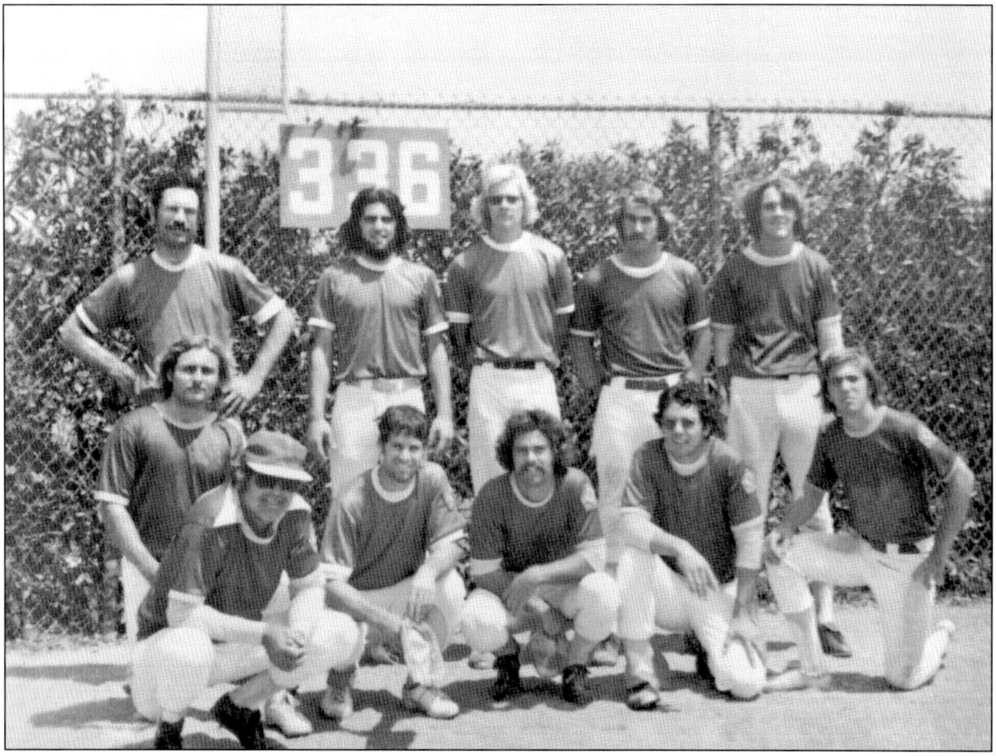

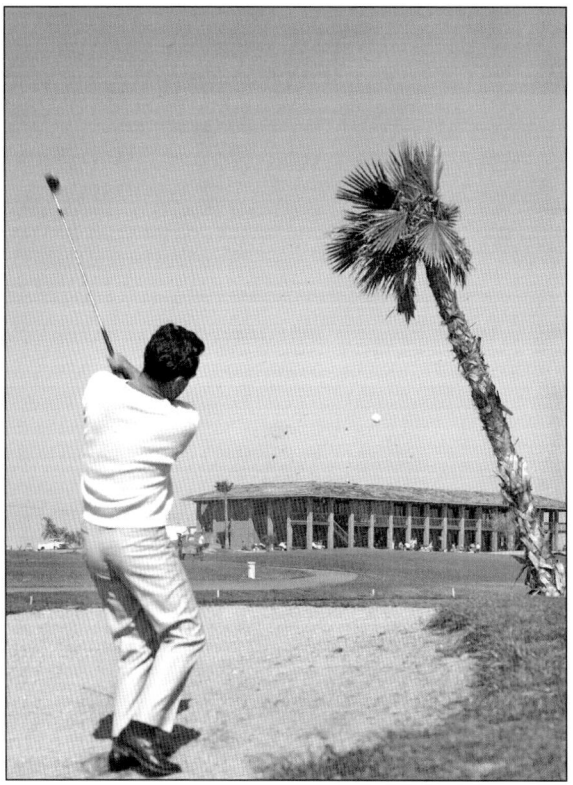

The Costa Mesa Comets semiprofessional baseball team was founded in 1964 by local businessman John Saint, shown here crouching down in the first row at far left. Saint was the team's coach and principal sponsor. The team was active in league competition at least until 1977, playing its home games at TeWinkle Park. John Saint was recognized for his work by a Costa Mesa City Council resolution in 1969 and by the Costa Mesa Chamber of Commerce in 1975. (Courtesy of Andrea Lennon.)

The city continued its focus on recreation by opening the 36-hole Costa Mesa Municipal Golf Course in July 1967. The 238-acre site surrounding Fairview State Hospital was leased from the State of California until it was purchased by the city in 1980 for $2.5 million—half of its appraised value—with the proviso that the land be kept as open space.

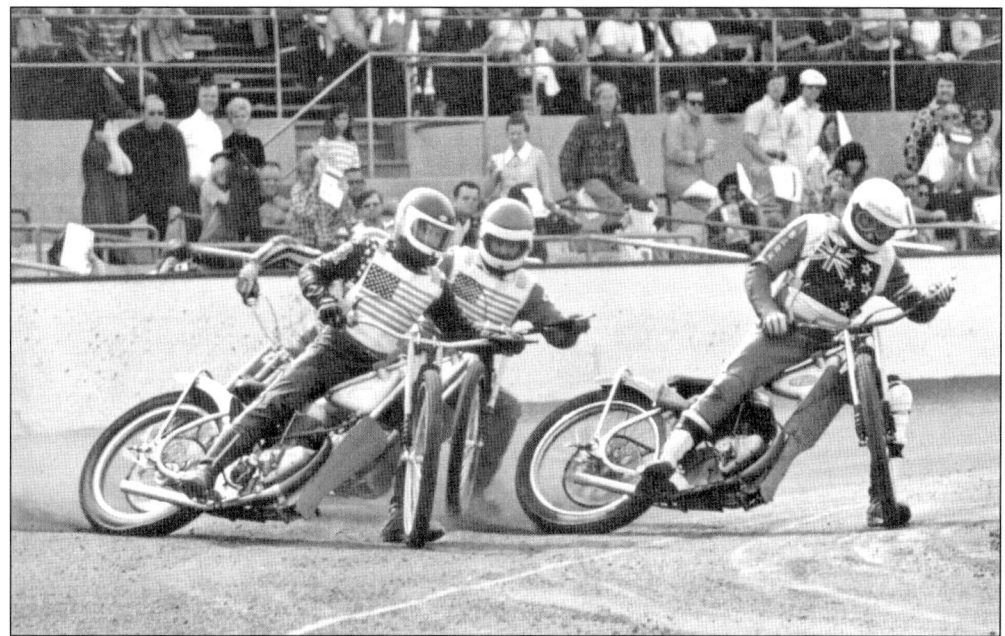

The construction of an arena with covered grandstand at the Orange County Fairgrounds provided a readymade home for the Costa Mesa Speedway. According to speedway publicity, the arena was home to the largest weekly motorsports event in North America. Capacity crowds jammed the tiny track every Friday night from April to November to watch the motorcycle races. Motorcycles such as these, pictured around 1970, burned exotic nitro-methane fuel and could accelerate from 0 to 60 miles per hour in three seconds flat.

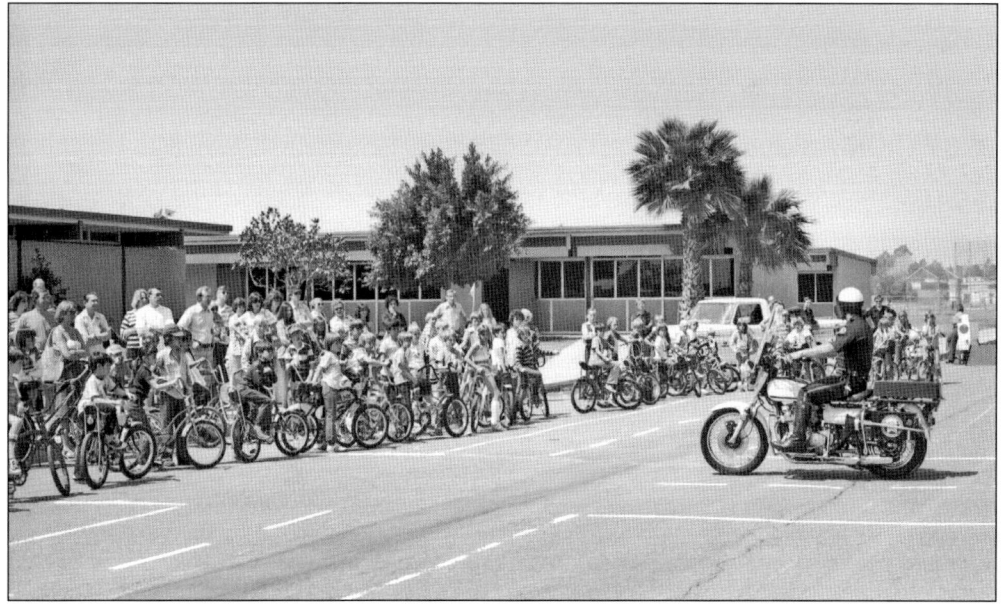

Community policing and community outreach continued as priorities for the Costa Mesa Police Department. Streets were busy with traffic, so bicycle rodeos were conducted at local schools to teach traffic awareness and safety. Competitive activities were held at the rodeos, such as this event in 1977, with trophies being awarded to top participants.

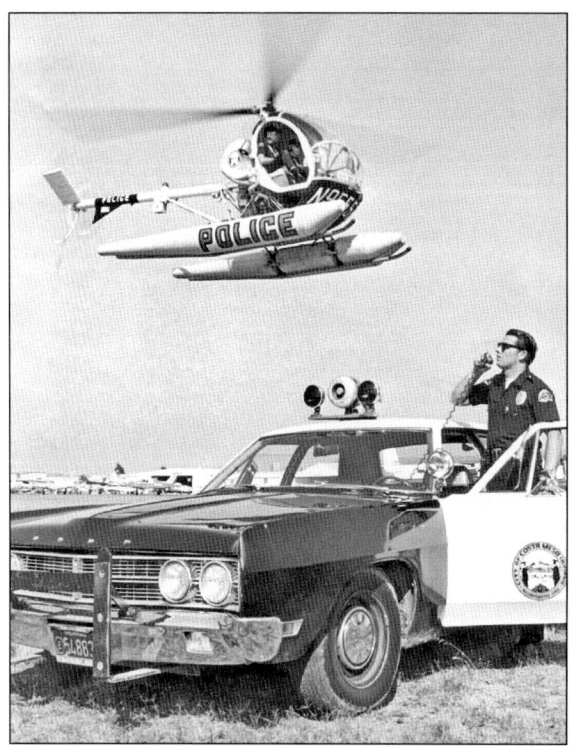

Costa Mesa became the second city in Orange County to add helicopter air support to its public safety capability, following Huntington Beach by just a few months. This 1970 photograph at Orange County Airport was taken in the early days of a program that ran for more than 40 years. An Airborne Law Enforcement (ABLE) joint powers program was formed with Newport Beach in 1997. Eventually, ABLE program costs resulted in the program being disbanded, and Huntington Beach was contracted to provide airborne support to Costa Mesa in lieu of the in-house program.

The Orange County Sheriff's Training Academy graduated its first class in 1965. Shown here in 1975 is the graduation ceremony for Sharon Lozzi, Costa Mesa's first female patrol officer. Lozzi was number one in her class.

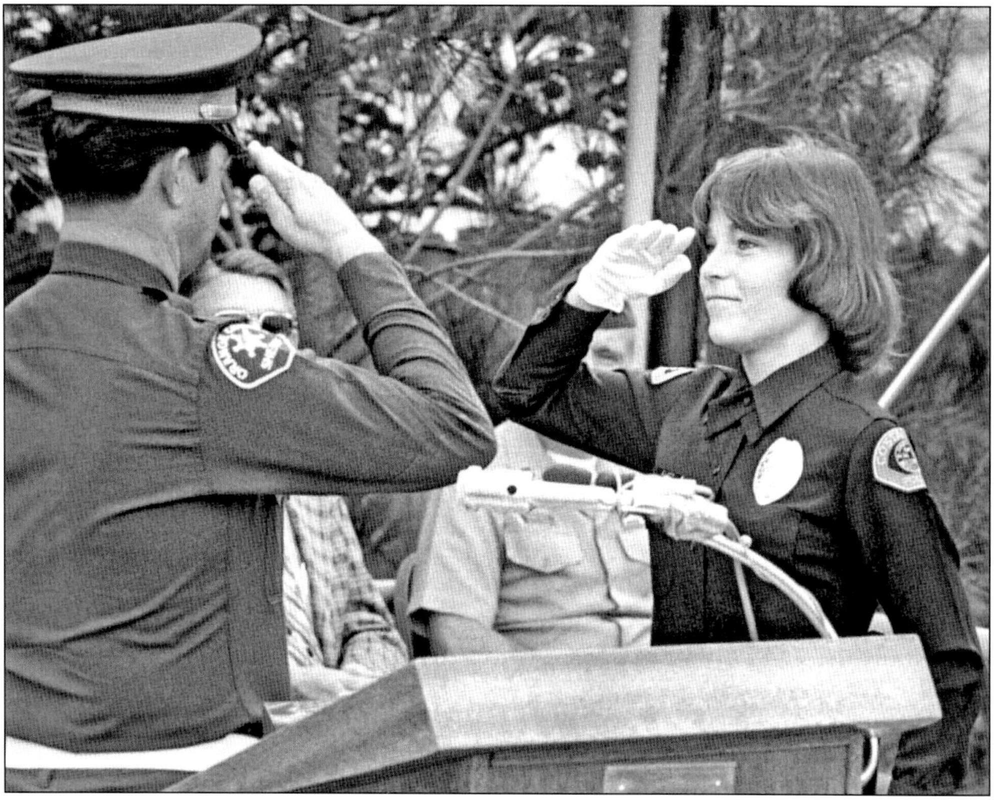

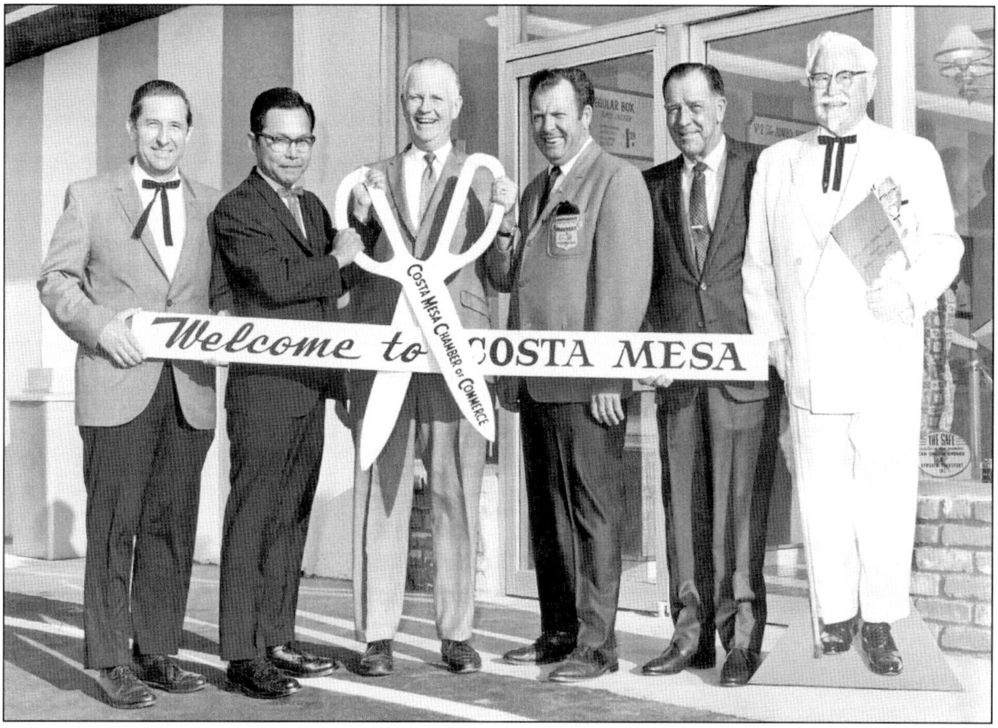

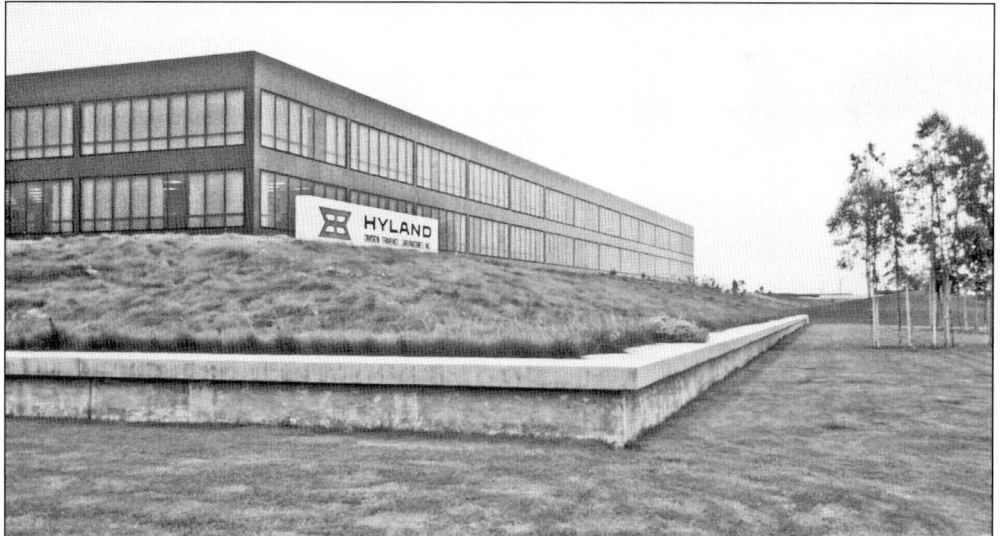

Fast food was no stranger to Costa Mesa. McDonalds had come to town, and in July 1969, Kentucky Fried Chicken opened at 2900 Harbor Boulevard. In this grand opening photograph, it appears that Colonel Sanders himself is present to assist local officials Mayor Alvin Pinkley (third from left) and Costa Mesa greeter Jack Hammett (fourth from left) with the ribbon-cutting.

In mid-December 1969, a new $6.6-million complex for the Hyland Division of Travenol Laboratories opened in the northwest commercial area of Costa Mesa. The building, located at 3300 Hyland Avenue, contained 162,000 square feet and employed 500 people in the pharmaceutical industry. Later, the building was occupied by ICN Pharmaceuticals and then Valeant Pharmaceuticals.

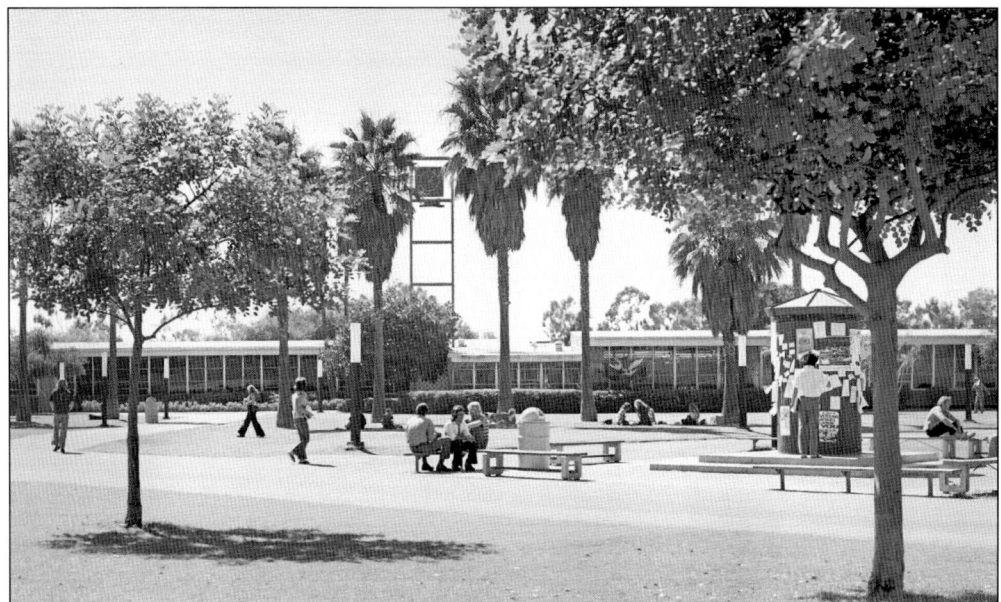

By its 20th anniversary in 1968, fall enrollment at Orange Coast College (OCC) had grown to 6,800 full-time day students and 9,000 night students. Ten years later, enrollment was approaching 30,000 students. Shown here is a view of the main quadrangle in 1973. The clock tower, appearing at center between palm trees, still watches over the quad today.

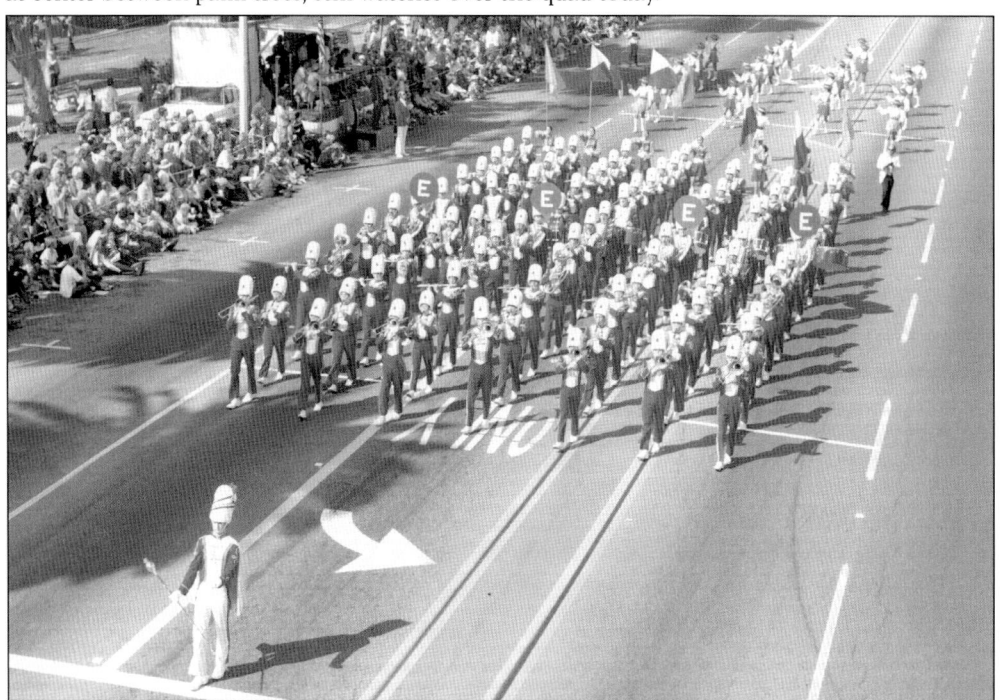

It was a banner year in 1975 for Estancia High School's marching band. Shown here is the Estancia Eagles Marching Band strutting its stuff in the 1975 parade competition sponsored by the Southern California School Band and Orchestra Association. The Eagles garnered the top score of 95.05 points. Way to go, Eagles!

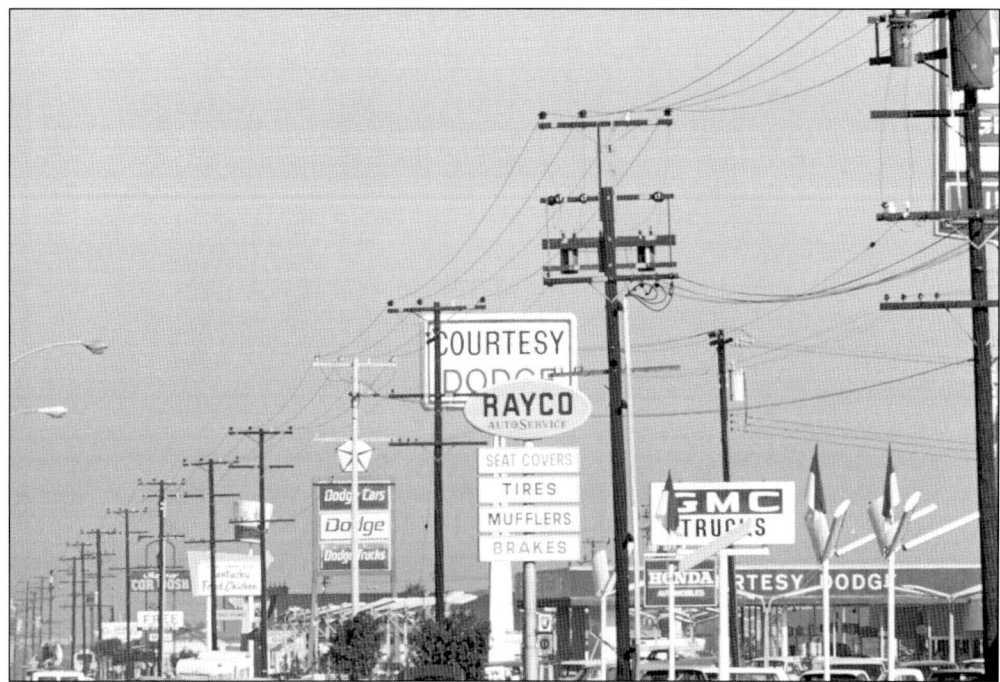

In December 1972, Costa Mesa was approaching its 20th anniversary. Population had grown to 75,710, and building permit valuations of $415 million had been issued, $54 million of which had been issued in 1972 alone. With such rapid growth, aesthetics had taken a back seat. The city Planning Department documented some of the scenes along major streets, such as this view looking north along the Harbor Boulevard of Cars.

The city council took action to beautify the city. In this 1974 photograph, Mayor Robert Wilson demonstrates his hands-on approach to city beautification as Southern California Edison moved its electrical lines underground and removed the overhead utility poles.

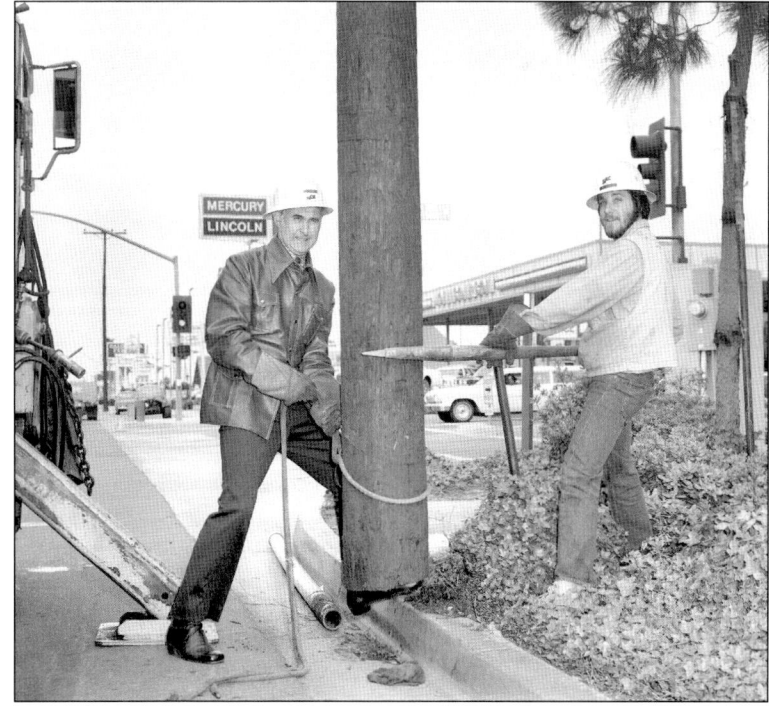

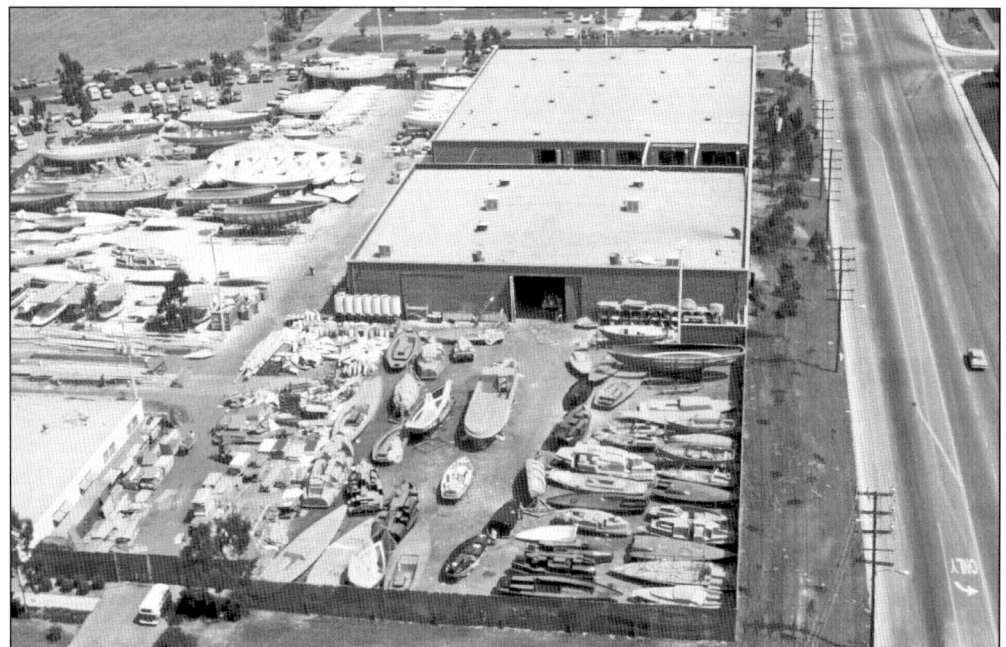

By the mid-1970s, fiberglass-based businesses were leaving town in droves. About 1970, Columbia Yachts had moved from West Eighteenth Street to the location shown here at 275 McCormick Avenue in Costa Mesa's airport industrial area. But that location was only a temporary stop on Columbia's journey to new headquarters in Virginia as a division of the Whittaker Corporation.

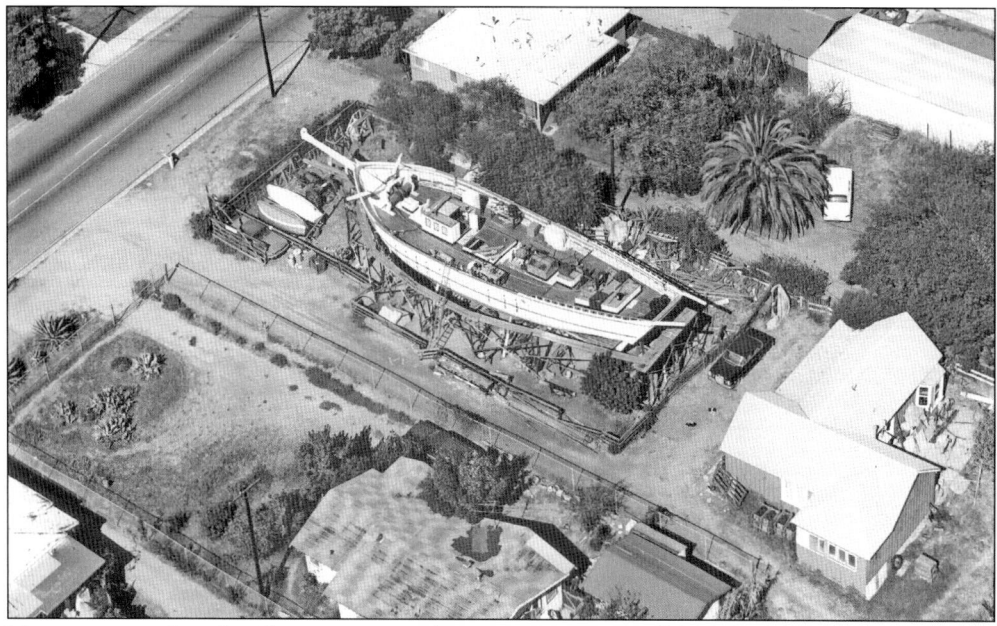

There was one boat building operation that was not going to be leaving town any time soon. Dennis Holland laid the keel of his Baltimore clipper on May 2, 1970. The tall ship was really taking shape at 2476 Santa Ana Avenue by the time this photograph was taken in 1975. Originally to be launched in time to participate in the nation's 1976 bicentennial, money problems delayed the launch of the *Pilgrim of Newport* another seven years until November 1983.

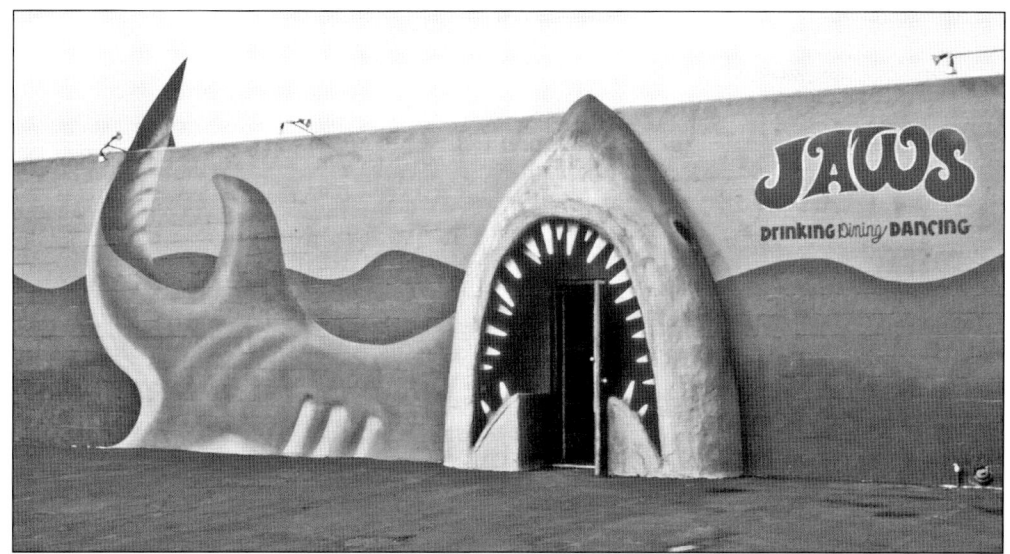

Costa Mesa had its share of turnovers in the commercial and retail business sector, but perhaps the record was held by a restaurant property located at 2285 Newport Boulevard. In 1974, Margarita's Mexican Restaurant was located at the site. Next, Margarita's became Spaghetti Joes', and then in 1975 it became Jaws, just a short time after the movie *Jaws* hit screens in June of that year. In 1977, Jaws became Desirees, a name that stuck for at least five years. By the early 2000s, the property had been reincarnated as Angels Auto Spa.

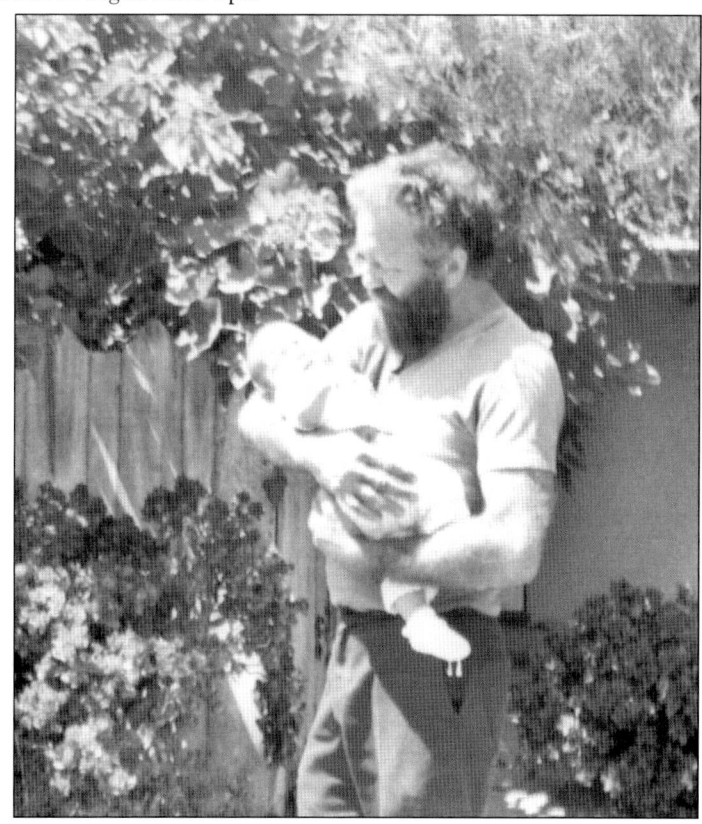

One restaurant businessman well known to municipal authorities in both Costa Mesa and Newport Beach was Sidney "Sid" Soffer, shown here in 1975 at his home at 900 Arbor Street, Costa Mesa. Soffer's concept of individual freedom and empathy for the underdog ultimately made him the area's best-known dissident. An extended cat-and-mouse scenario with code enforcement efforts eventually led to Soffer's emigration to Las Vegas, where he continued to run his local restaurant business by remote control until his death in 2007. (Courtesy of Shima Soffer Behrend.)

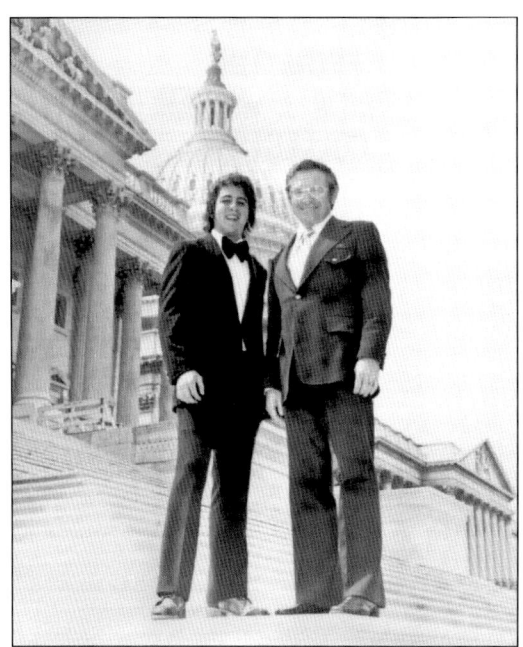

With the approach of the nation's bicentennial, Costa Mesa civic leaders swung into action. Donald Bull headed the Bicentennial Committee. The Costa Mesa Jaycees collaborated with the Bicentennial Committee to publish an updated edition of Edrick Miller's 1970 book on Costa Mesa history, *A Slice of Orange*. The committee also sponsored an essay contest. Shown here is the 1974 contest winner, Jim Scott Jr., with Congressman Andrew Hinshaw.

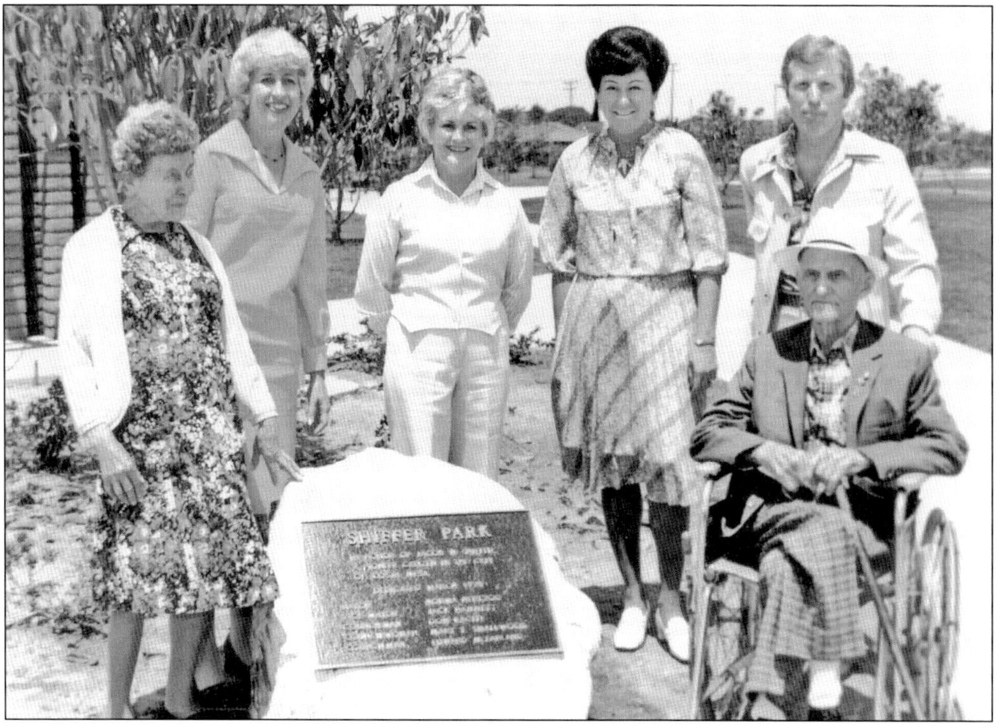

Costa Mesa continued to add neighborhood parks for the enjoyment of residents. On May 20, 1978, city council members dedicated Shiffer Park in honor of one of the pioneer families in the area. Shown here at the park dedication are, from left to right, Grace Shiffer, Norma Hertzog (councilmember), Mary Smallwood (vice mayor), Arlene Schafer (councilmember), Edward "Ed" McFarland (mayor), and Jacob "Jake" Shiffer. Hertzog and Smallwood were the first and second women respectively to be elected to the Costa Mesa City Council.

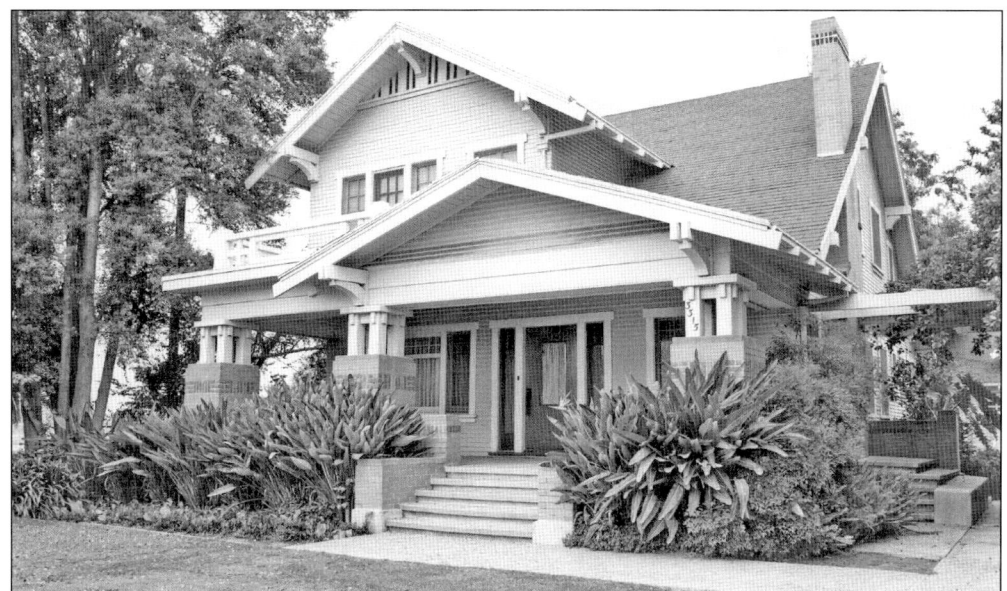

The Segerstrom Home Ranch house, shown here in 1977, was built in 1915 in the Craftsman bungalow style. Located at 3315 Fairview Road, the house is still used for special events and is occasionally opened to the public. From this property, the Segerstrom family acquired land and became the largest independent producer of lima beans in the United States. But third-generation Henry Segerstrom had a different vision: development of retail and high-rise office space.

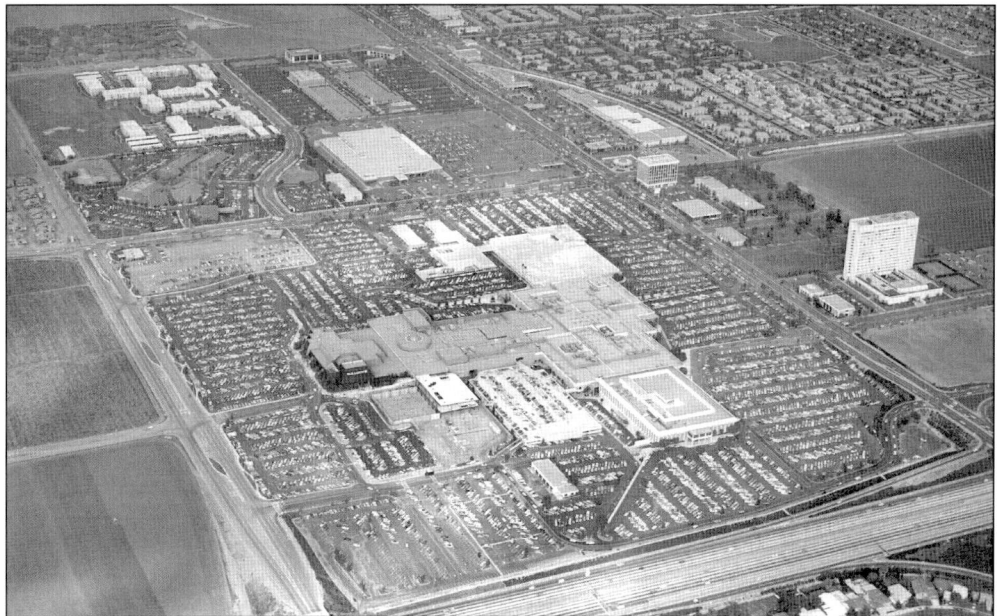

South Coast Plaza opened its doors in 1966 and held a grand opening in 1967 (see pages 66 and 67.) Just 10 years later, on Black Friday, November 26, 1976, this aerial photograph captured the scene. The 405 Freeway runs across the bottom, with Bear Street at left and Bristol Street at right. South Coast Plaza Village appears at top center and left, while the future location of Crystal Court appears as farm fields at left. At right behind the South Coast Plaza Hotel are farm fields that would soon become the site of Orange County's premier performing arts complex.

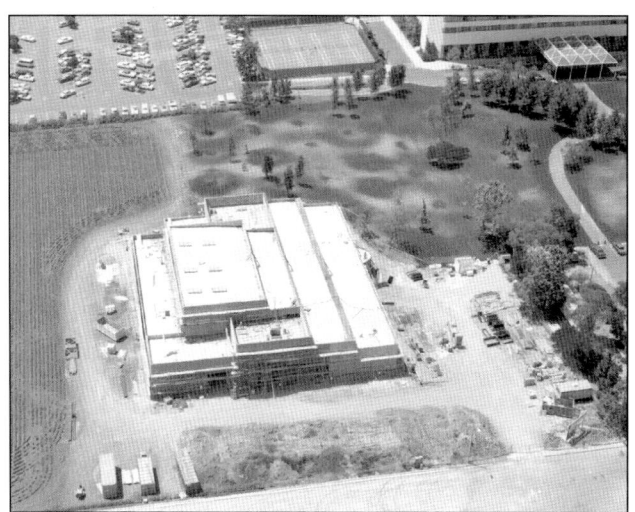

The first performing arts venue to sprout up from a Segerstrom farm field was South Coast Repertory's fourth-step theater, which opened in 1978. South Coast Rep was the vision of David Emmes and Martin Benson, who started the group with a "ragtag" production in 1964 and planned the group's four-step growth on the back of a napkin. The fourth step, a fully equipped permanent theater staging professional productions, was taking shape in this aerial photograph taken in June 1978.

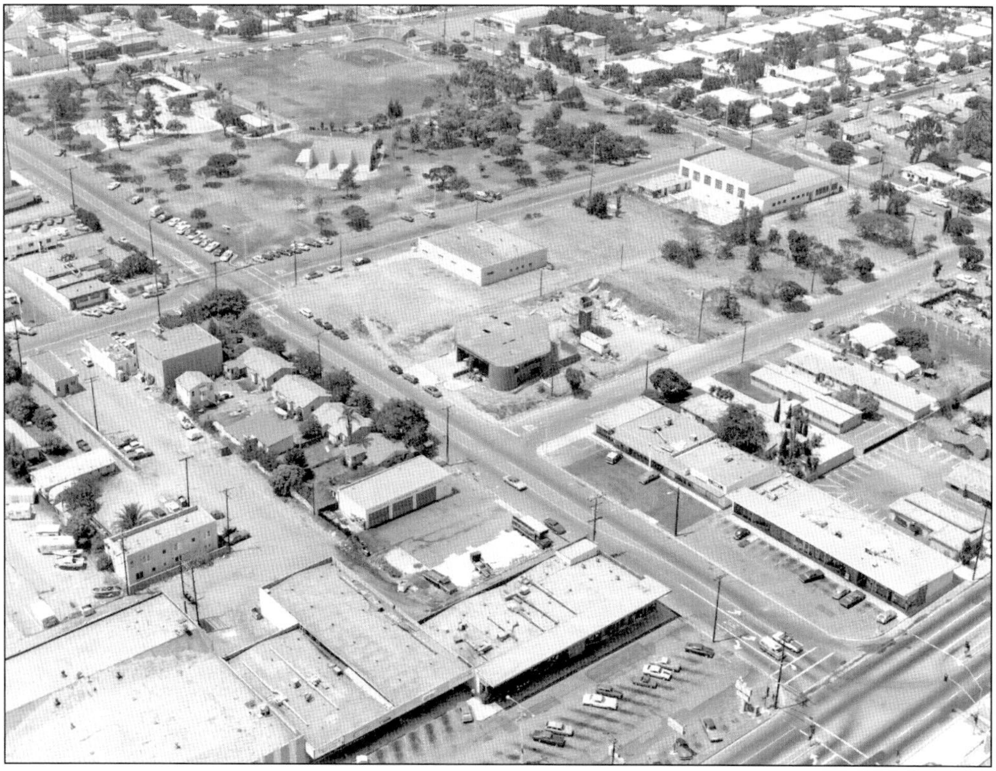

Although Costa Mesa had formed a redevelopment agency in 1972, it took a few years for results to become visible. In this June 1978 aerial photograph, Park Avenue runs upward to the left, starting from West Nineteenth Street in the lower right. The new Fire Station No. 3, at 1865 Park Avenue, is at center. The surrounding area to the left of Park Avenue became Costa Mesa Courtyards, while the area to the right between the fire station and West Nineteenth Street became the Park Center Place apartment complex.

Five
REDEVELOPMENT AND SOUTH COAST METRO

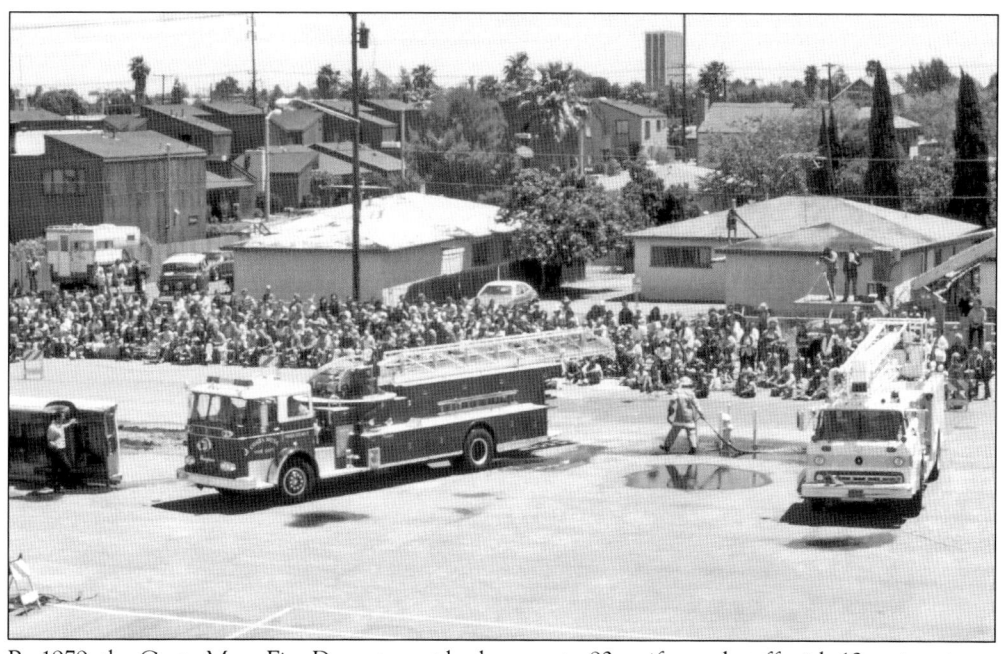

By 1979, the Costa Mesa Fire Department had grown to 93 uniformed staff with 12 major pieces of equipment. Some of the most recent equipment additions were demonstrated to the public at Fire Station No. 4, at 2300 Placentia Avenue, in May 1980. At left is a Seagrave 100-foot aerial ladder truck, while at right is a Crown Pumper with a 50-foot boom, known as the "White Knuckler." The department's fledgling paramedic operation proved successful, with a second medic truck added in 1983.

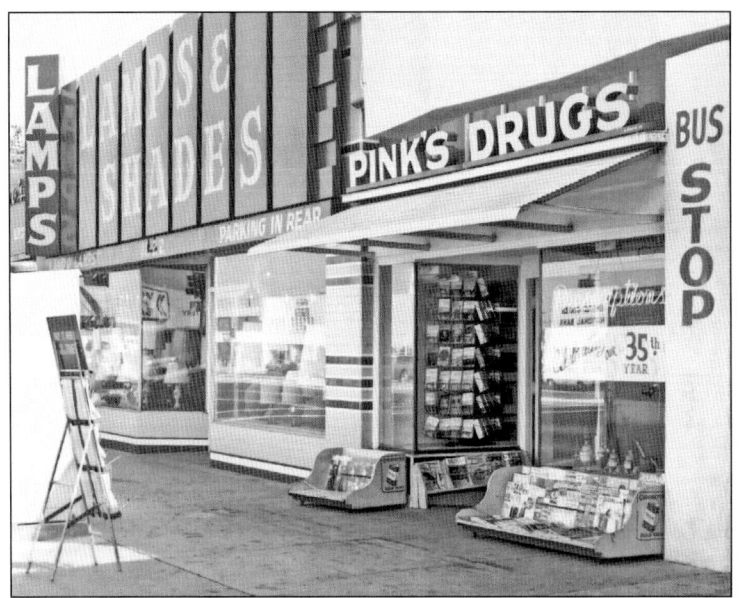

Pink's Drugs at 1820 Newport Boulevard had been in business for 35 years when this photograph was taken in 1968. The drugstore featured not only a soda fountain but also several large racks of comic books that attracted local youth. Owner Alvin "Pink" Pinkley also served for 22 years on the Costa Mesa City Council and held so many civic positions that he has often been remembered as "Mr. Costa Mesa."

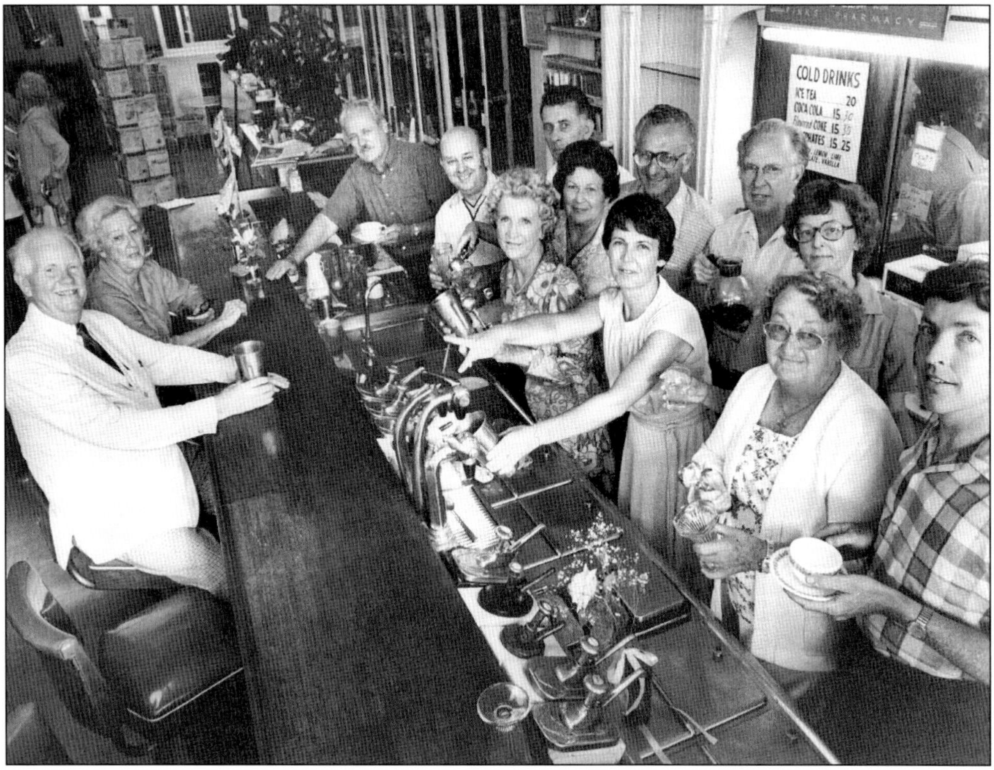

Last call at Pink's Drugs occurred in July 1979, when, after nearly 46 years in business, the Pinkleys retired. Pictured here are members of the Costa Mesa Historical Society serving the Pinkleys, seated at the drugstore's soda fountain. From left to right are Alvin "Pink" Pinkley, Lucille Pinkley, Harold "Bud" Hohl, John Lillycrop, Joyce Martin, Edrick "Ed" Miller, Betty Beecher, Gertrude "Trudy" Ohlig, Henry "Hank" Panian, Charles Beecher, Mildred Fisher (front), Mary Ellen Goddard (rear), and Robert Wolf.

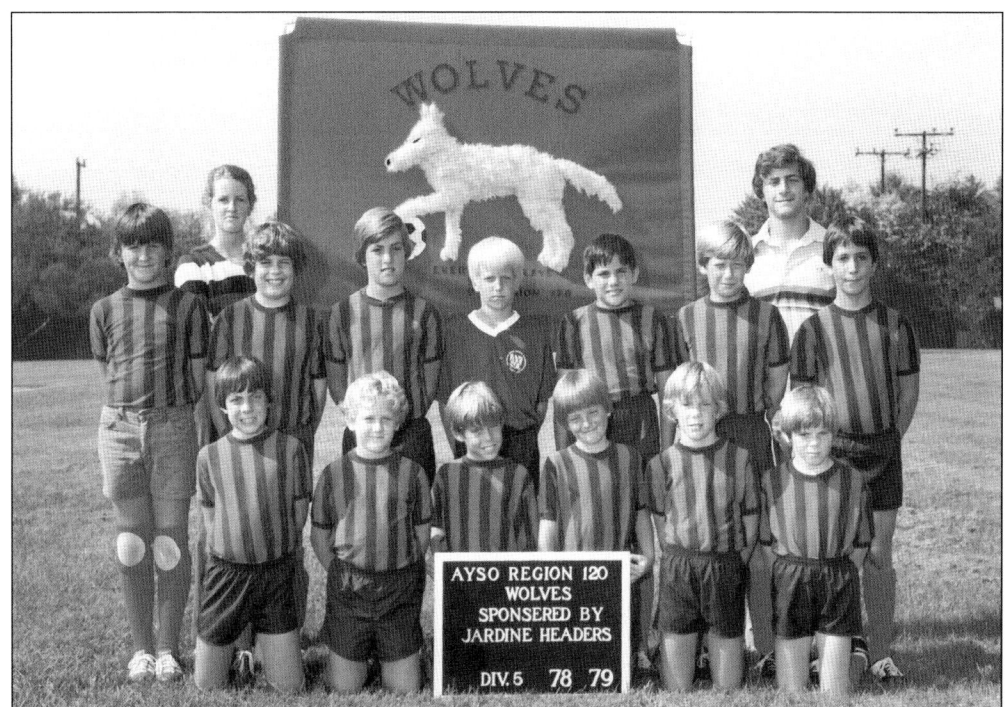

Costa Mesa's focus on parks and recreation featured a special emphasis on youth sports, an emphasis that continues to the present. More than a dozen leagues were active in the city, encompassing soccer, rugby, baseball, football, skateboarding, and softball. In addition, the city's recreation program provided youth sports programs in basketball, swimming, volleyball, flag football, baseball, and track and field. Shown here in 1979 are the Wolves, a Division 5 team in American Youth Soccer Organization (AYSO) Region 120.

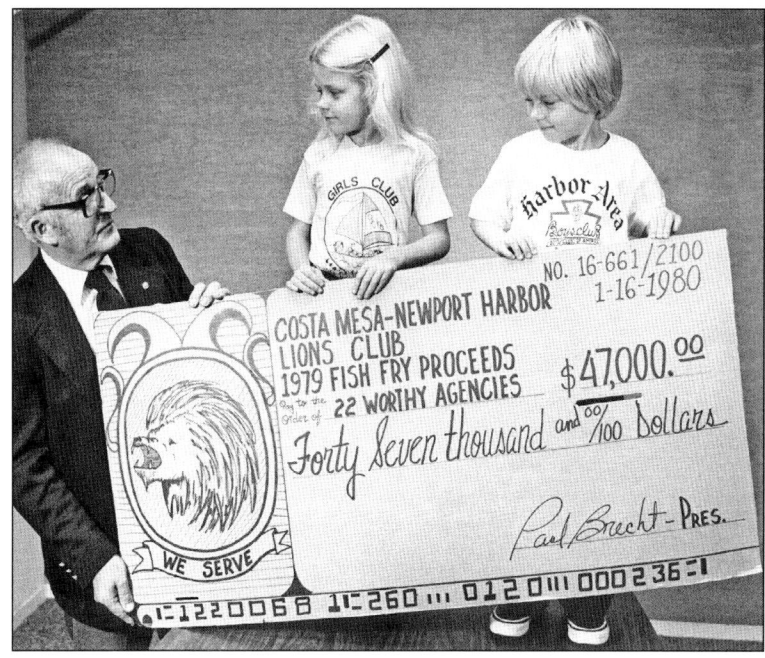

In January 1980, Lions Club president Paul Brecht presented the proceeds from the 1979 fish fry to 22 community organizations, including the Girl's Club and Boys' Club of the Harbor Area. Brecht also was known for his Orchid Garden business at 1989 Harbor Boulevard.

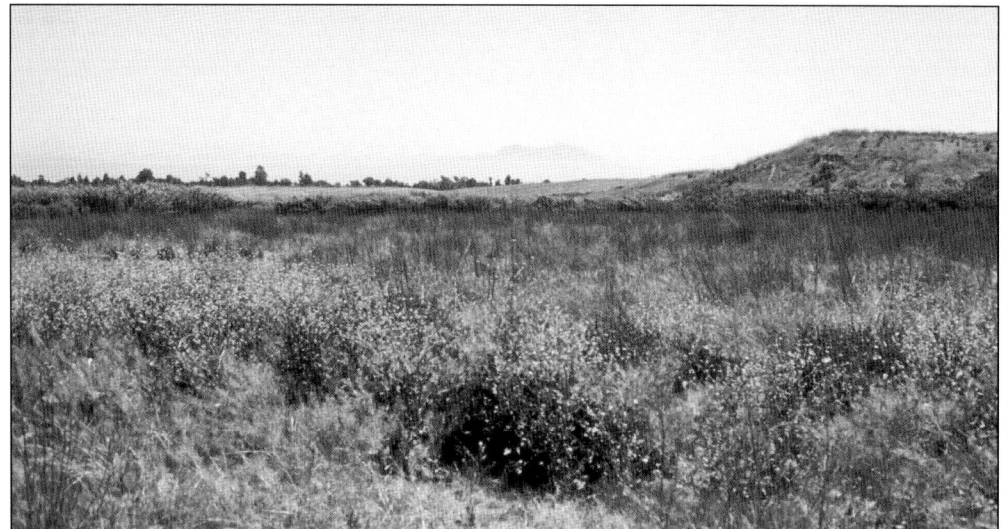

Fairview Park is one of the few remaining open spaces in Costa Mesa. The park includes Native American sites as well as bluffs, native grasslands, coastal sage, scrub, and wetlands that attract and support a wide variety of wildlife. Shown here in May 1986, the park is overseen by Saddleback Mountain in the distance. Native Americans called the mountain Kalawpa, the resting place of the great god Chimingchinish who watched over the people in the valleys below. Of the 219 images in this book, this is the only one in which the hand of man does not appear.

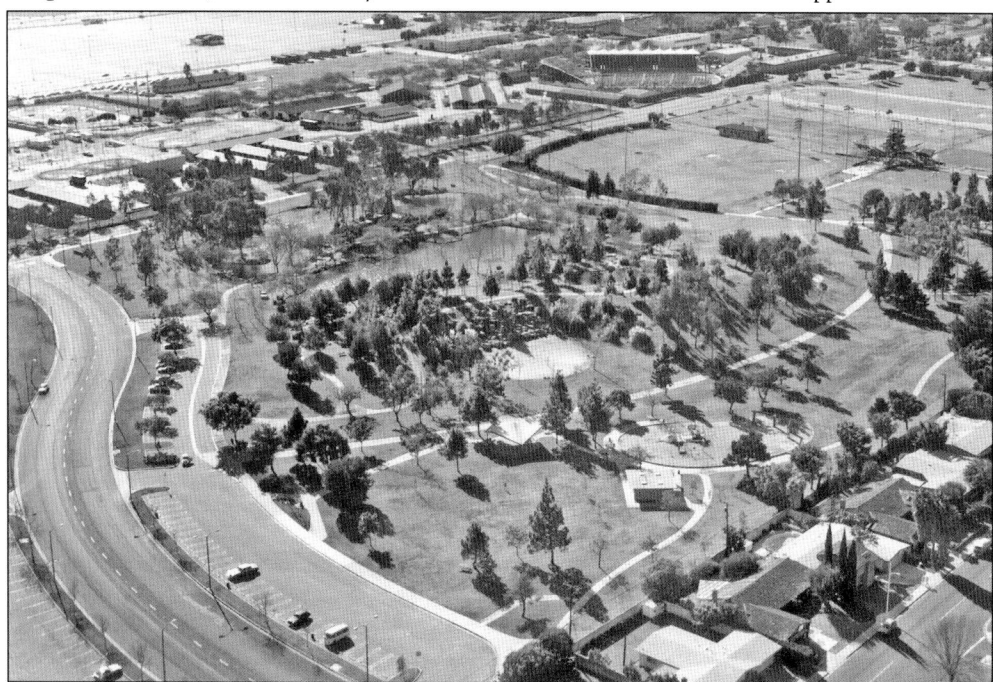

By the 1980s, TeWinkle Park had added several amenities, such as restrooms, lighting, sports fields, tennis courts, playgrounds, barbecues, picnic tables, shelters, a duck pond, and an amphitheater. In this aerial view, Junipero Drive curves at left, Arlington Drive runs diagonally across the top, and a short length of Presidio Drive appears at bottom right. Nearby Bark Park opened in 1994 and Volcom Skate Park of Costa Mesa opened in 2005.

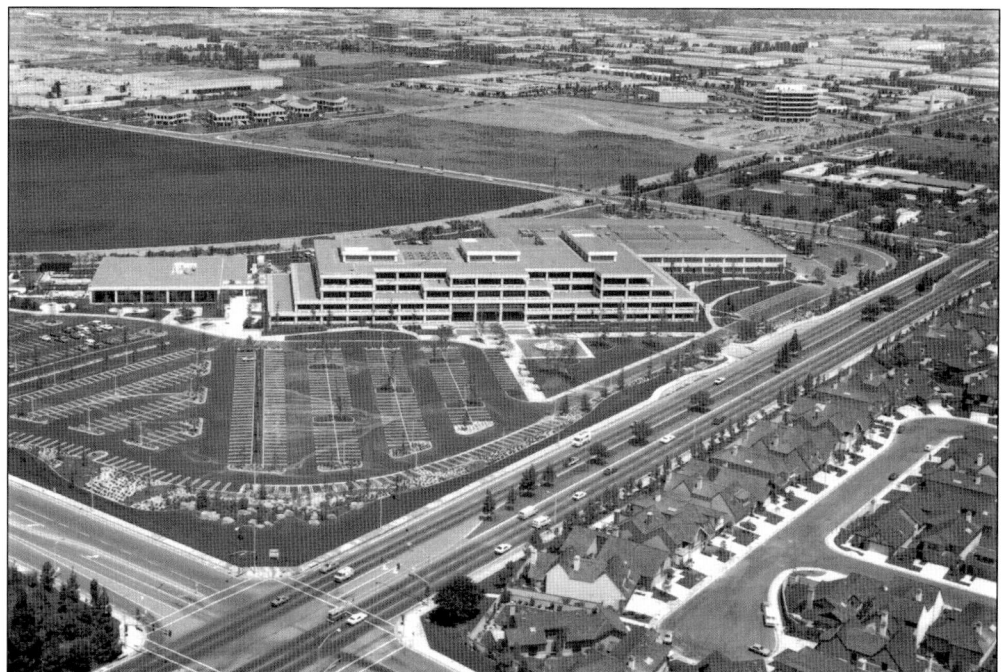

The Automobile Club of Southern California opened this processing center at 3333 Fairview Road in 1982, becoming one of Costa Mesa's largest employers. In this July 1982 view looking northwest, Fairview Road runs diagonally from lower left to upper right, while South Coast Drive crosses at lower left. Wimbledon Village appears at lower right.

The Automobile Club building appears at top left in this c. 1983 aerial view of the future site of the Segerstrom Home Ranch project. The 405 Freeway curves at right, while South Coast Drive runs diagonally from lower left and Harbor Boulevard runs horizontally across the bottom. A large IKEA store would later occupy the center farm field, while Emulex Corporation and the Providence Park gated community were built in the field at upper left, just beyond the *Los Angeles Times* printing facility at left center.

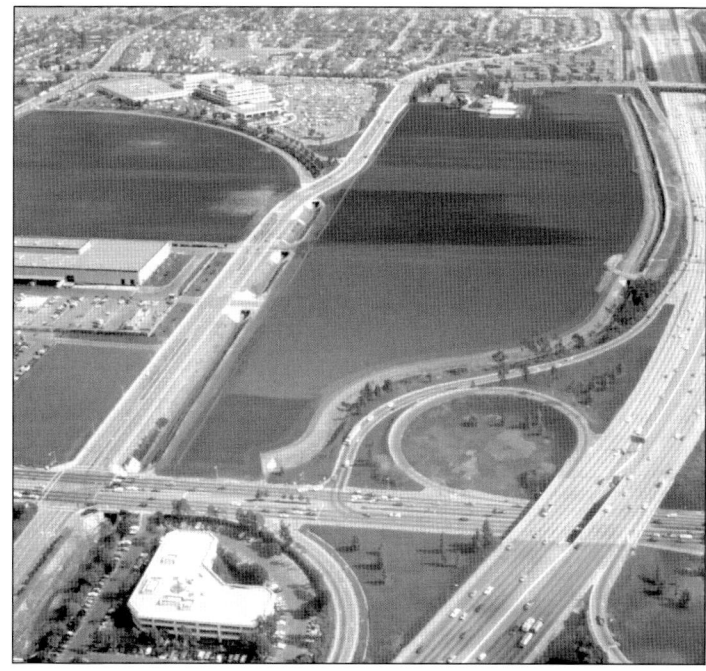

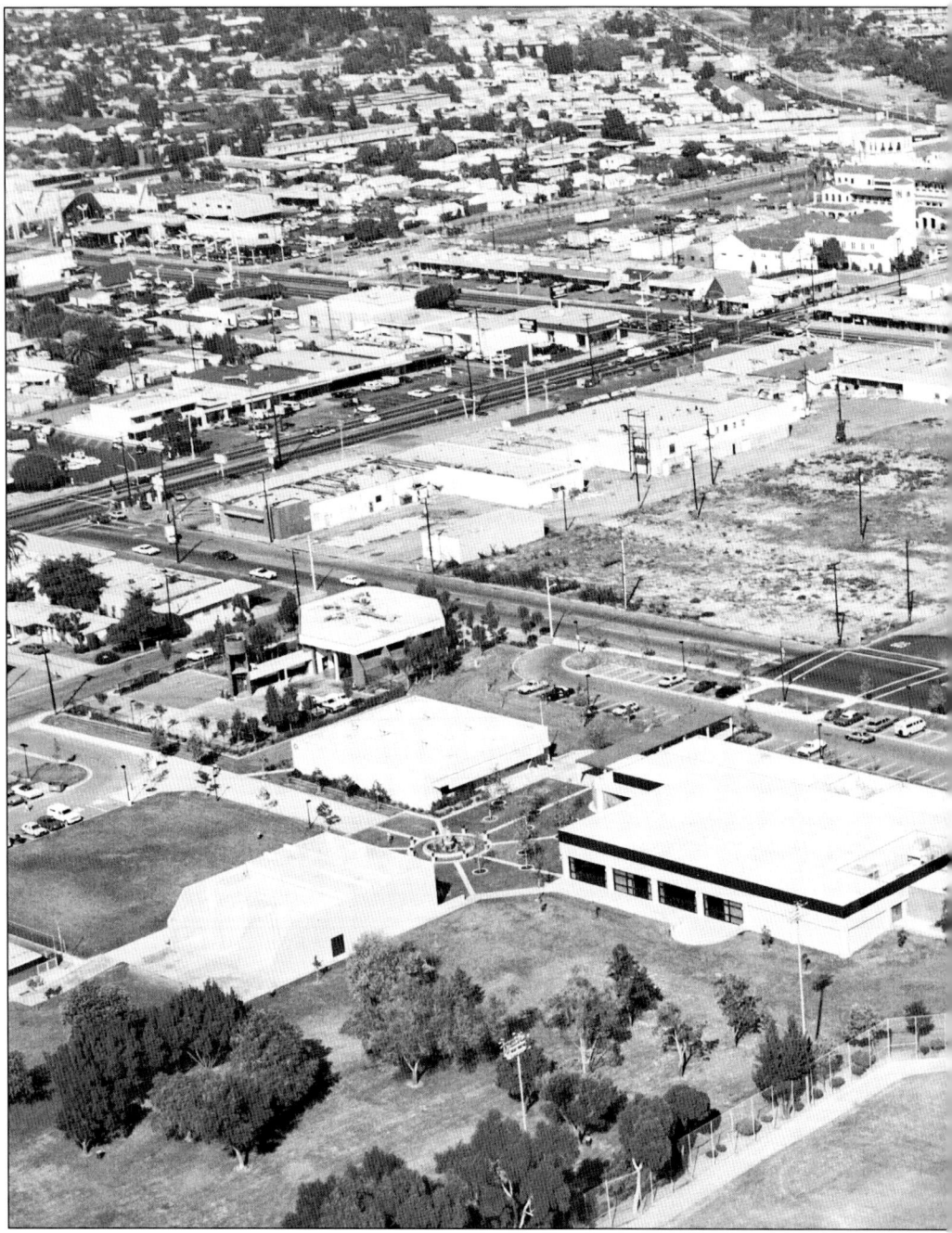

Not to be outdone by new development in North Costa Mesa, the traditional downtown area was due for revamping, according to the Downtown Costa Mesa Redevelopment Project adopted by the city's redevelopment agency in 1973 and amended in 1977, 1980, 1984, and 1986. The redevelopment area covered 195 acres and included both residential neighborhoods and commercial corridors. In this 1982 aerial view looking northeast, Newport Boulevard runs diagonally from center right to top center, West Nineteenth Street runs from top center diagonally to center left, and Park Avenue runs from center left diagonally to lower right. Visible projects include Fire

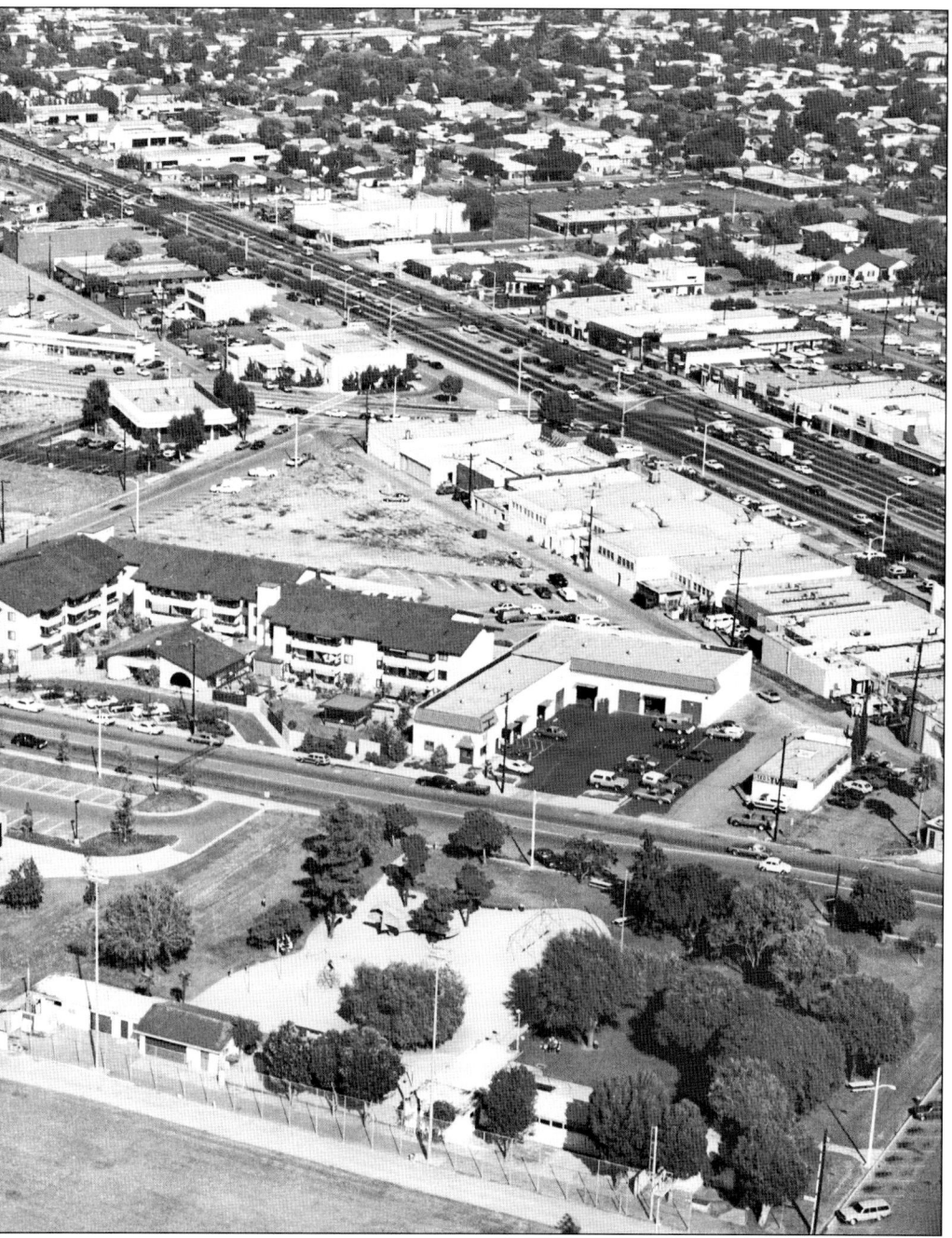

Station No. 3 and the Neighborhood Community Center (Park Avenue, left-hand page), Casa Bella Apartments (Park Avenue, right-hand page), and Pacific Savings Plaza (Spanish Colonial Revival building at top center, adjacent to church). Projects yet to be started are Costa Mesa Courtyards (opened 1985), Donald Dungan Library (opened 1987), Demonstration Block (mid-1980s), and Triangle Square (opened 1992). The city's redevelopment plan was to have a duration of 40 years, ending in December 2013.

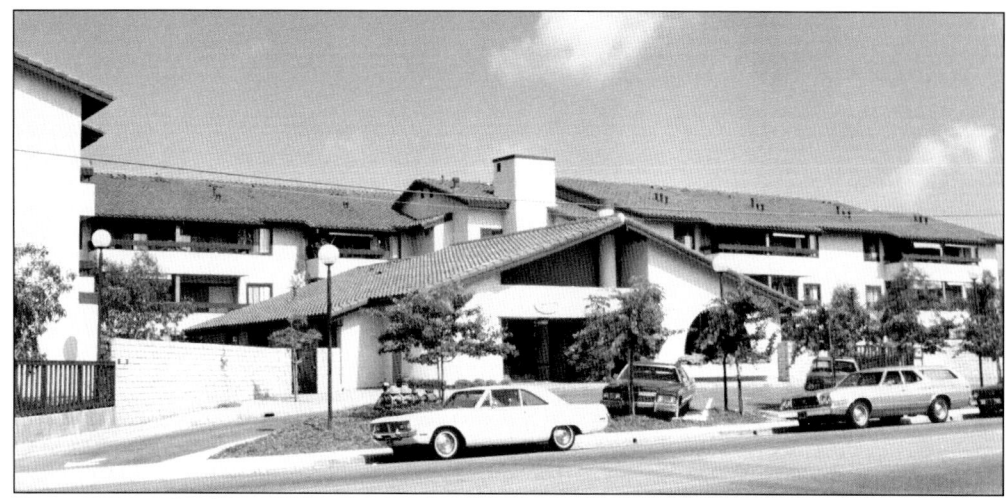

Downtown Redevelopment Project No. 2, Casa Bella Apartments, contained 75 one-bedroom apartments for senior citizens. Rents would be subsidized per Section 8 of the 1974 Federal Housing Act so that residents would pay no more than 25 percent of their income for rent. Just before opening in late 1980, the city's housing office sifted through 1,500 applications for the 75 apartments. After expiration of the initial long-term Section 8 contract, Casa Bella's rental subsidies were subject to short-term contract renewals.

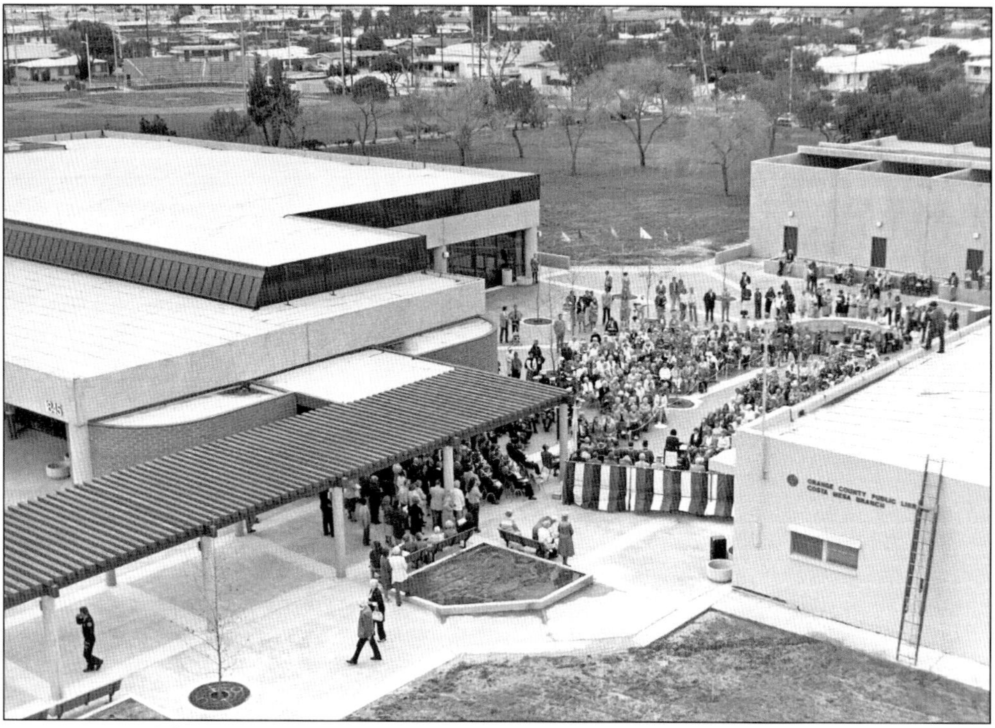

Project No. 1 of the Downtown Redevelopment Plan included Fire Station No. 3 (completed 1979), Neighborhood Community Center (completed 1981), and Donald Dungan Library (completed 1987). Shown here is the opening ceremony for the Neighborhood Community Center, held in March 1981. The Costa Mesa Branch Library building appearing here at lower right was demolished in 1987 after the Donald Dungan Library opened.

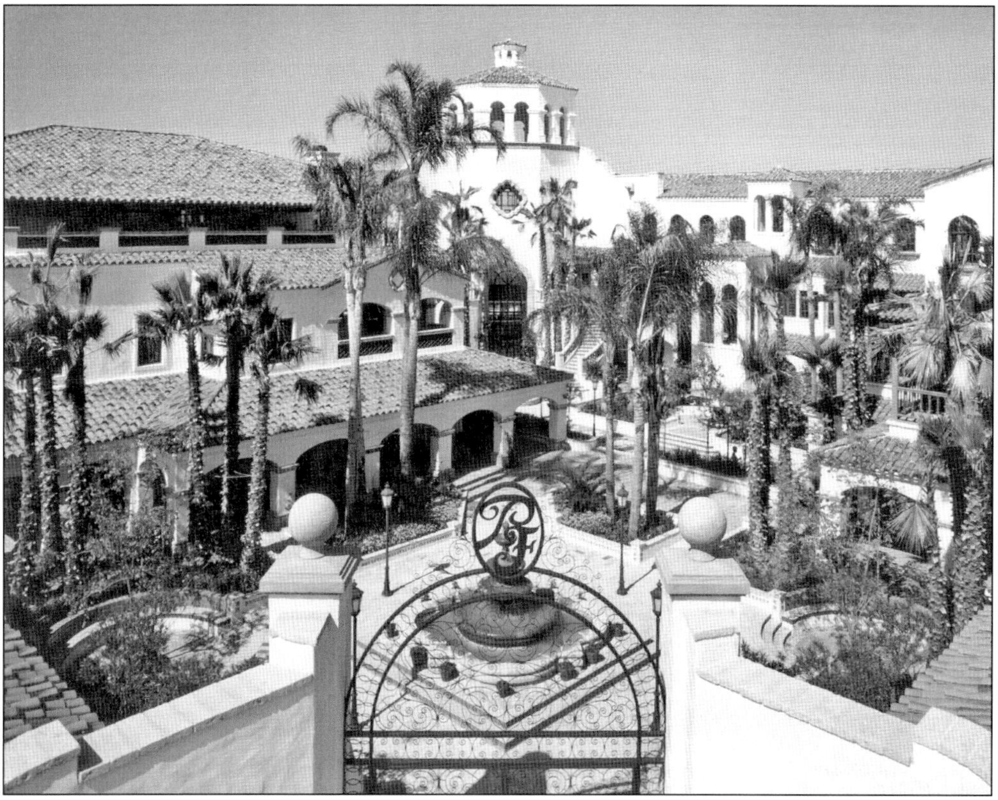

The Pacific Federal Savings Plaza, shown here around 1983, was Downtown Redevelopment Project No. 7. The plaza offered 125,000 square feet of office space highlighted by attractive Spanish Colonial Revival architecture. Located at 1901 Newport Boulevard, the new plaza was situated at ground zero for the downtown district. But Pacific Savings went bust during the Savings & Loan crisis of the mid-to-late 1980s, and the building sat empty for nearly 10 years before being purchased by new owners.

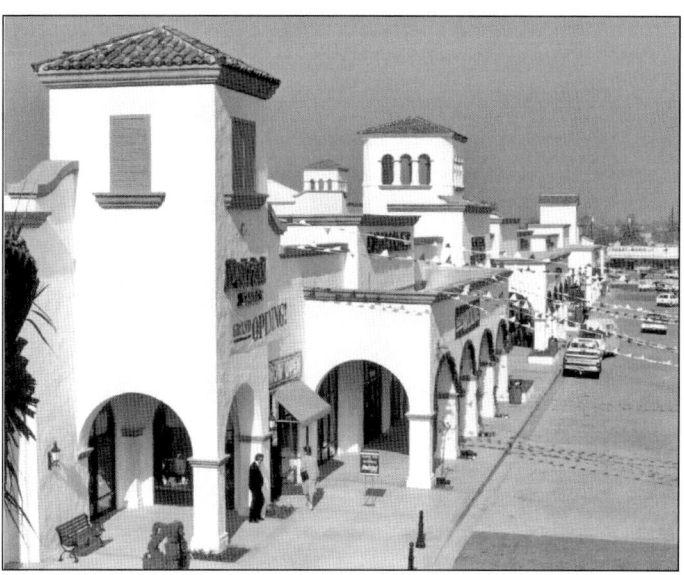

Downtown Redevelopment Project No. 3, Costa Mesa Courtyards, offered 185,000 square feet of retail and office space on a parcel bounded by Harbor Boulevard, West Nineteenth Street, Park Avenue, and Newport Boulevard. Shown here during its grand opening in 1985, the Costa Mesa Courtyards continued as a hub of downtown business activity.

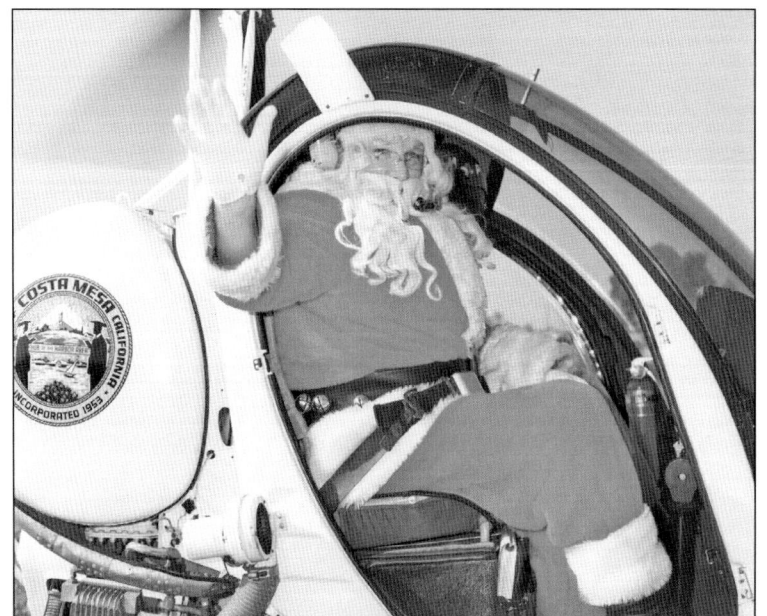

Costa Mesa's community policing effort took to the air to assist Santa in delivering candy canes and hugs to local schoolchildren. Shown here in December 1982, Sgt. Mike Bechtel waves to school kids who reportedly did not mind Santa Claus arriving without his reindeer.

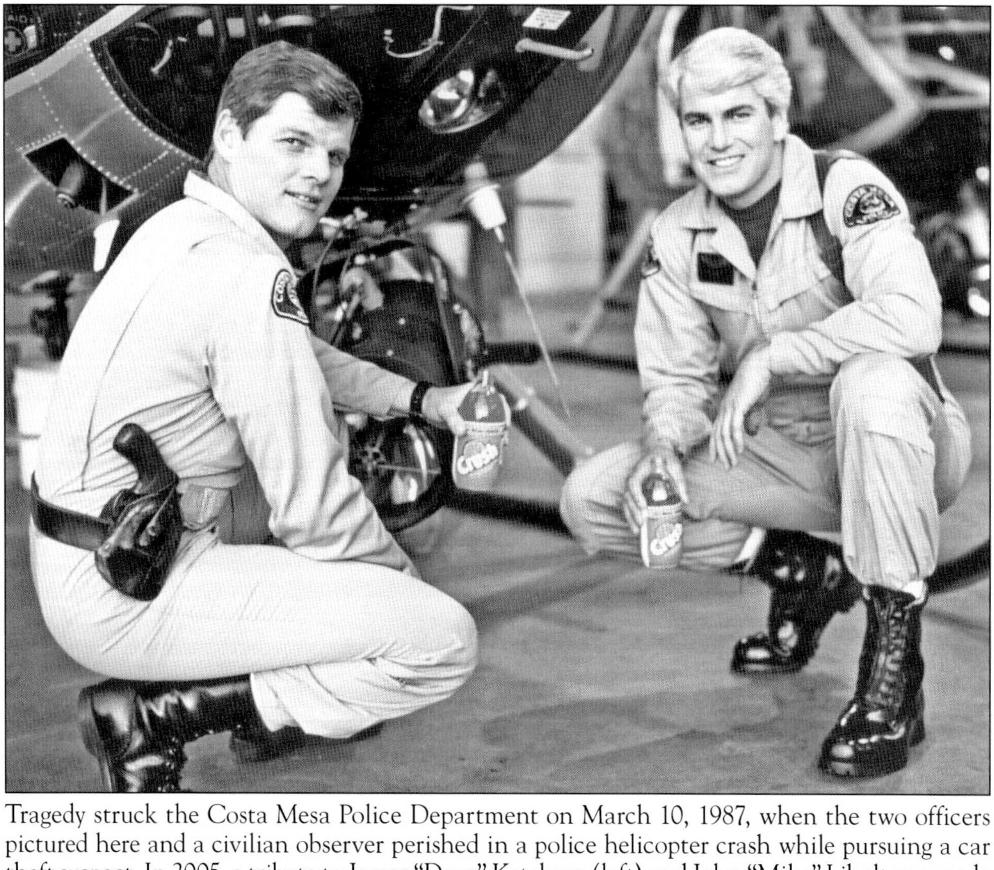

Tragedy struck the Costa Mesa Police Department on March 10, 1987, when the two officers pictured here and a civilian observer perished in a police helicopter crash while pursuing a car theft suspect. In 2005, a tribute to James "Dave" Ketchum (left) and John "Mike" Libolt was made with the dedication of Ketchum-Libolt Park at 2150 Maple Street.

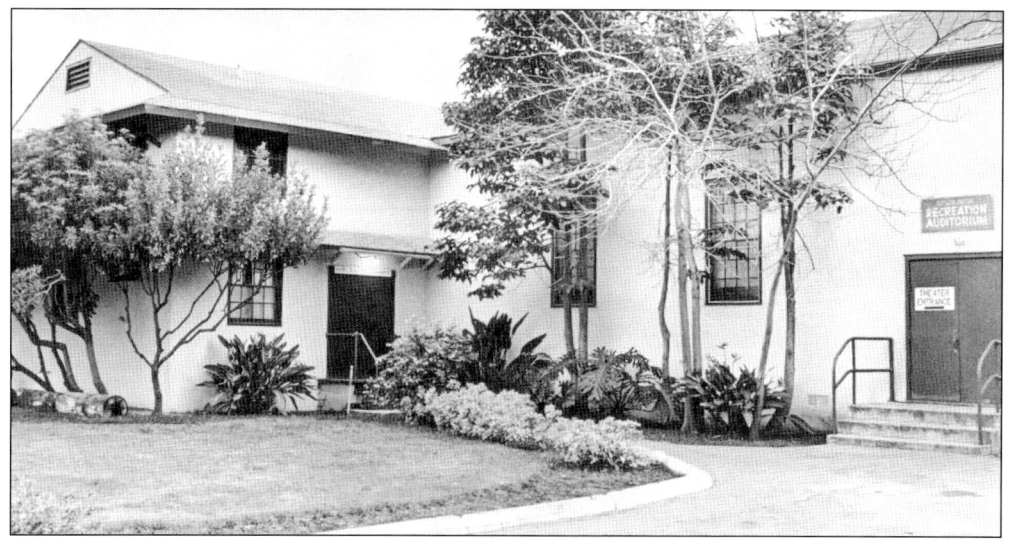

Shown here in 1983, the Costa Mesa Community Center was housed in a former Santa Ana Army Air Base building on the west side of the Orange County Fairgrounds next to the newly built Pacific Amphitheater. The Costa Mesa Civic Playhouse staged its first production in this building in June 1965 under the direction of Patti Tambellini. The group soldiered on at this location until 1983, when noise from the amphitheater drowned it out. The city participated in a deal to move the Costa Mesa Civic Playhouse to Rea School, where the group continues to stage high-quality community theater productions.

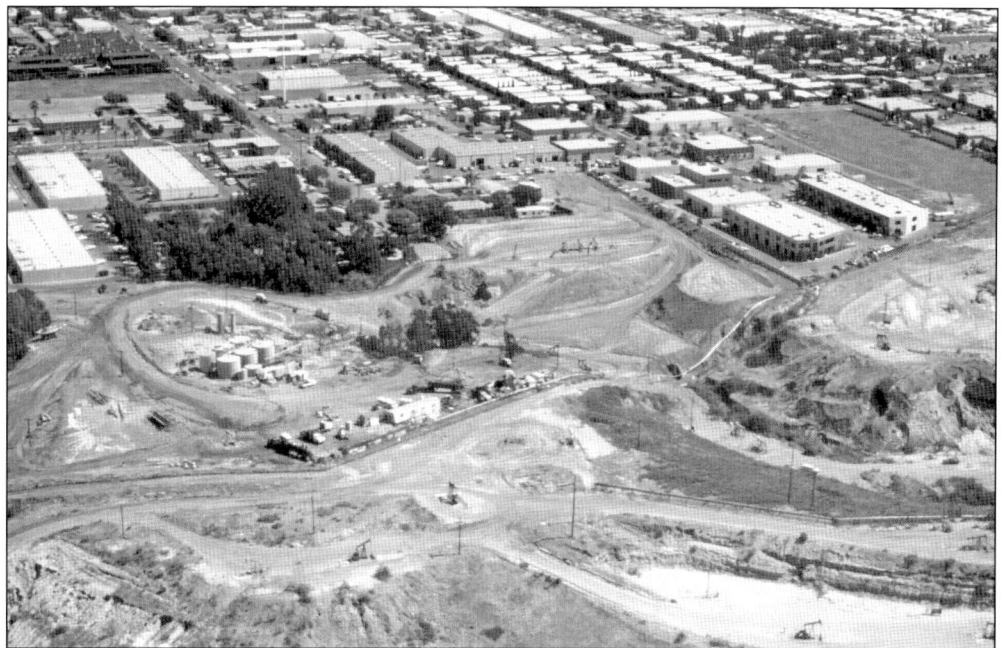

Although the Keys Marina was a no-go (see page 56), the city moved forward with development of a gated housing project on former oil company land adjacent to Banning Ranch. In this 1984 aerial view looking southeast, West Eighteenth Street runs from top left toward the center, while the border with Newport Beach runs diagonally from center right to lower left. By 1990, California Seabreeze Homes were built on the area at center left where the storage tanks and field office appear.

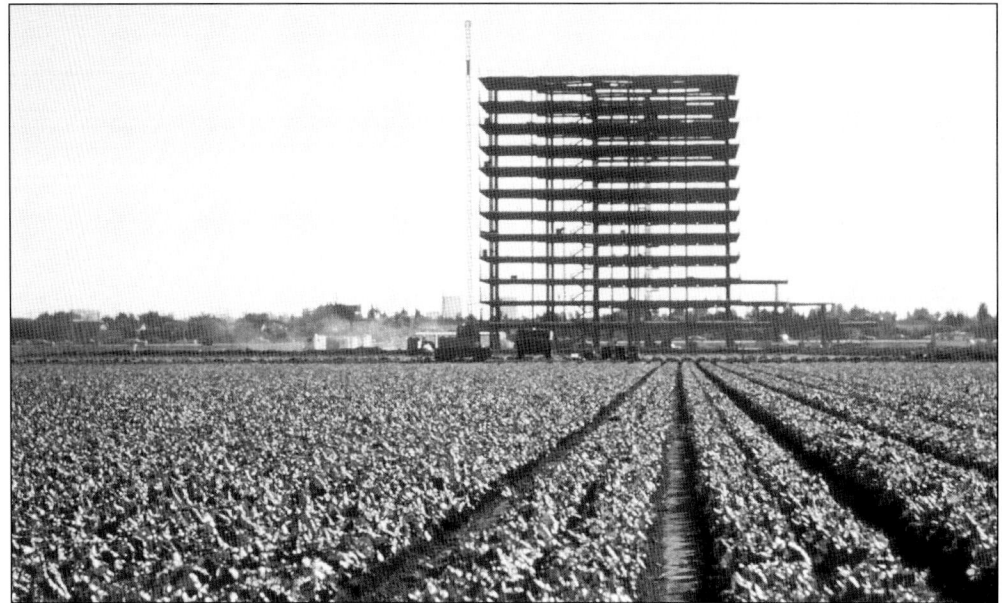

This January 1984 photograph captures the action as a new city center is born. Springing up from a farm field, the first phase of the Sakioka development was to feature high-rise office towers in a complex named Metro Center at South Coast.

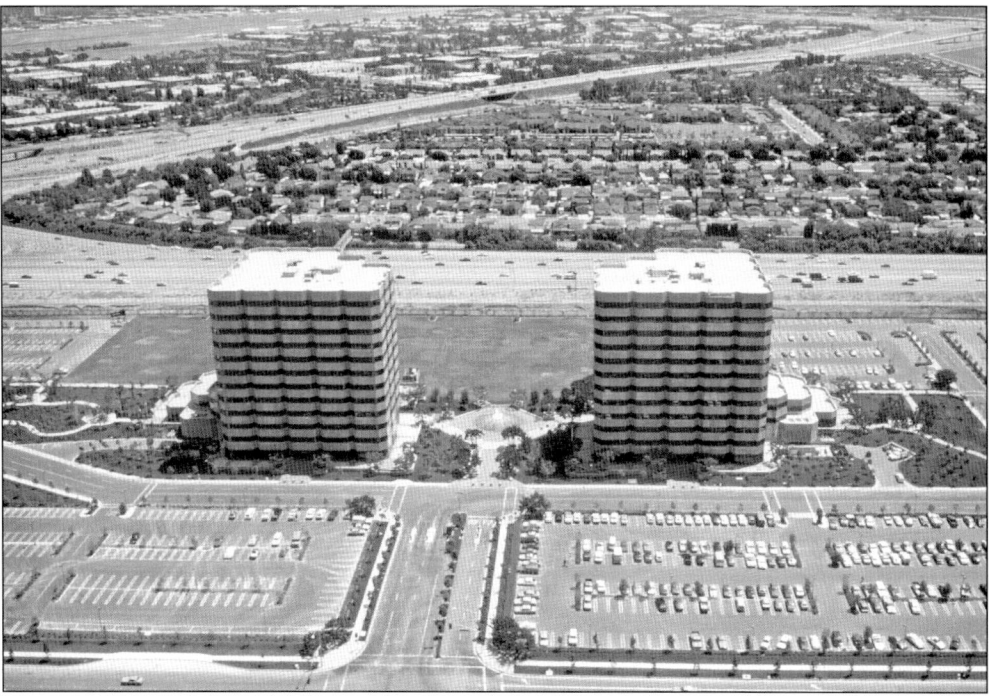

By 1986, the same site pictured above had grown to two office towers with associated parking lots. In this view looking south, Anton Boulevard runs horizontally across the bottom, while the 405 Freeway runs horizontally across the center, with State Route 55 and Orange County Airport running diagonally at upper left towards the center. Metro Center at South Coast is located at 535–575 Anton Boulevard.

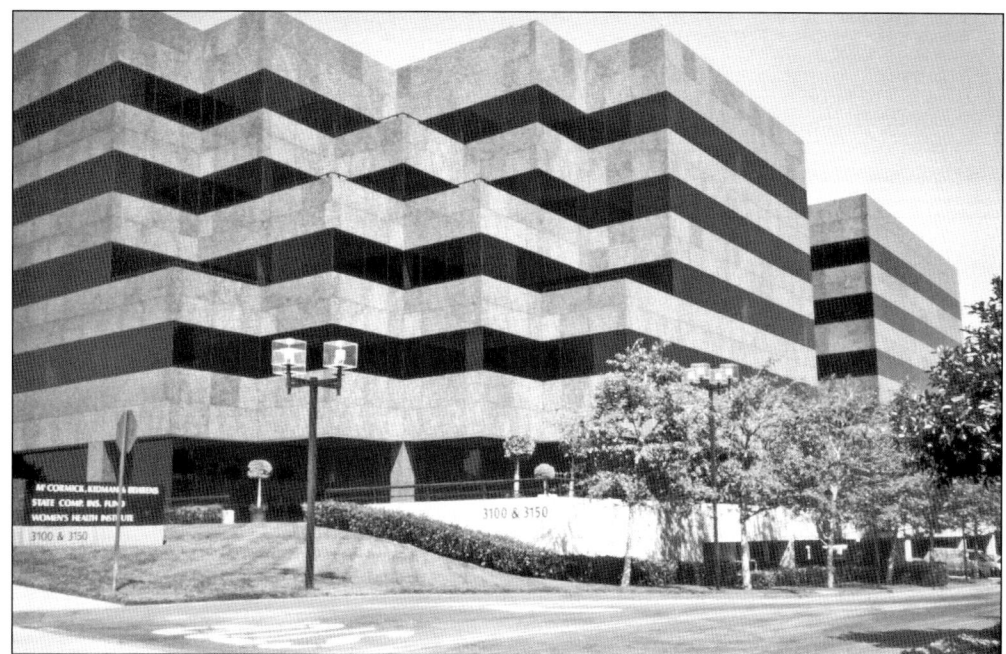

South Coast Executive Center, at 3100–3150 Bristol Street, was built on a parcel adjacent to the former White Front store location shown at the top of page 76. What a change in architecture and land use! The executive center is part of North Costa Mesa known today as South Coast Metro.

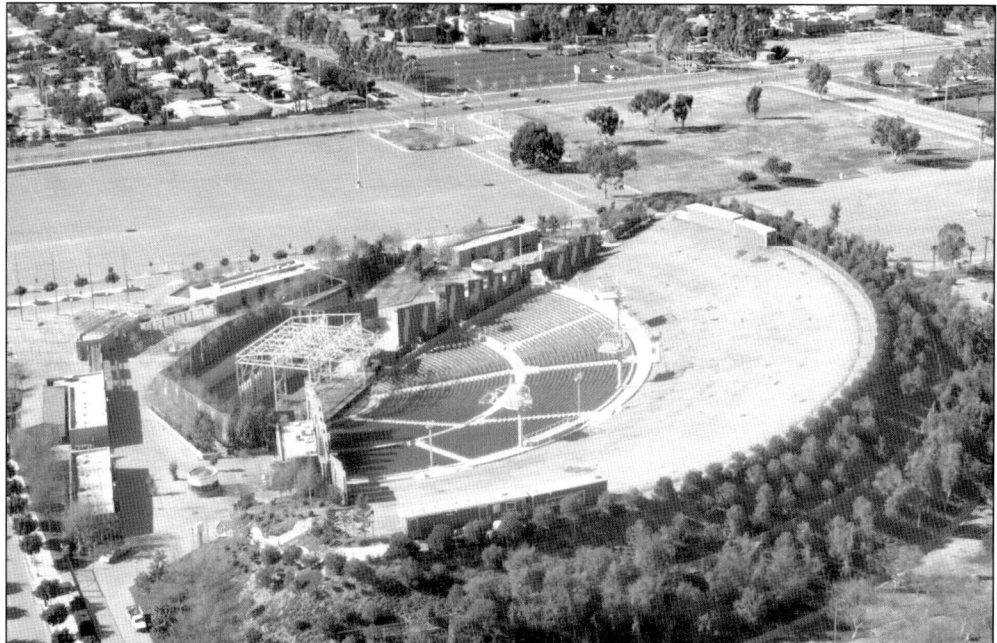

The Pacific Amphitheater was a controversial project from the beginning. In 1979, the courts ruled that the Orange County Fair Board did not have to submit its plans for future development to the city. The 18,800-seat amphitheater shown here opened in 1983, and a homeowner group sued over the noise levels from concerts by bands such as Guns 'N' Roses. The amphitheater was closed in 1995 and reopened during the 2003 Orange County Fair.

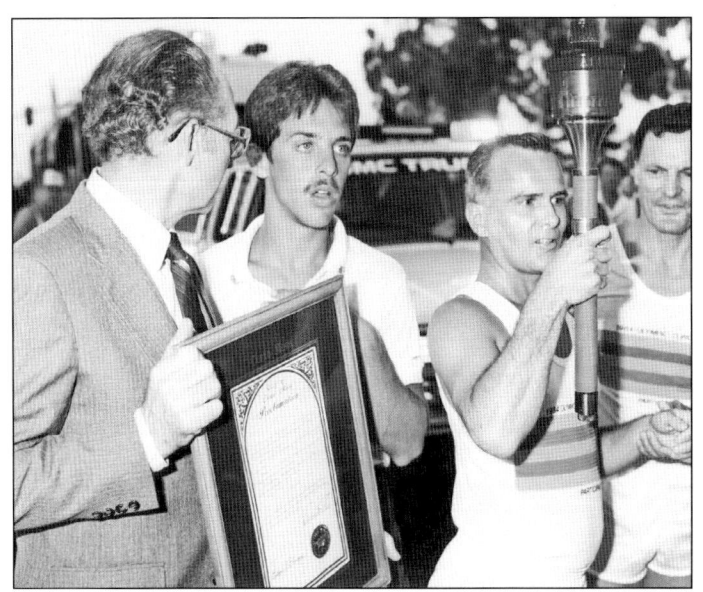

Despite the boycott of the 1984 Summer Olympic Games by Eastern Bloc countries, Costa Mesans were excited to be so close to the center of Olympic action in Los Angeles and Orange County. The Olympic torch relay was run from May 7 to July 28. The route covered 9,300 miles across the United States and involved over 3,600 torchbearers. Shown here is Costa Mesa mayor Donn Hall holding the city's proclamation as the torch relay passed through town.

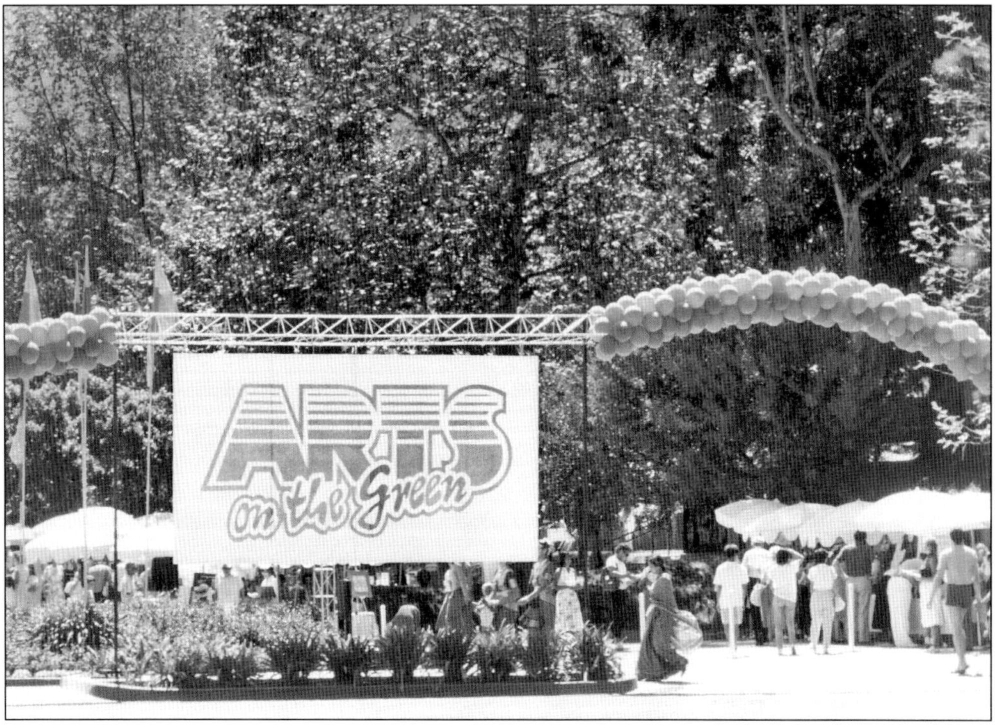

Costa Mesa continued its focus on arts with the fourth annual Arts on the Green event in Town Center Park, located between the South Coast Repertory Theater and the Westin South Coast Plaza Hotel. This event, hosted by the Costa Mesa Chamber of Commerce, was held in September 1987.

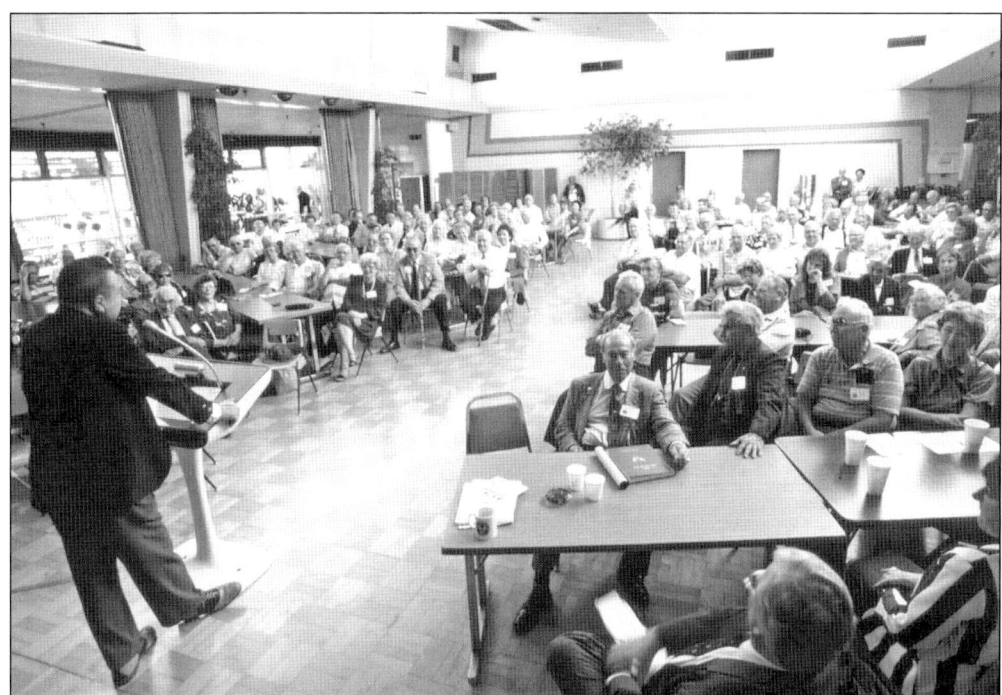

Beginning in 1972, the Costa Mesa Historical Society held annual reunions for former cadets and staff of the Santa Ana Army Air Base. Seven years later, the Society formed the SAAAB Wing, a group much like an alumni association. Membership grew to 2,500, and the reunions gained in popularity, reaching a peak about the time of the 1988 reunion, shown here. (Courtesy of Orange County Archives.)

Mickey Mouse's 60th birthday provided an opportunity for Costa Mesa Day at Disneyland, located just 10 miles north of Costa Mesa. This photograph, taken in summer 1988, shows Mayor Mary Hornbuckle (first row, second from left) with city staff and a group of children from Girls Inc. enjoying their visit to the "happiest place on earth."

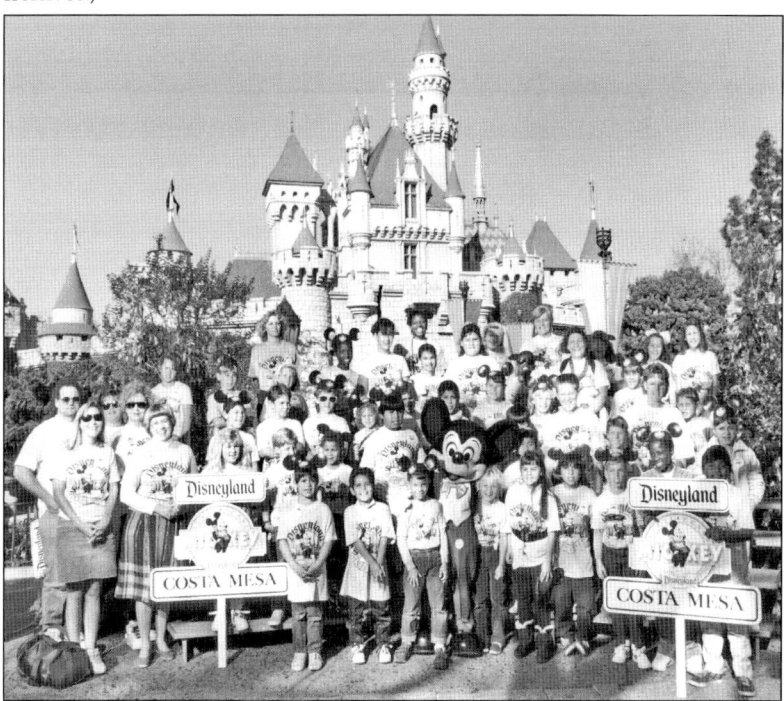

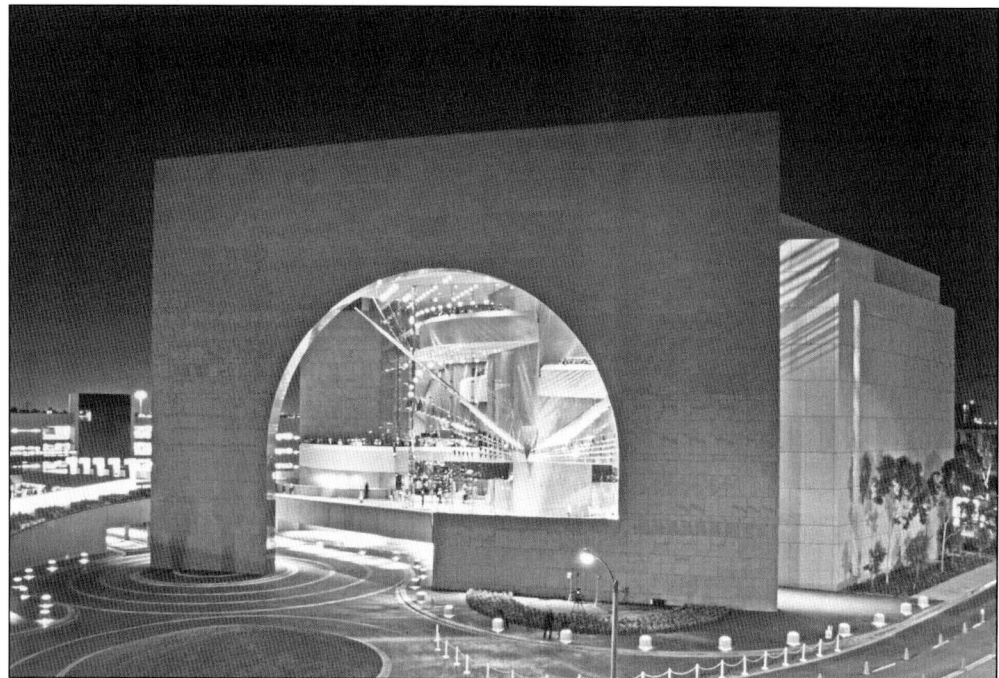

The Orange County Performing Arts Center looked very much as shown here when it officially opened on September 29, 1986. The center was built on a Segerstrom lima bean field and signified the urbanization and coming of age of Costa Mesa. The center also became a symbol of Orange County's aspirations and cultural independence from Los Angeles. Prominently featured in the notched archway is the *Fire Bird* sculpture, a work of public art designed by Richard Lippold.

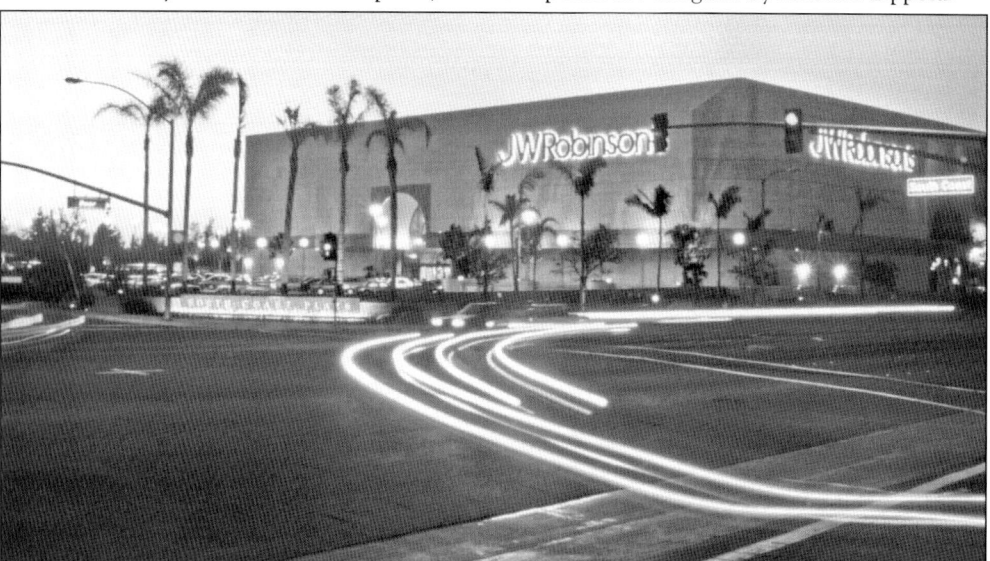

South Coast Plaza's largest expansion came in 1986, first with the opening of an upsized Nordstrom store and then with the opening of a new wing across Bear Street called Crystal Court. Shown here in 1988, Crystal Court was anchored by J.W. Robinson's and the Broadway. The 1986 expansion is often viewed as marking South Coast Plaza's growth from a regional mall to a nationwide shopping destination.

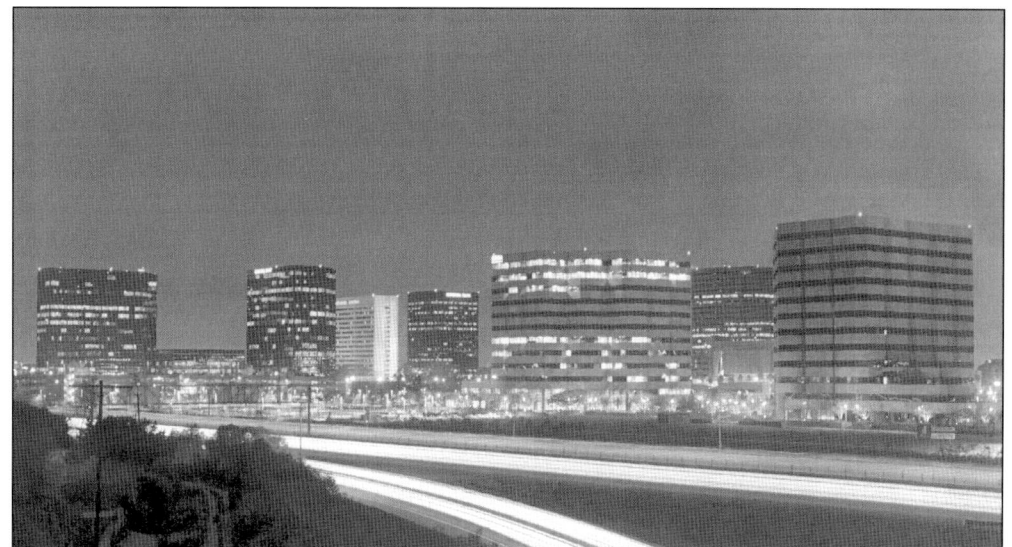

Looking at this 1987 cityscape, one can only marvel at the transformation of the farm fields that characterized the area in the preceding decades. South Coast Metro had arrived! The three buildings on the left comprise the Pacific Arts Plaza. Next to the right is the Westin South Coast Plaza Hotel, and then Park Tower, located at 695 Town Center Drive. The building cluster on the right is Metro Center at South Coast (see page 100).

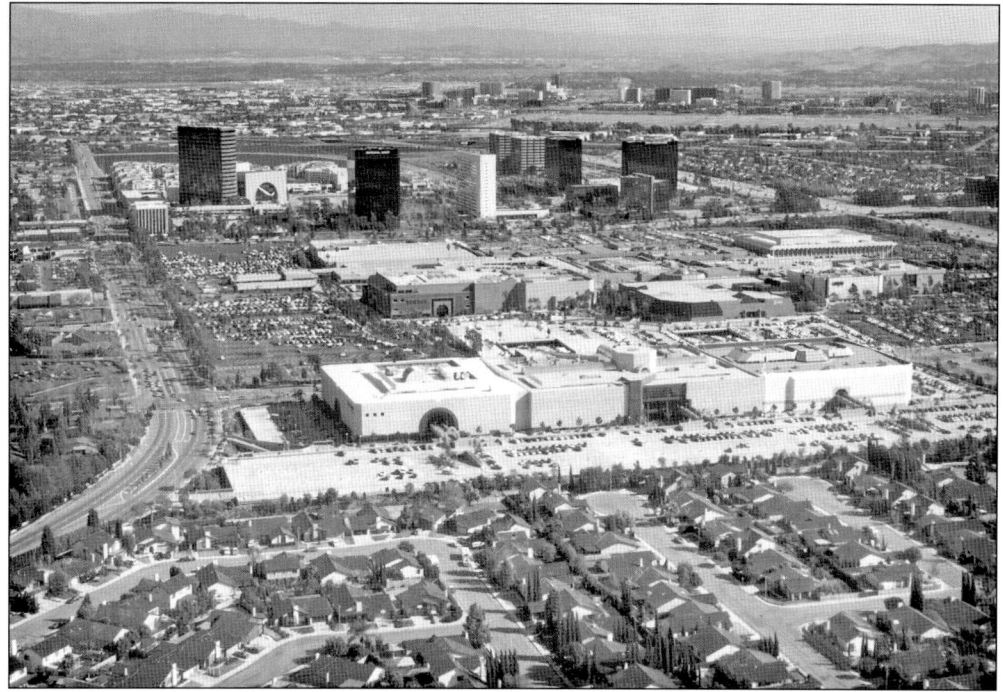

In his 1991 book *Edge City*, Joel Garreau states, "Americans are creating the biggest change in a hundred years in how we build cities." This 1988 aerial view of South Coast Plaza, Town Center, and the surrounding area appears to confirm Garreau's point. Ample leasable office and retail space, more jobs than bedrooms, and perception as one place qualify the area shown here as an edge city.

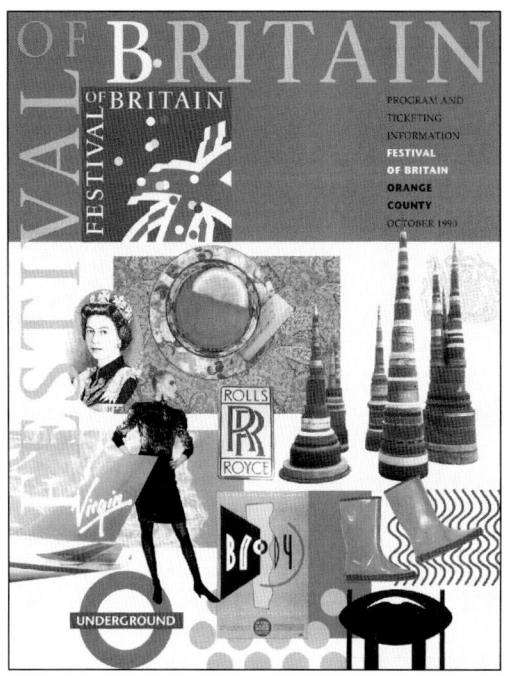

The Festival of Britain, held in October 1990, was a major promotional effort by South Coast Plaza. Henry Segerstrom said, "One of the purposes of the festival is to bring us in closer touch with contemporary Britain." The festival included nearly 20 arts events and featured guests such as Princess Alexandra, actors Michael Caine and Patrick Stewart, and even a dinner with Margaret Thatcher. (Courtesy of Werner Escher, South Coast Plaza.)

British culture notwithstanding, another Segerstrom gift to the community, the Diego Sepulveda Adobe, was engaged here in introducing Costa Mesa's Hispanic heritage to local schoolchildren. Since its dedication in 1966, the adobe has served as a local resource in support of California's Fourth Grade Mission Project, a requirement of California's fourth-grade curriculum.

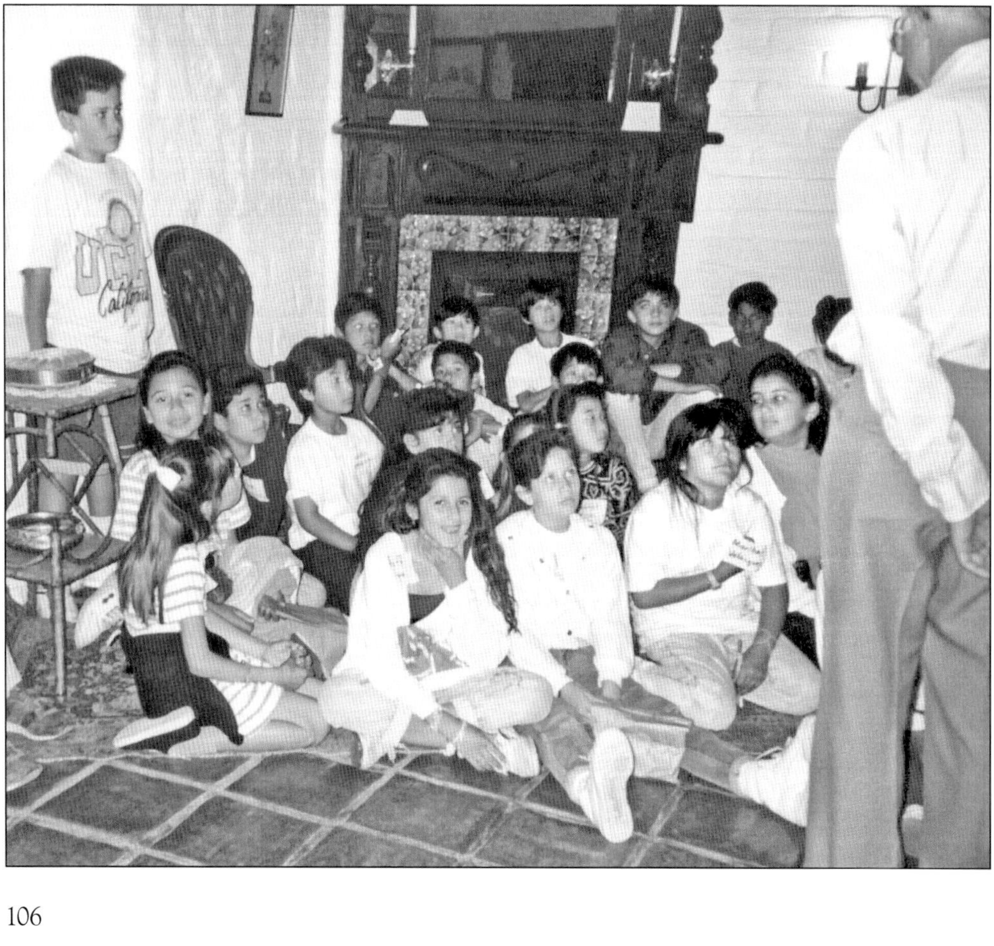

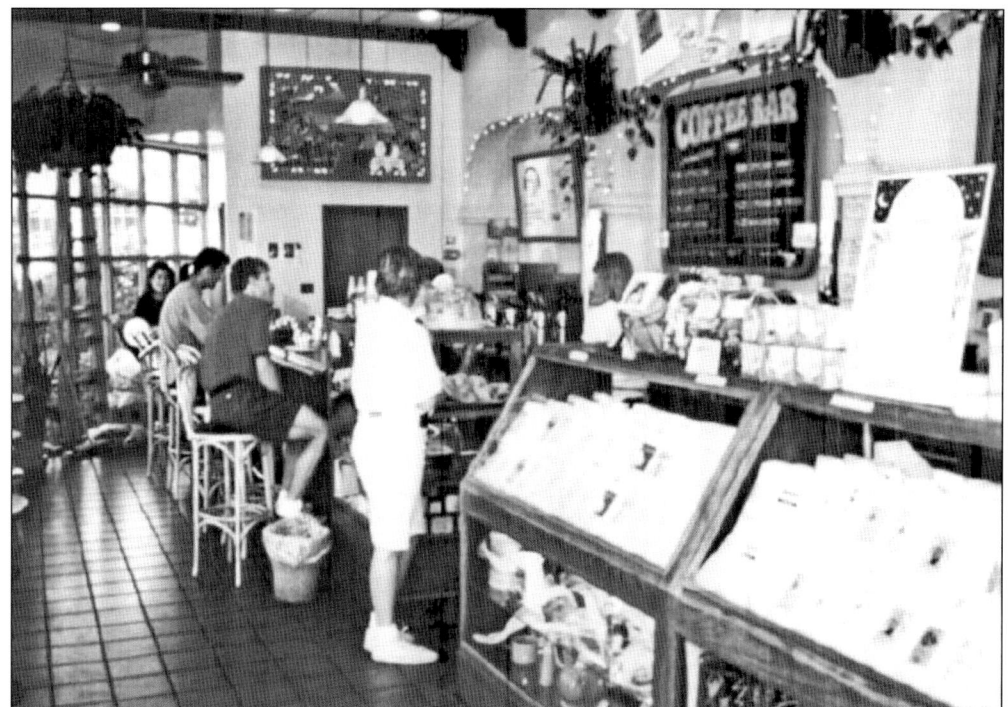

One of Costa Mesa's venerable family-owned businesses was Diedrich Coffee. Starting on a coffee plantation in Antigua, Guatemala, Carl Diedrich developed a new roasting machine and in 1972 moved his roasting operation to Costa Mesa. Shown here around 1989 is the family's third store, Diedrich Coffee & Espresso Bar, located at 474 East Seventeenth Street. The company went public in 1996 and was sold in 2009, but the Diedrich family tradition lives on at Kéan Coffee.

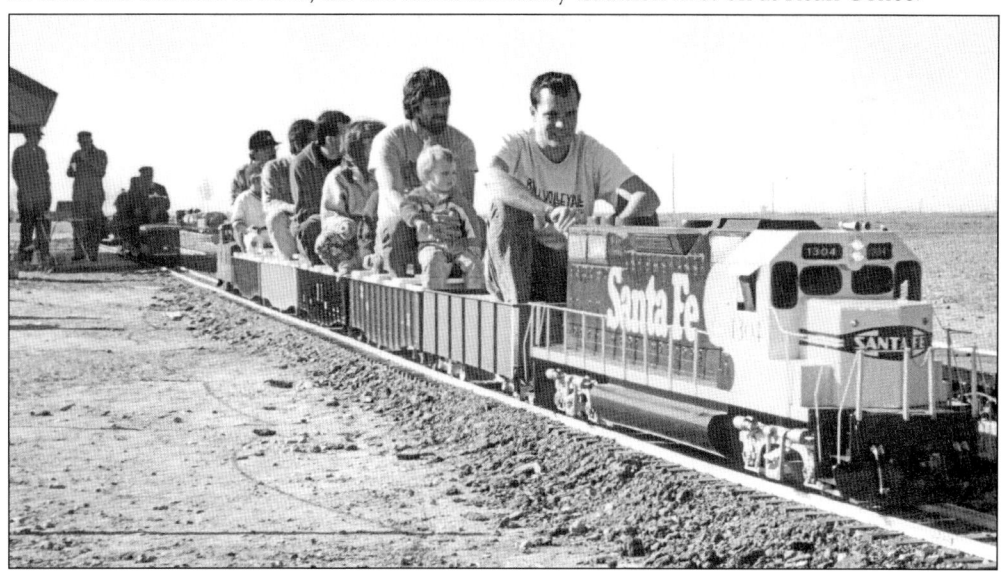

The Orange County Model Engineers (OCME) group had been looking for a permanent home for more than a decade before it entered into a 25-year lease for a site in Costa Mesa's Fairview Park in 1988. Shown here in March 1991, Santa Fe GP-38 No. 1304 departs from the Goat Hill Junction station for an excursion along OCME's newly opened phase one rail line.

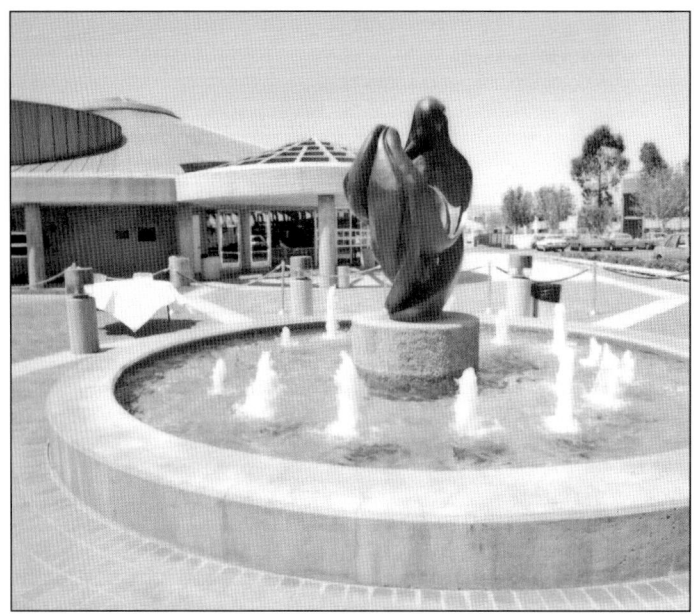

When the Donald Dungan Branch Library opened in 1987, the north area of Lions Park had become a mini–civic center, containing Fire Station No. 3, the Neighborhood Community Center, the Costa Mesa Historical Society, and the Downtown Community Center (formerly Boys' Club). Pictured here are the library in the background and a fountain in the foreground featuring the sculpture *Mother and Child*, created by Robert Ortlieb in 1982.

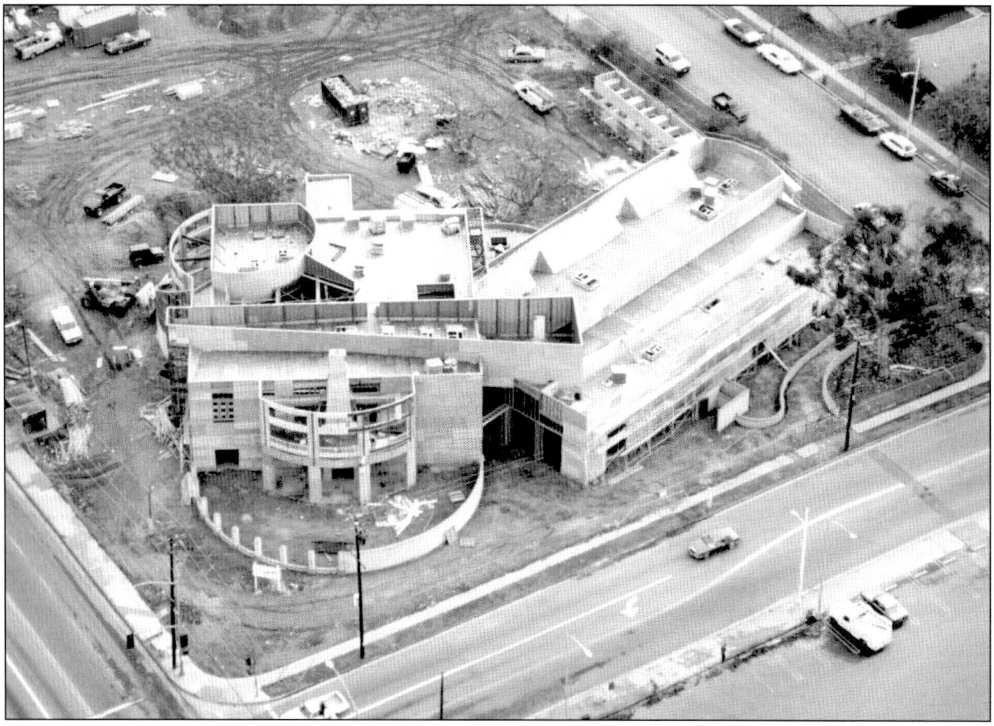

The old city hall at 695 West Nineteenth Street served as the Mardan School for 20 years before the building was demolished to make way for a new Costa Mesa Senior Center. Pictured here in December 1991, the new senior center building was built in proximity to two of Costa Mesa's senior housing projects, Bethel Towers and Casa Bella Apartments. Before the new facility opened in 1992, senior activities were available at the Golden Timers Senior Citizen's Center at 114 East Nineteenth Street as well as at the Neighborhood Community Center and Rea Community Center.

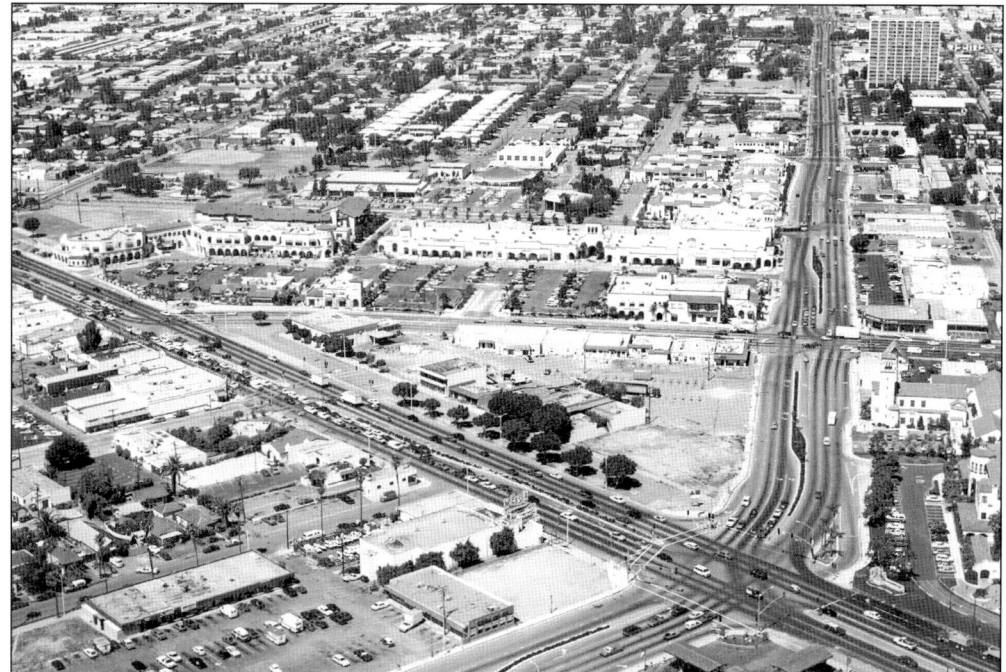

One of the last elements of Costa Mesa's Downtown Redevelopment Plan was Project No. 5, Triangle Square, which was to provide 185,000 square feet of retail space with underground parking. In this summer 1990 view looking west, Newport Boulevard runs diagonally from lower right to center left, while Harbor Boulevard runs horizontally across the center to meet West Nineteenth Street running vertically at right. The three streets enclose the project's triangular footprint.

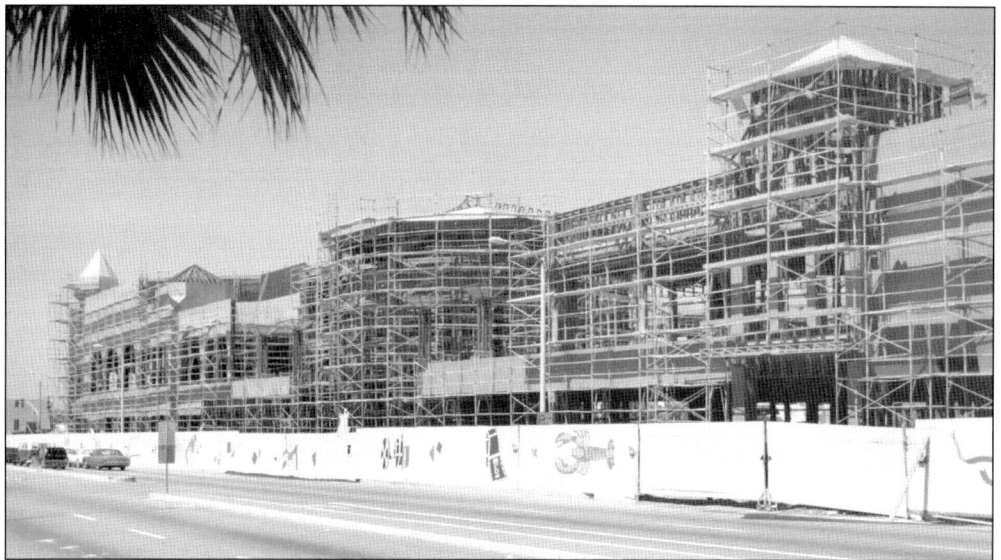

By July 1991, substantial progress had been made in constructing Triangle Square. This view looking northeast shows the 1870–1890 Harbor Boulevard block. At completion, the redevelopment project cost $62 million. The first business to open at the new center was Edwards Triangle Square, featuring an eight-screen movie theater complex and advertising "plush seating and a spacious café."

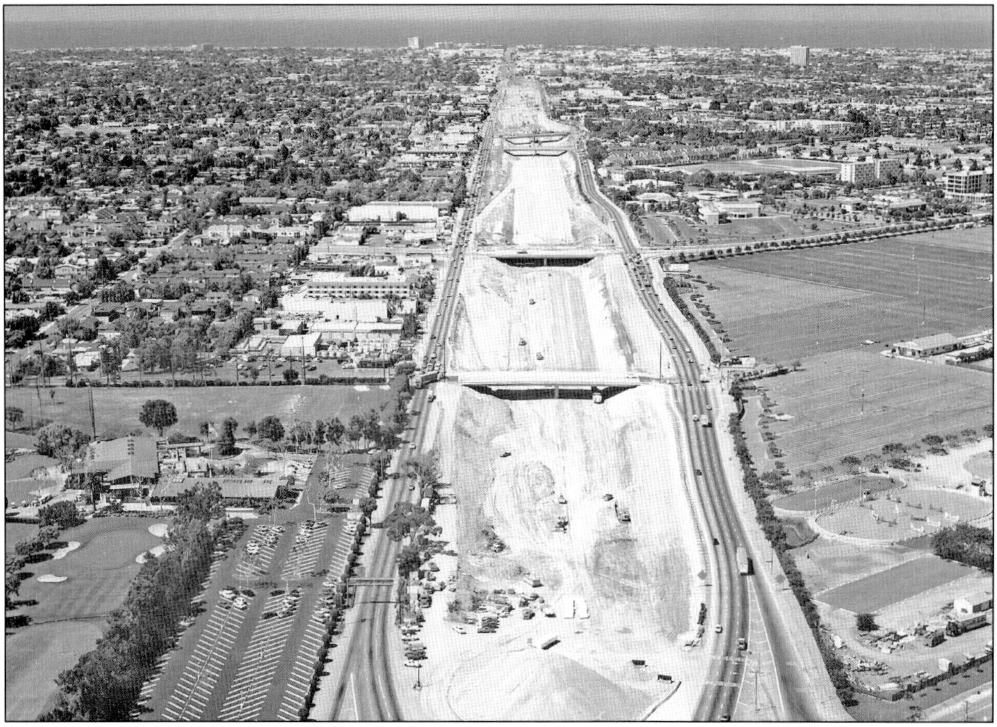

Known to decades of Costa Mesans as "the Ditch," the roadbed for the segment of State Route 55 from the 405 Freeway to Nineteenth Street in Costa Mesa was used over the years for the storage of nursery stock and construction equipment. After years of delay, construction on the highway was in full swing when this aerial photograph looking southwest was taken in the summer of 1990.

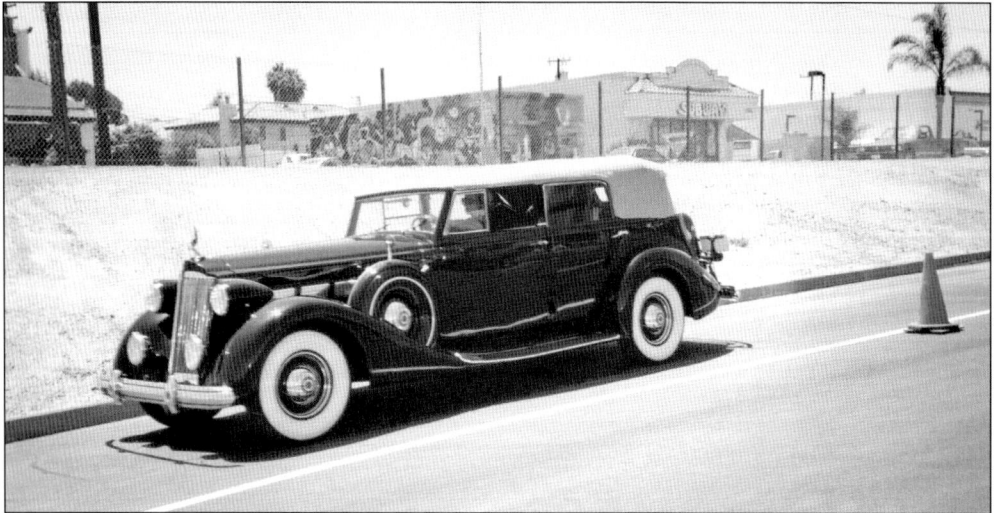

Conversion of the Ditch into a freeway was completed and a grand opening held on June 30, 1992. Shown here is the lead car, a 1937 Packard Phaeton, headed north from the freeway terminus at Costa Mesa's Nineteenth Street. In 1971, voters in the charter city of Newport Beach passed a freeway poison pill, virtually assuring that the 55 Freeway would not connect with Pacific Coast Highway, thus leaving to Costa Mesa the consequence of holding backed-up traffic awaiting access to the beach.

Six

CostaMazing

When Orange County voters approved Measure M in 1990, $340 million was to be set aside for urban light rail. Studies conducted over the next seven years identified an initial 28-mile rail segment connecting Fullerton to Irvine. At least two of the options would provide a station in Costa Mesa's Town Center area. As the initial Measure M expired in 2011, voters approved a 30-year continuation known as Measure M2.

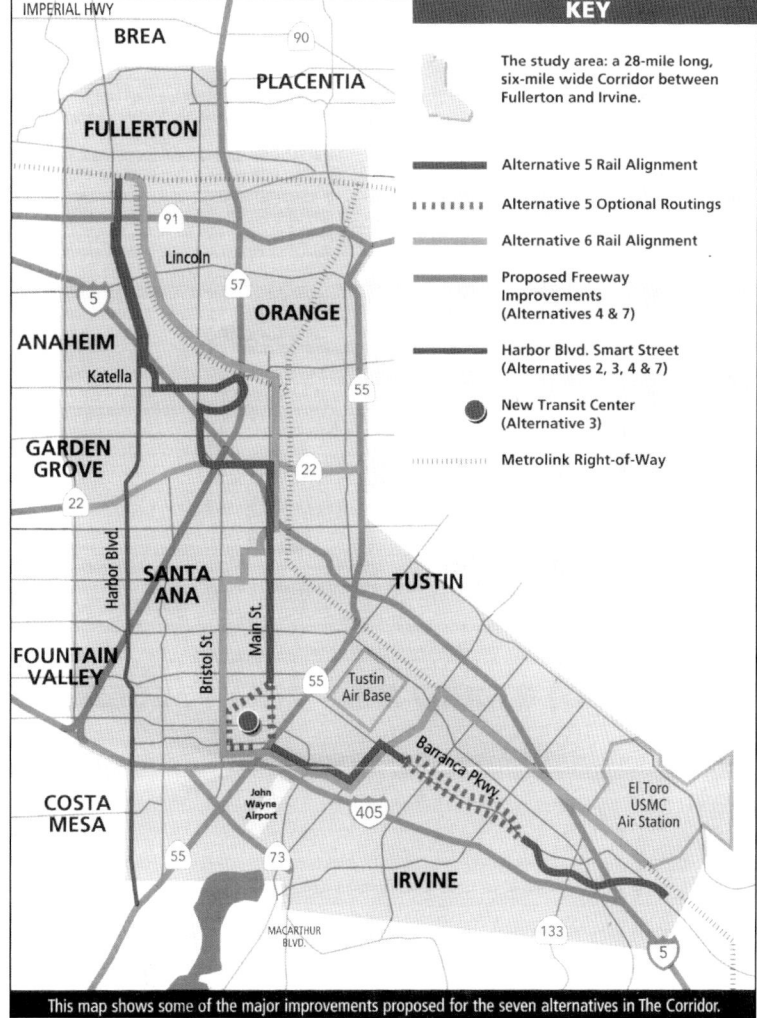

This map shows some of the major improvements proposed for the seven alternatives in The Corridor.

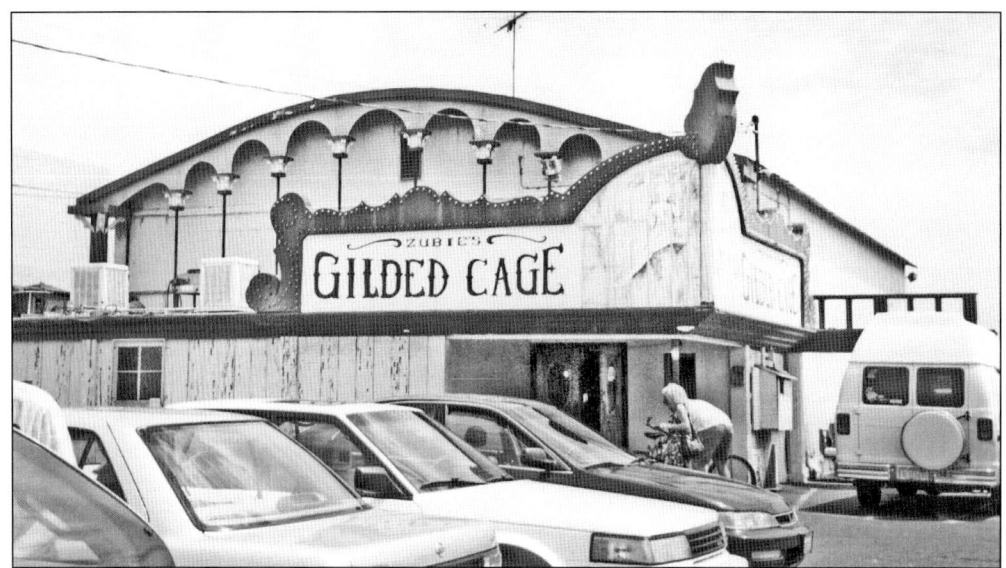

As North Costa Mesa was experiencing urban growth, other areas were being revamped, and familiar haunts were disappearing. Zubie's Gilded Cage at 1714 Placentia Avenue was near the end of its run when this photograph was taken in August 1998. Urban cowboy patrons of Zubie's sometimes had run-ins with the younger punk rock crowd at the Cuckoo's Nest next door.

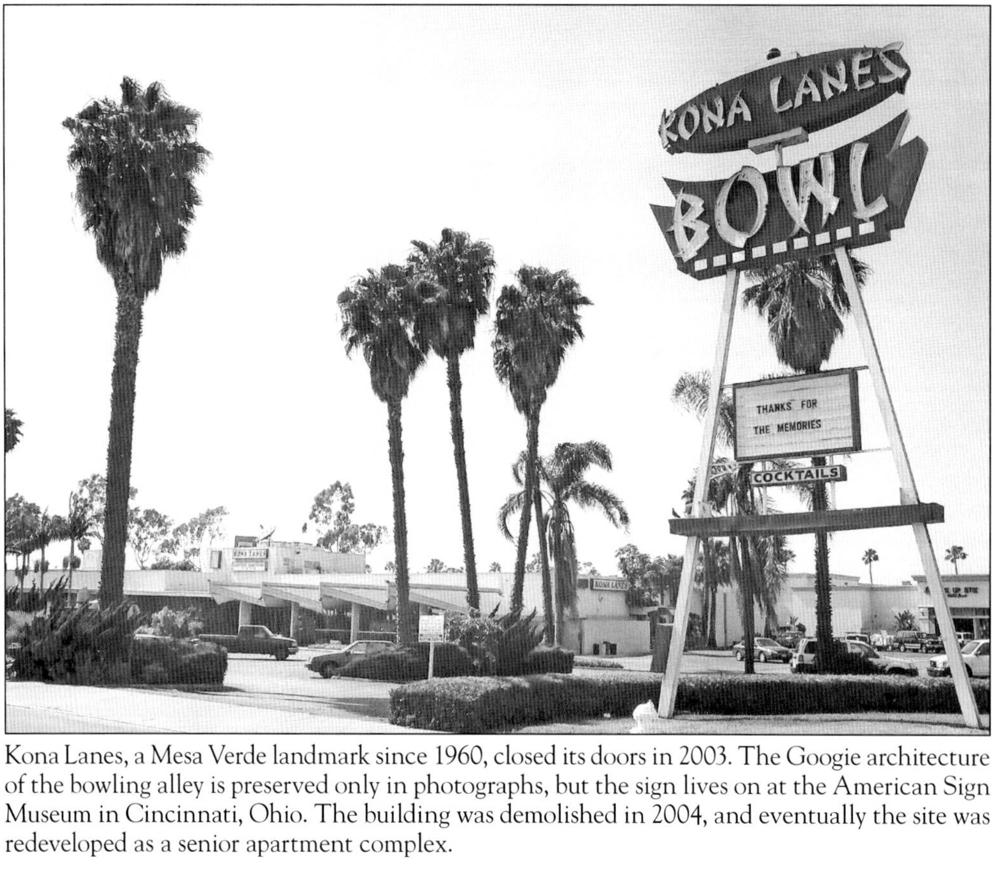

Kona Lanes, a Mesa Verde landmark since 1960, closed its doors in 2003. The Googie architecture of the bowling alley is preserved only in photographs, but the sign lives on at the American Sign Museum in Cincinnati, Ohio. The building was demolished in 2004, and eventually the site was redeveloped as a senior apartment complex.

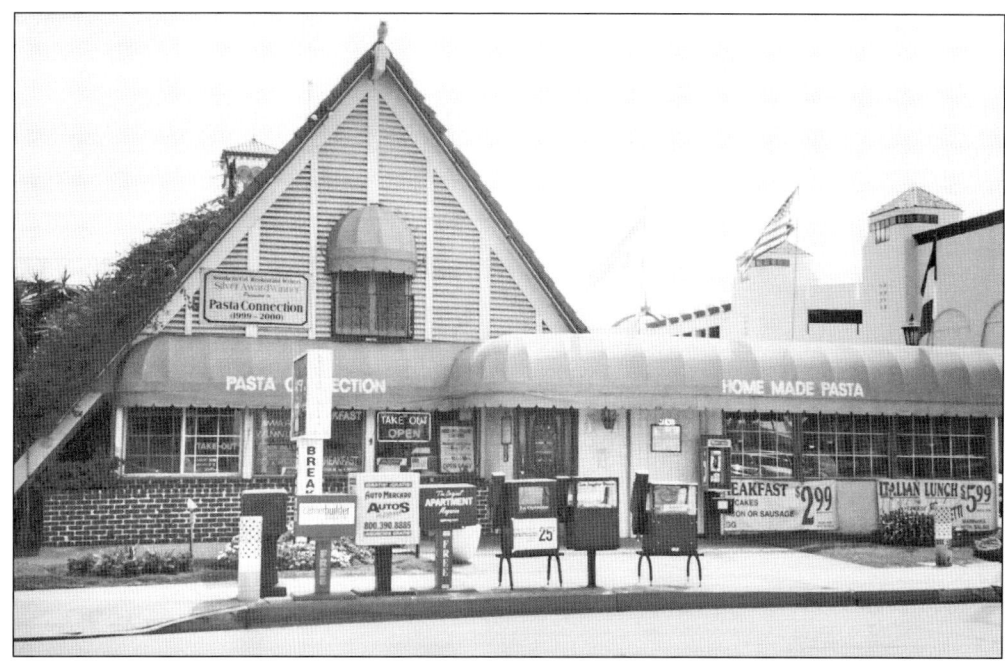

One of several A-frame buildings in the 1900 and 2000 blocks of Harbor Boulevard, the Pasta Connection opened in 1984 at 1902 Harbor Boulevard. The menu featured "authentic Italian pasta with Argentinian flavor." When this photograph was taken around 2001, Triangle Square, visible at right, had been open almost 10 years. By 2008, Pasta Connection had moved a few blocks north to 1969 Harbor Boulevard, while the A-frame was demolished and replaced by a new building.

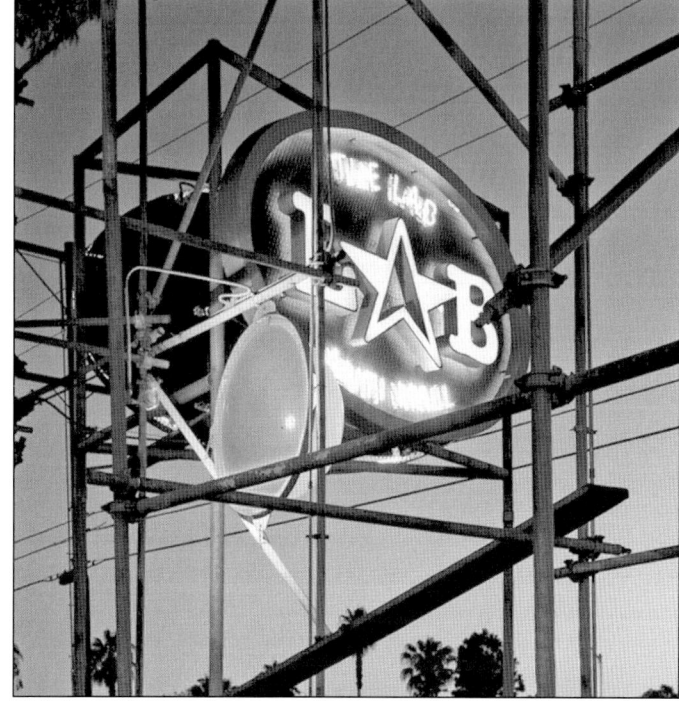

While old landmarks were disappearing, new businesses and new concepts were developing. One successful venture was the LAB Anti-Mall, established by Shaheen Sadeghi in 1993. The LAB, standing for Little American Business, provided a youth-driven shopping experience that offered an outlet for students and emerging artists and featured compatible boutiques and restaurants. Built in an abandoned factory, the anti-mall offered a contrast to upscale South Coast Plaza, located less than a mile away. (Courtesy of Shaheen Sadeghi, LAB Anti-Mall.)

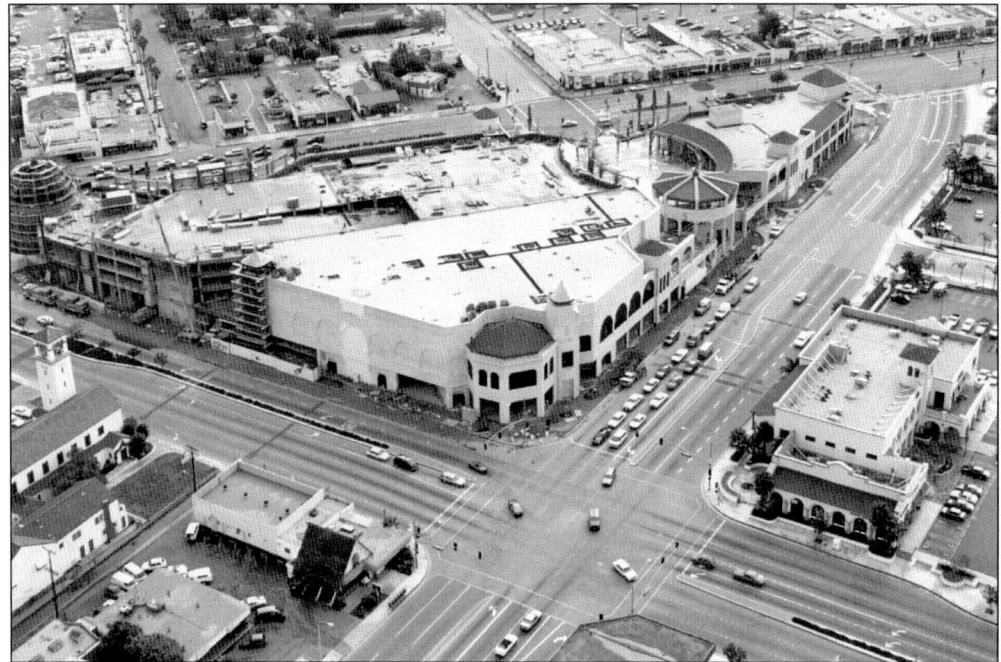

When this photograph was taken in December 1991, Triangle Square was progressing rapidly towards an initial opening in June 1992 and additional openings throughout the fall and winter. In this aerial view, West Nineteenth Street runs diagonally from left center to lower right, and Harbor Boulevard runs from bottom center to upper right, where it intersects Newport Boulevard. The center experienced changes of ownership and a steady exodus of anchor tenants. In 2010, the center was sold again and rebranded as a restaurant and entertainment hub called the Triangle.

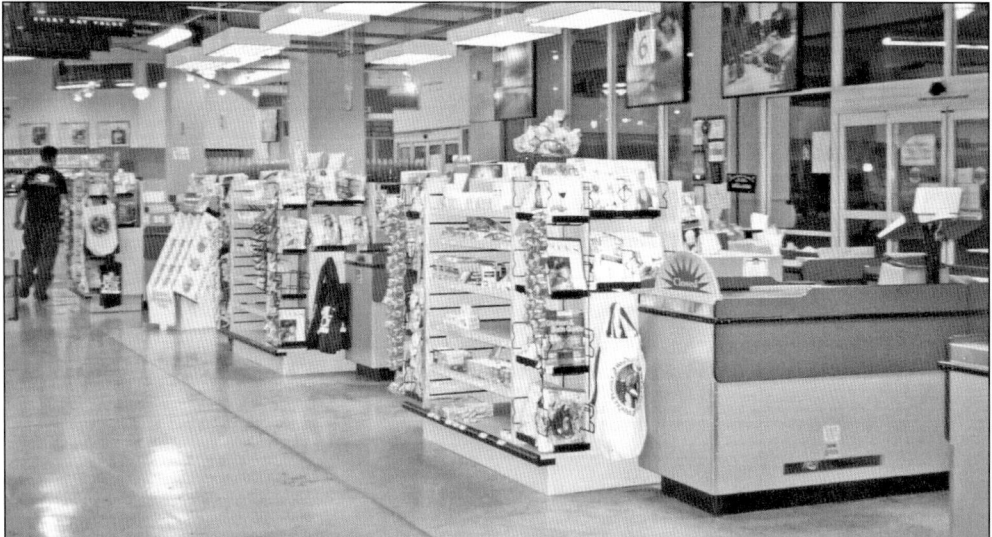

One of the original anchor stores in Triangle Square was Ralph's supermarket, which opened in September 1992. One unique feature of the store was its subterranean location, adjacent to underground parking. Ralph's was gone by October 1998, and Whole Foods moved in. When this photograph was taken in 2001, Whole Foods was near the end of its run. The store closed in April 2002. In November 2011, 24-Hour Fitness held a grand opening at the location.

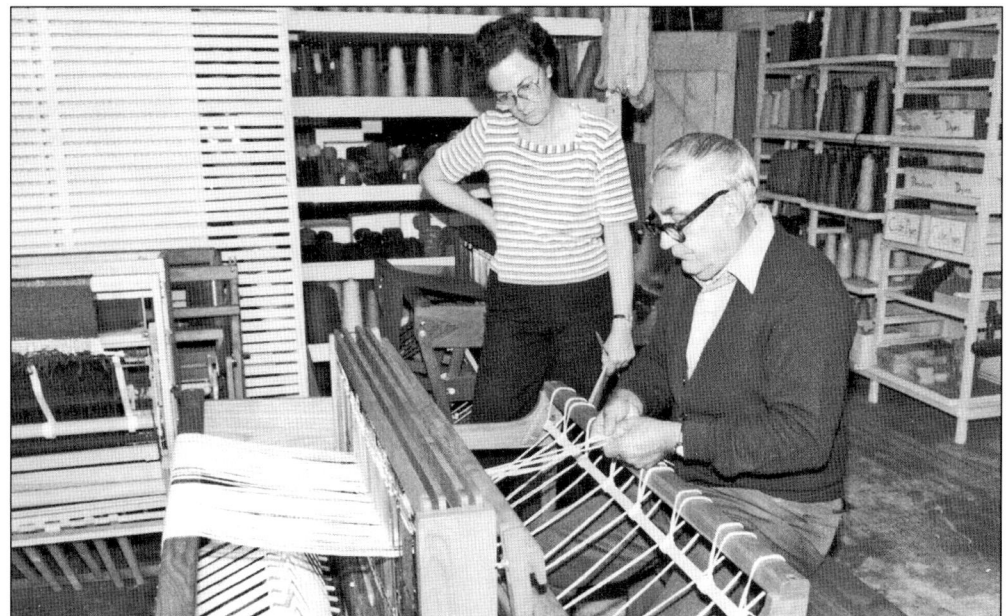

In the midst of redevelopment and growth, family-owned businesses continued to thrive in Costa Mesa. Pictured here in the 1990s is Gerald "Jo" Dendel (right) demonstrating how to warp a handloom at Denwar Studios, located at 236 East Sixteenth Street. Denwar started in Costa Mesa in 1947, using patterns, colors, and concepts inspired by African art. The Denwar legacy lives on through the Artistic License Fair held in Costa Mesa annually on the last full weekend in October.

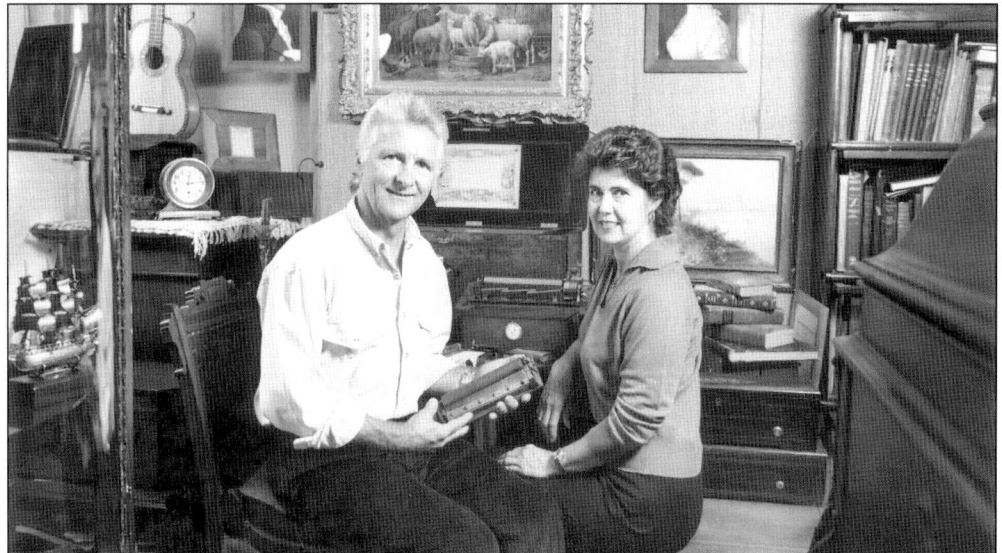

One of fewer than a dozen music-box restoration businesses in the world is owned and operated by Christian Eric and his wife, Kathleen, pictured here in 1998 in their shop at 1825 Placentia Avenue. The Erics started their business, Antique Music Box Restoration, as a sideline in 1967 but went fulltime as Christian's music performing career began to take too great a toll. Their craftsmanship is in demand across the globe among museums and collectors. The Erics also are known for their community service in civic groups and city committees.

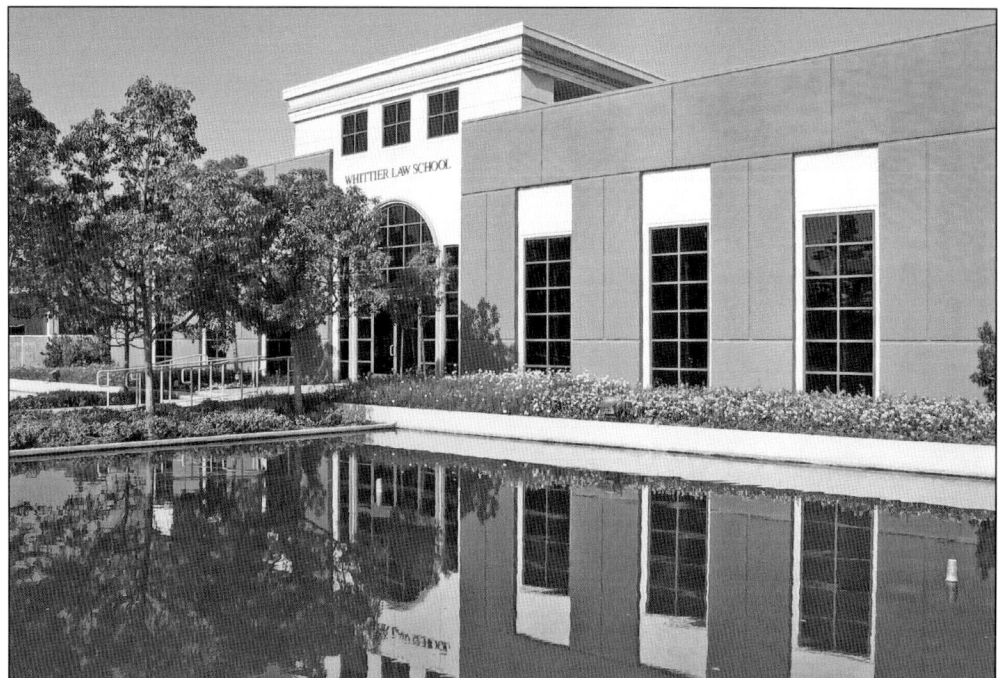

The Whittier Law School, part of Whittier College, began moving to a 14-acre campus at 3333 Harbor Boulevard in 1996. Supreme Court associate justice Anthony Kennedy was the main speaker at the school's opening ceremony in 1997. The property was originally developed for Atlantic Research Corp. Systems Division in 1966 and changed hands to Brunswick Corp. Defense Division in 1977.

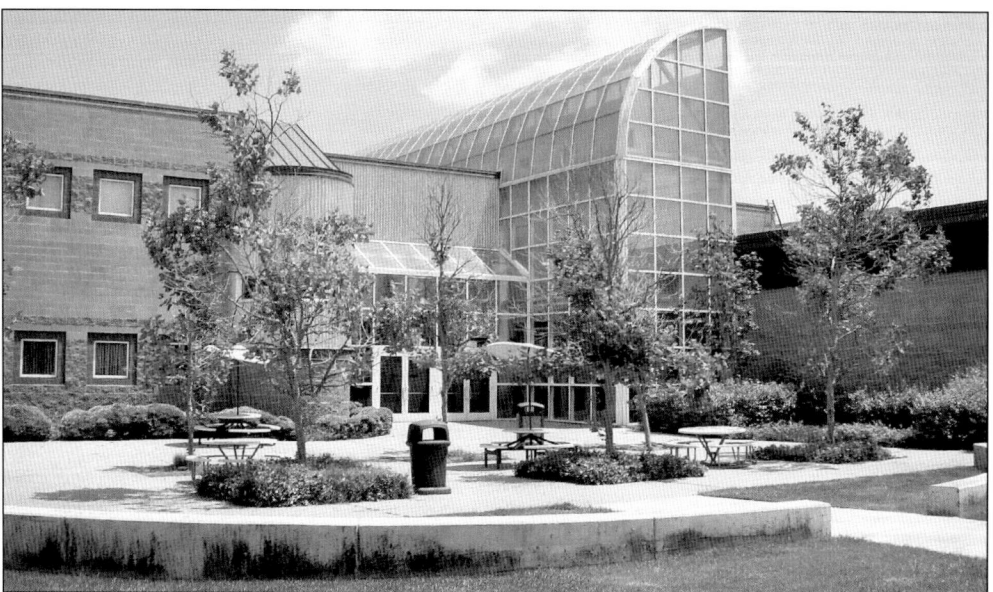

When the $8.6-million Orange Coast College (OCC) Technology Center opened in September 1994, it was the largest tech center in any community college west of the Mississippi River. The 78,000-square-foot facility replaced seven buildings that dated from OCC's beginning in 1948. OCC continued to plan for the future by developing a Vision 2020 Facilities Master Plan.

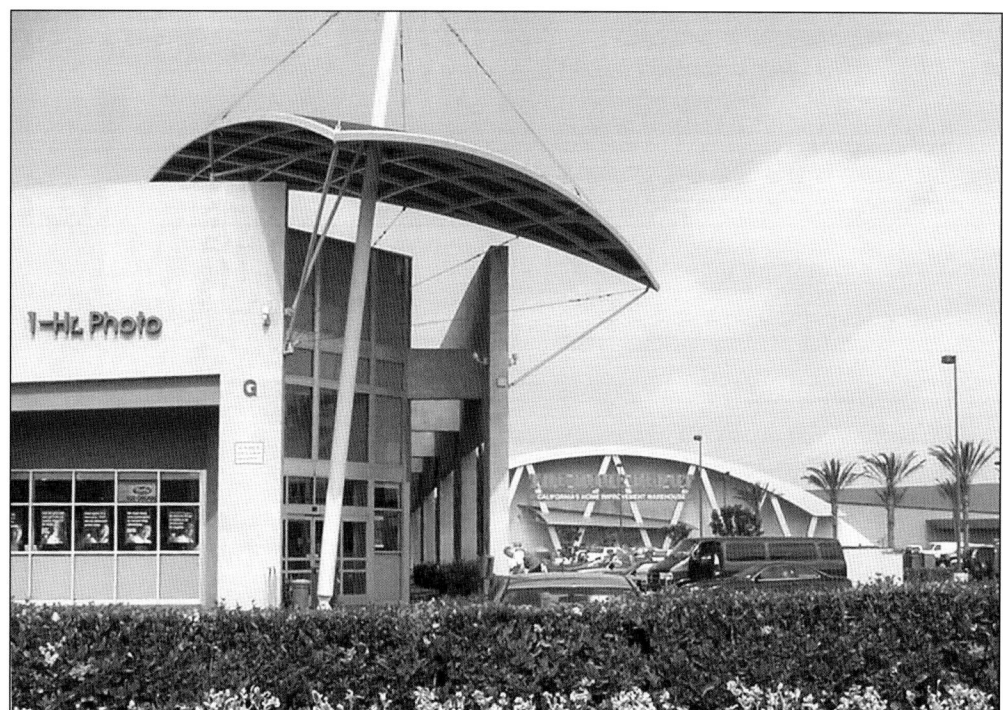

By the late 1990s, Harbor Shopping Center was ready for a makeover. The spruced-up center attracted national and regional brands such as Home Depot, Albertson's, T.J. Maxx, Big 5, and Chuck E. Cheese. Thrifty Drug stayed, as did a popular family-owned restaurant, Nick's Pizza. Gone were Woolworth's, Sears, Singer, and JC Penney, among others. Compare this 2002 photograph to the mid-1960s view on page 55.

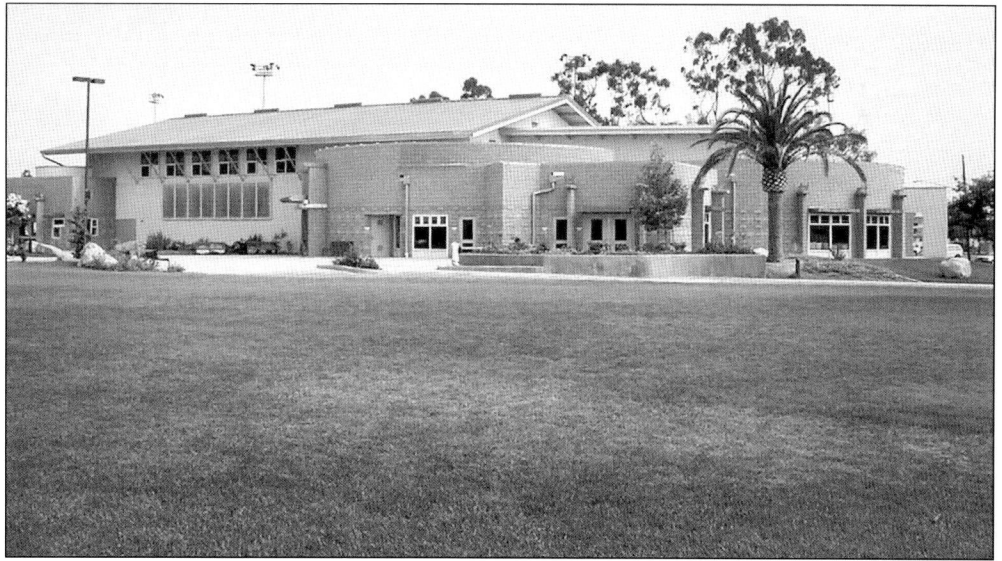

Costa Mesa's Downtown Recreation Center, at 1860 Anaheim Avenue, opened in the fall of 2001. The new facility replaced the Downtown Community Center that had provided more than 60 years of service to the community (see page 14). The new facility included amenities such as an indoor gym, 25-yard outdoor pool, and multipurpose rooms.

facilities map

"RECREATE AND MEET NEW FRIENDS"

1	Balearic Center	1975 Balearic Dr.
2	Bark Park	970 Arlington
3	Brentwood Park	265 E. Brentwood
4	Canyon Park	970 Arbor St.
5	Civic Center	77 Fair Dr.
6	C.M. Golf & Country Club	1701 Golf Course Dr.
7	C.M. Tennis Club	880 Junipero
8	Corporation Yard	2310 Placentia
9	Del Mesa Park	2080 Manistee Dr.
10	Downtown Center	1860 Anaheim
11	Estancia High School	2323 Placentia
12	Estancia Park	1900 Adams
13	Fairview Park	2525 Placentia
14	Gisler Park	1250 Gisler St.
15	Harper Park	425 E. 18th St.
16	Heller Park	257 16th St.
17	Lindbergh Park	220 E. 23rd St.
18	Lions Park	570 W. 18th St.
19	Marina View Park	1035 W. 19th St.
20	Mesa Verde Park	1795 Samar Ave.
21	Moon Park	3377 California St.
22	Neighborhood Center	1845 Park Ave.
23	Paularino Park	1040 Paularino Ave.
24	Pinkley Park	360 E. Ogle
25	Senior Center	695 West 19th Street
26	Shiffer Park	3134 Bear St.
27	Smallwood Park	1656 Corsica Pl.
28	Suburbia I Park	3302 Alabama
29	Tanager Park	1780 Hummingbird Dr.
30	TeWinkle Park	970 Arlington
31	Vista Park	1200 Victoria St.
32	Wakeham Park	3400 Smalley St.
33	Willard T. Jordan Park	2141 Tustin Ave.
34	Wilson Park	360 Wilson
35	Wimbledon Park	3440 Wimbledon Way

Costa Mesa's fall 1999 Recreation Review booklet listed 35 facilities across the city. Costa Mesa had established a network of 26 neighborhood parks and nine facilities and fields. Parks and recreation had become a major focus for the city, operating under the motto, "We create community through people, parks and programs." In 2006, three of Costa Mesa's fields were lighted, and action was taken to add lighting to two more. By 2015, there were 29 parks and 37 facilities and fields listed in the city's recreation guide booklet.

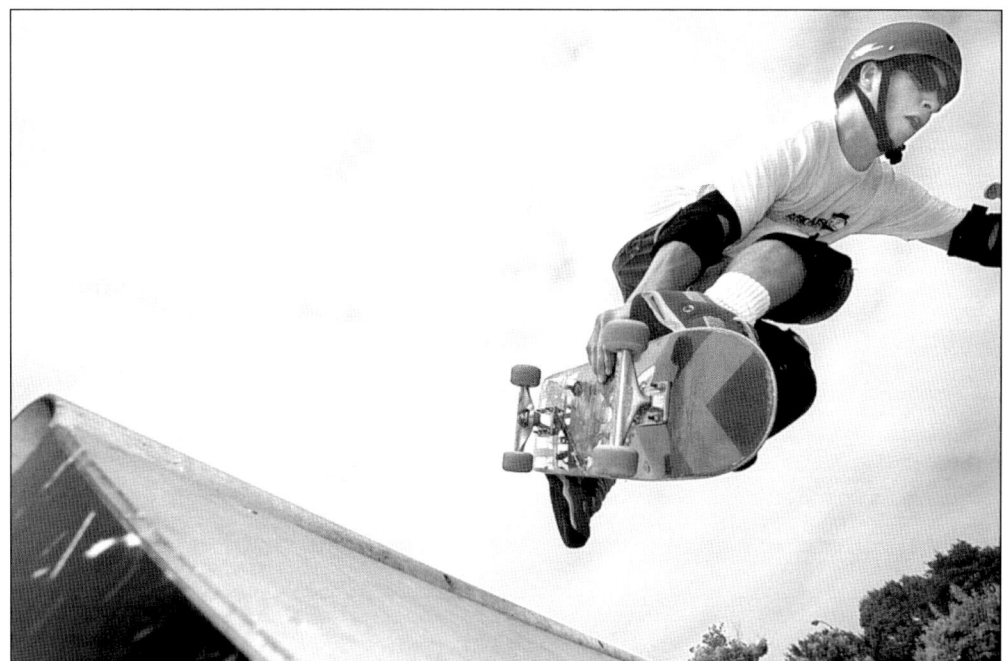

After years of looking for a location for a permanent skate park, Costa Mesa officials hit upon the idea of a mobile facility that could be set up at various parks on a regular schedule. The mobile skate park program kicked off in May 2001 and ran until the summer of 2005, when Volcom Skate Park of Costa Mesa opened. (©2003, *Orange County Register*. Reprinted with permission.)

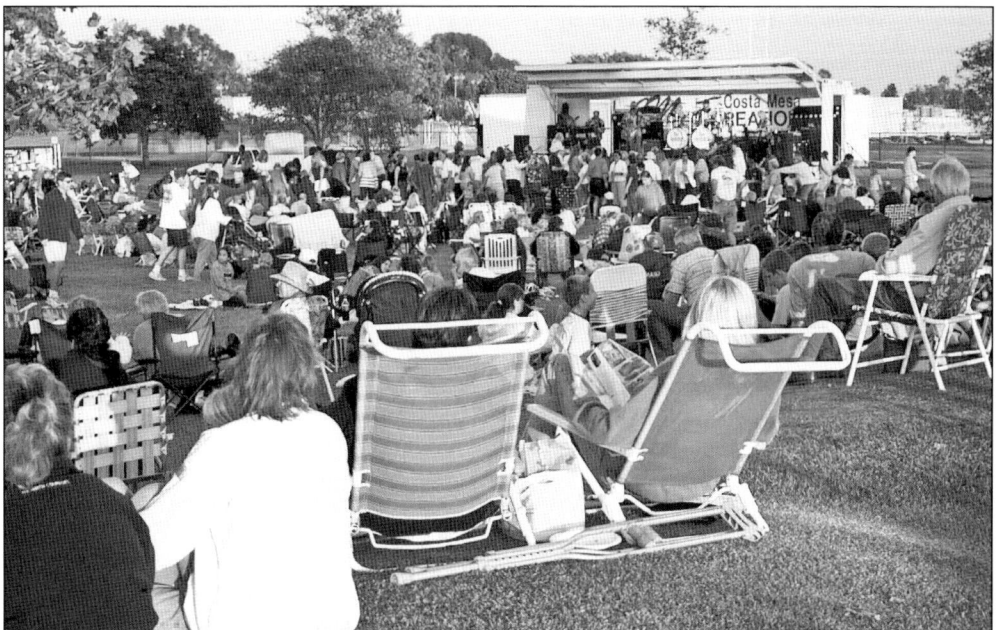

The popularity of Costa Mesa's Concerts in the Park program can be seen in this image of a summer 2002 concert. The city sponsored these events until 2010, when the Costa Mesa Community Foundation took the lead. The free concerts were another way to build community in Costa Mesa.

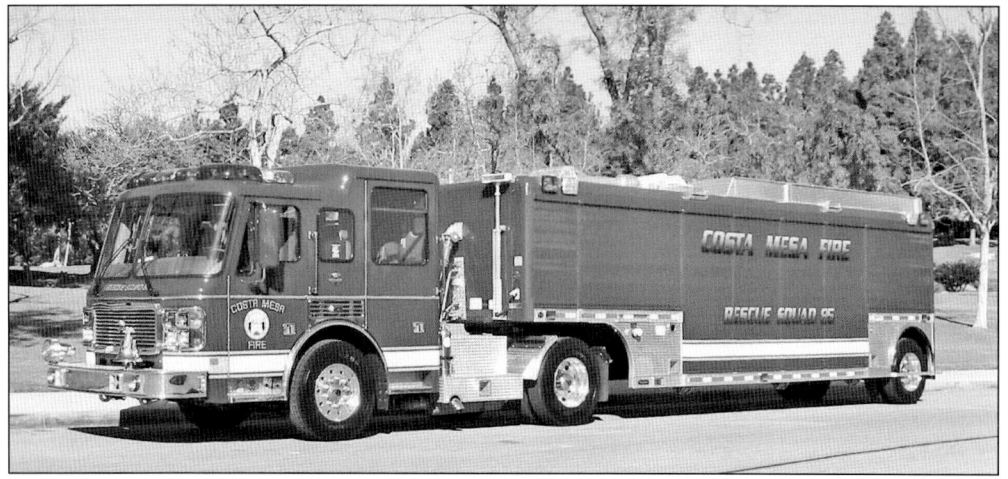

Rescue Squad 85 entered service in the fall of 2002. This unit was designed to respond to fires and heavy rescues such as vehicle extrication, building collapse, and confined space rescues using equipment such as the jaws of life, winches, jacks, cutting torches, and circular saws. Costa Mesa's first responders were now even better equipped. Rescue Squad 85 later was renamed Urban Search and Rescue (USAR) 84.

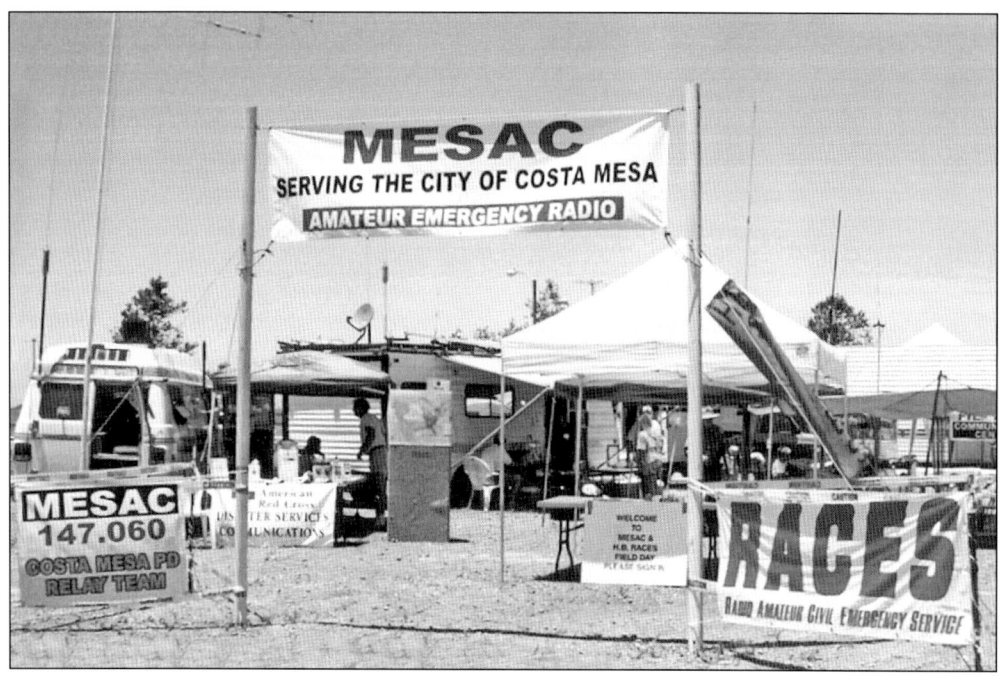

Over the decades, Costa Mesa's citizens have provided volunteer service to public safety as volunteer firemen, police reserves, Explorer Post, and volunteer communicators. Shown here is an amateur radio station set up in Fairview Park for an annual communications exercise known as Field Day. This volunteer group, known as Mesa Emergency Services Amateur Communications (MESAC), began serving the community in the 1980s. (Courtesy of Gordon West.)

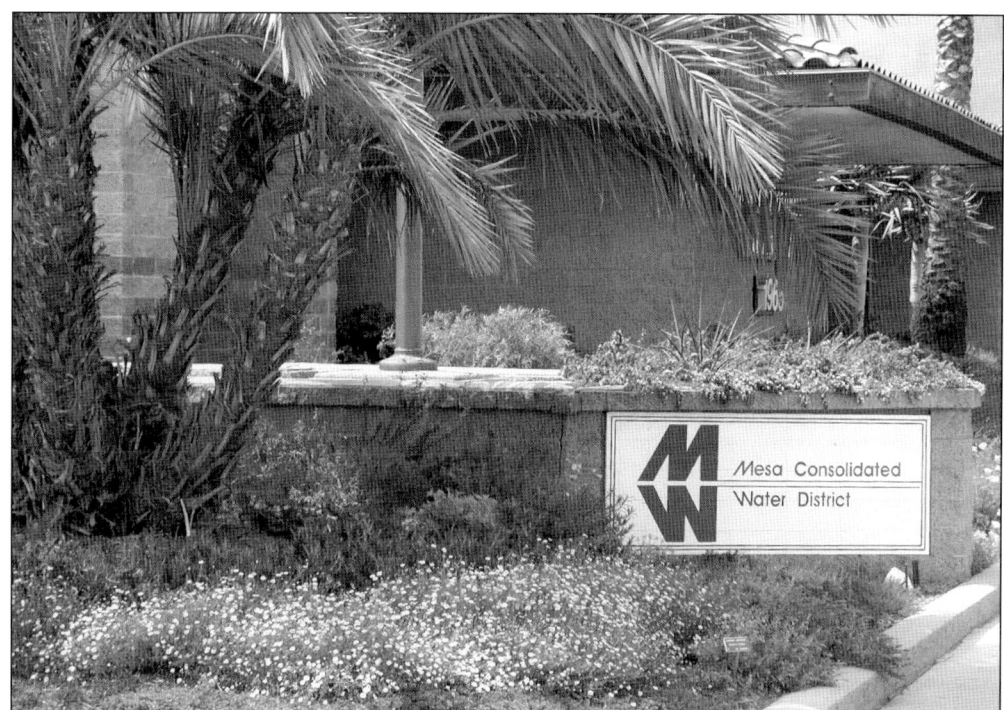

The Costa Mesa County Water District was formed in 1960 and was renamed the Mesa Consolidated Water District in 1978. By that time, emphasis had shifted from imported water to water independence provided by deep wells. After an extended period of drought in the early 1990s, attention turned to conservation. The district planted this demonstration garden to show customers just how attractive drought-tolerant, California-friendly plants could be. (Courtesy of the Mesa Consolidated Water District.)

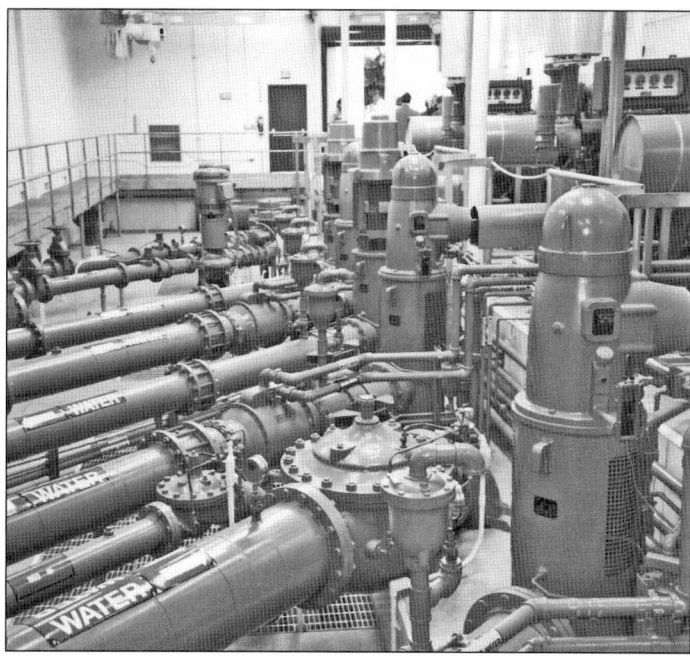

Mesa Consolidated Water District's Reservoir One was dedicated in May 1990. The 10-million-gallon water storage facility helped the district to wean itself away from expensive imported water. Shown here is the pumping plant at Reservoir One. The plant provided a 10,000-gallon-per-minute capacity and used both natural gas and electric-powered pumps for reliability. A second reservoir, named after long-term general manager Karl Kemp, was completed in 1995. (Courtesy of the Mesa Consolidated Water District.)

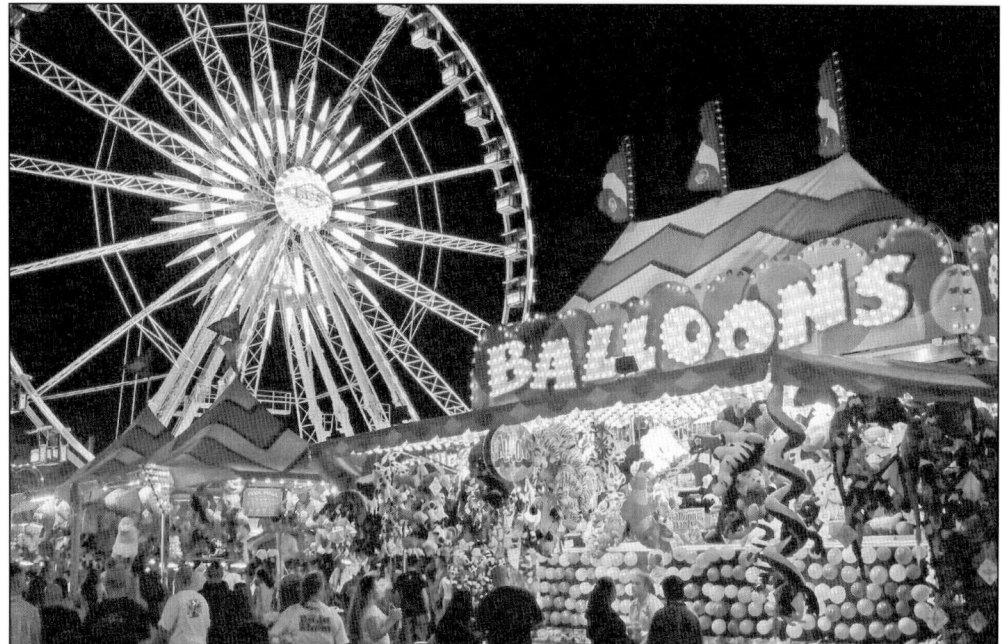

Attendance at the 2003 Orange County Fair reached nearly 900,000 under the new format of a 21-day fair (closed Mondays). The 2005 fair was the first to break the one-million mark. The carnival midway continued to be popular, as did foods both familiar and exotic, especially to those fairgoers not counting calories.

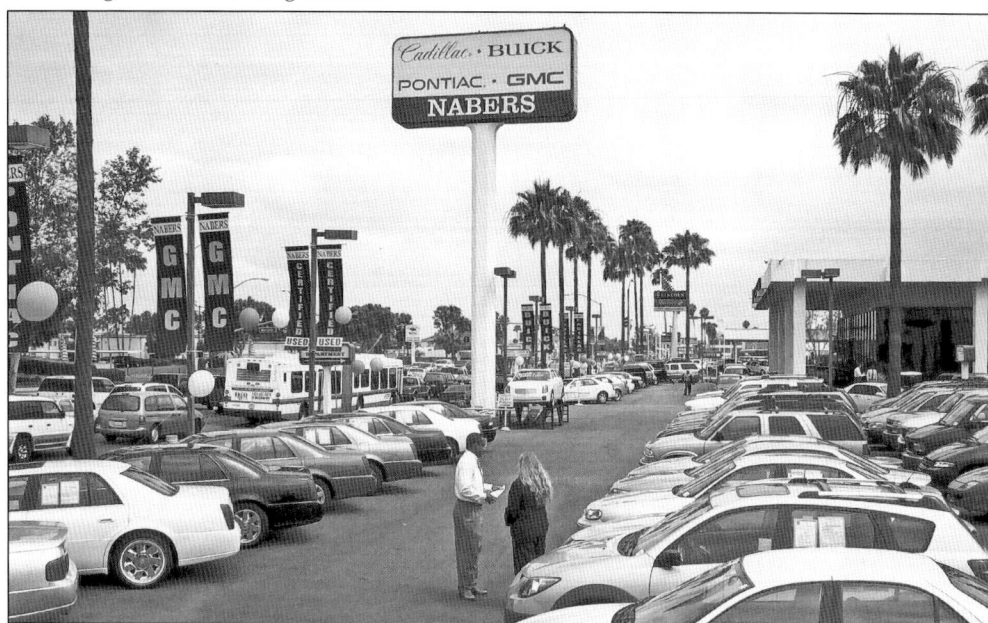

Since the 1960s, the Harbor Boulevard of Cars had been a reliable source of sales tax revenues to the city. Shown here in 2003, the Nabers dealership at 2600 Harbor Boulevard had been in business since 1968. Additional General Motors brands were added to the original Cadillac brand, but Oldsmobile was finished by 2004. After the automobile industry crisis and bail-out of 2009, General Motors dropped Pontiac. Nabers sold the business in 2012.

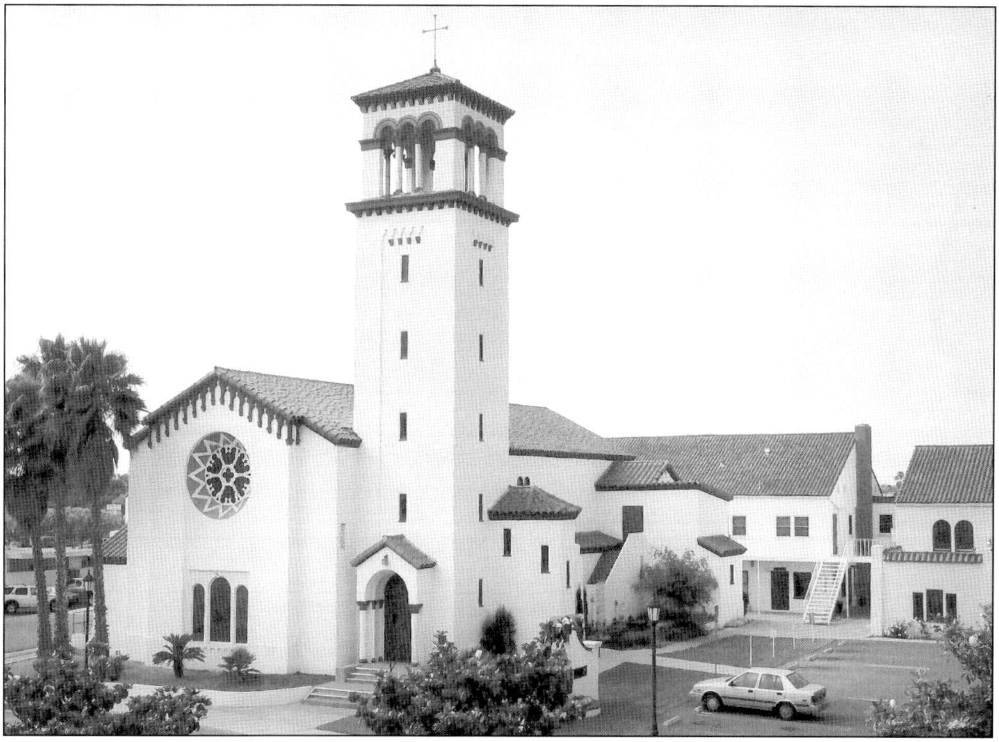

The First United Methodist Church at 420 West Nineteenth Street is one of five sites identified by the 2000 Costa Mesa General Plan as eligible for listing in the National Register of Historic Places. The Spanish Colonial Revival structure, built in 1928, served as an anchor point downtown during the area's transition from farming to unincorporated city. The church, which survived a magnitude-6.3 earthquake in 1933, now finds itself hemmed in by surrounding development.

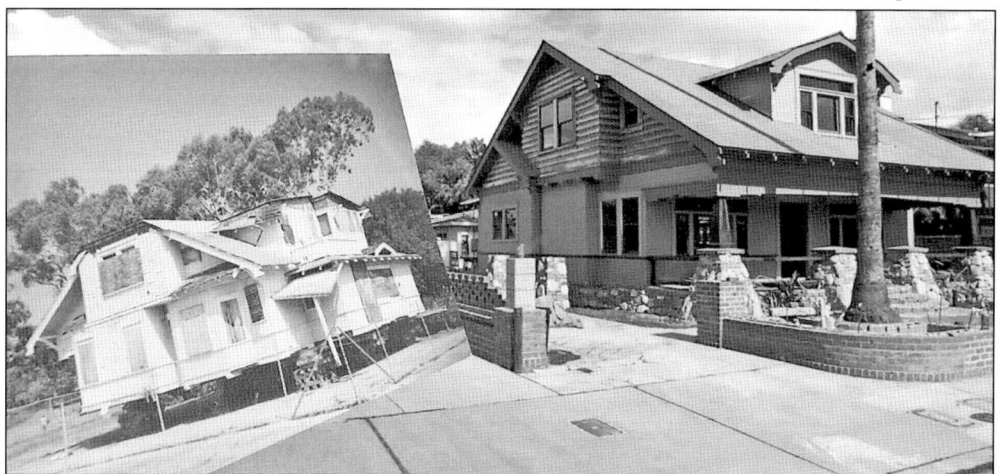

The 2000 Costa Mesa General Plan identifies 24 sites eligible for listing in the local register of historic places. One of those is the 1915 Huscroft House, shown here in a then-and-now format. After being moved from Santa Ana to Costa Mesa in 1954, the house was moved to temporary storage in TeWinkle Park in 1999 (left) before being rescued and relocated to Bernard Street in 2004 (right). The Huscroft House qualified for property tax relief under California's Mills Act in 2007. (Photograph by Kent Treptow, ©2005, *Los Angeles Times*. Reprinted with permission.)

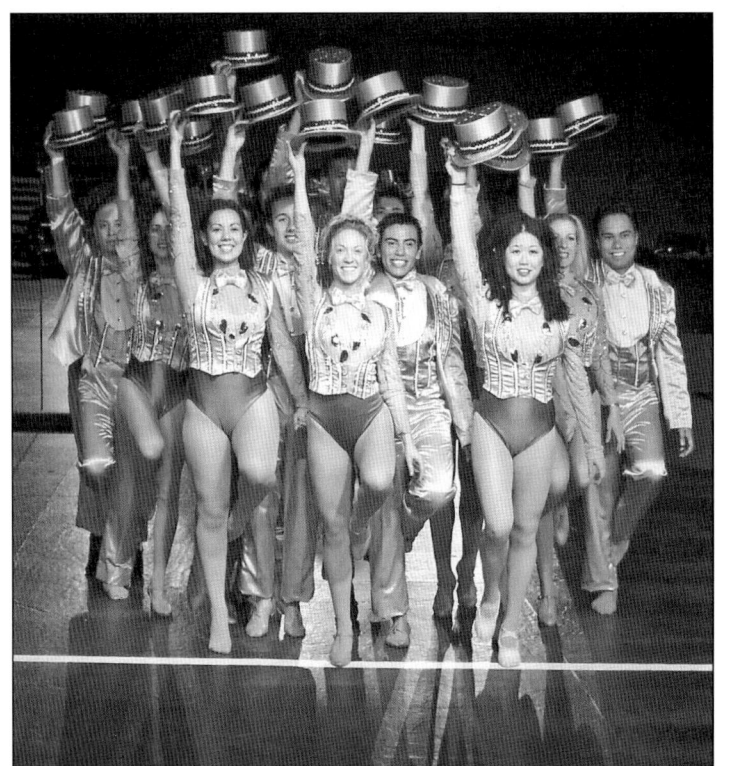

The combination of early city encouragement and private philanthropy gave Costa Mesa a big boost in the performing arts and led the city to officially change its motto to "City of the Arts" in 1999. One of the beneficiaries of city support and encouragement was the Costa Mesa Civic Playhouse. Shown here is the cast of *A Chorus Line*, which was staged in June 2002 at the nonprofit group's new 73-seat theater at Rea School, 661 Hamilton Street. (Courtesy of Costa Mesa Civic Playhouse.)

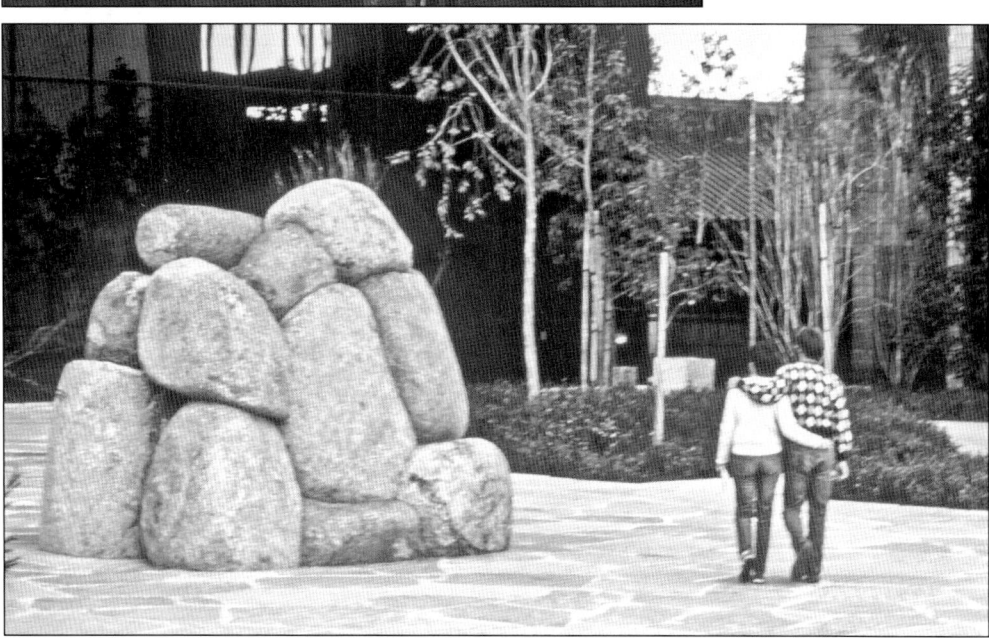

Part of Costa Mesa's claim to be the "City of the Arts" was based on public artworks situated in the Theater and Arts District, located across Bristol Street from South Coast Plaza. Shown here in the mid-1980s is a portion of *California Scenario* by Isamu Noguchi. The sculpture to the left of the couple is titled *Spirit of the Lima Bean* in recognition of the Segerstrom family's farming enterprise that led to the development of the Theater and Arts District.

By 2003, South Coast Repertory (SCR) had celebrated its 40th anniversary and had just completed an expansion of its fourth-step theater to three stages with a total seating of more than 900 theatergoers. With strong philanthropic support and the directorial leadership of David Emmes and Martin Benson, SCR became one of the most influential regional theaters in the United States. Emmes and Benson retired from active directing in 2011 and became founding artistic directors.

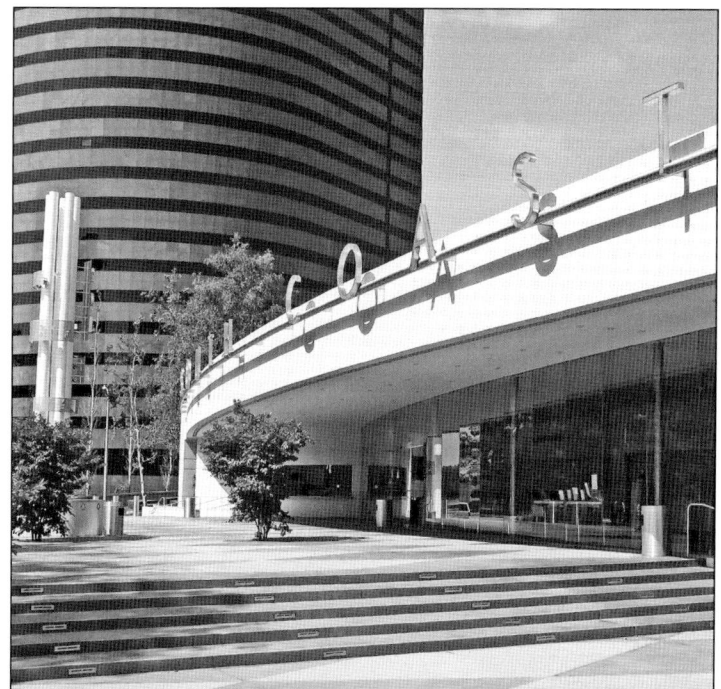

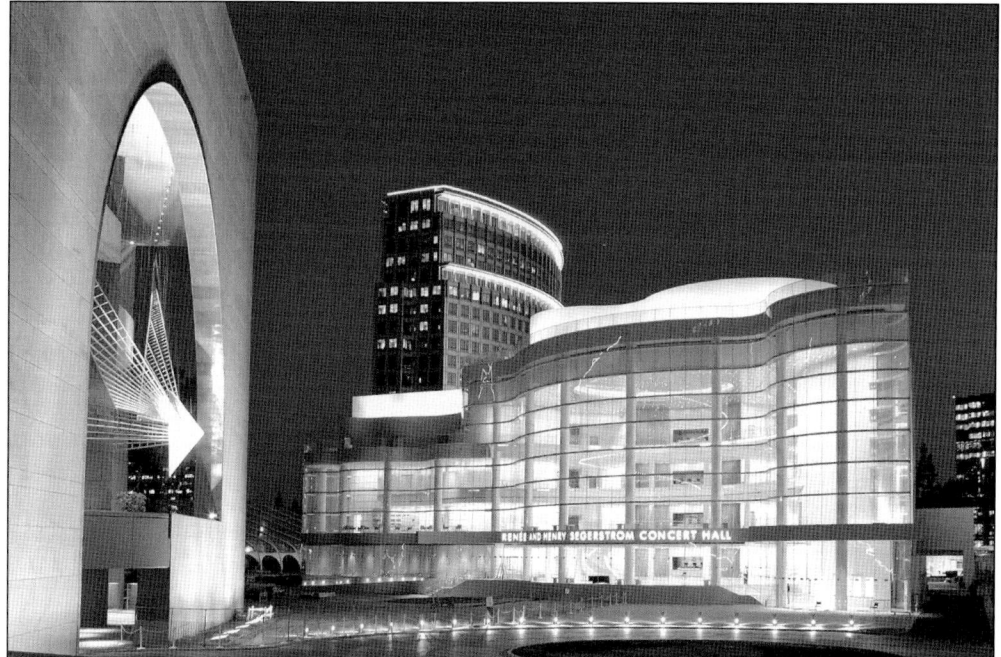

When Costa Mesa celebrated its 50th anniversary in June 2003, plans were made and a capital campaign was underway to build the Renée and Henry Segerstrom Concert Hall. The nearly 2,000-seat venue opened on September 15, 2006. The new facility became the resident home for the Pacific Symphony, Philharmonic Society of Orange County, and Pacific Chorale. Shown here is a portion of the Segerstrom Center for the Arts, with Segerstrom Hall on the left and the new concert hall at center. (Courtesy of South Coast Metro Alliance.)

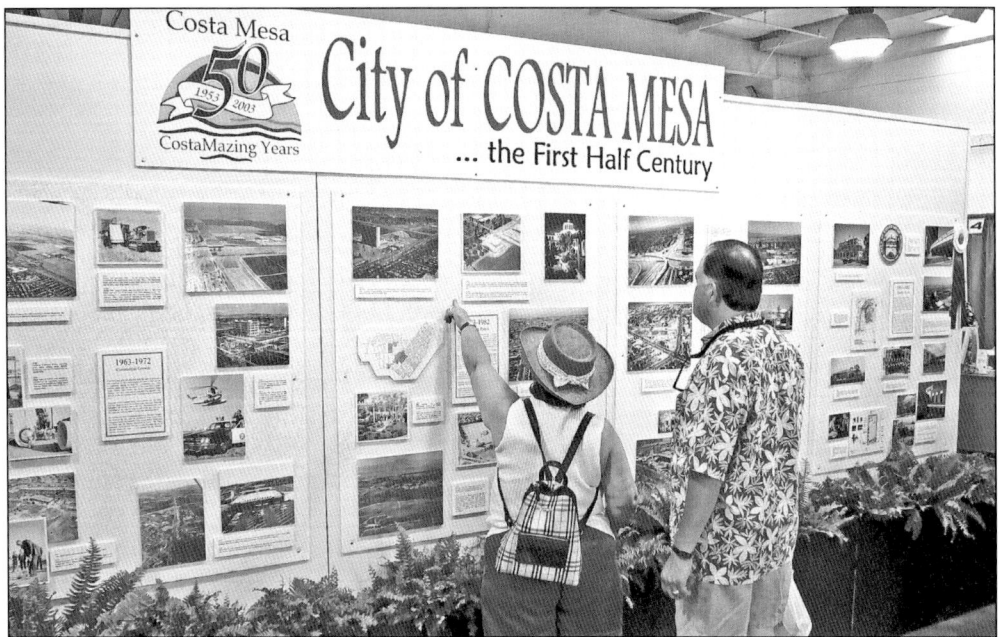

Costa Mesa's 50th anniversary, named "CostaMazing," was celebrated over a one-year period beginning in June 2003. One of the anniversary events was a major exhibit placed at the entrance to the Orange County Exhibit Building at the 2003 Orange County Fair. Covering the transformation of Costa Mesa from early communities to a modern city, the exhibit garnered special recognition from the fair's judges. See the image at bottom of page 10 for a listing of other 50th-anniversary events.

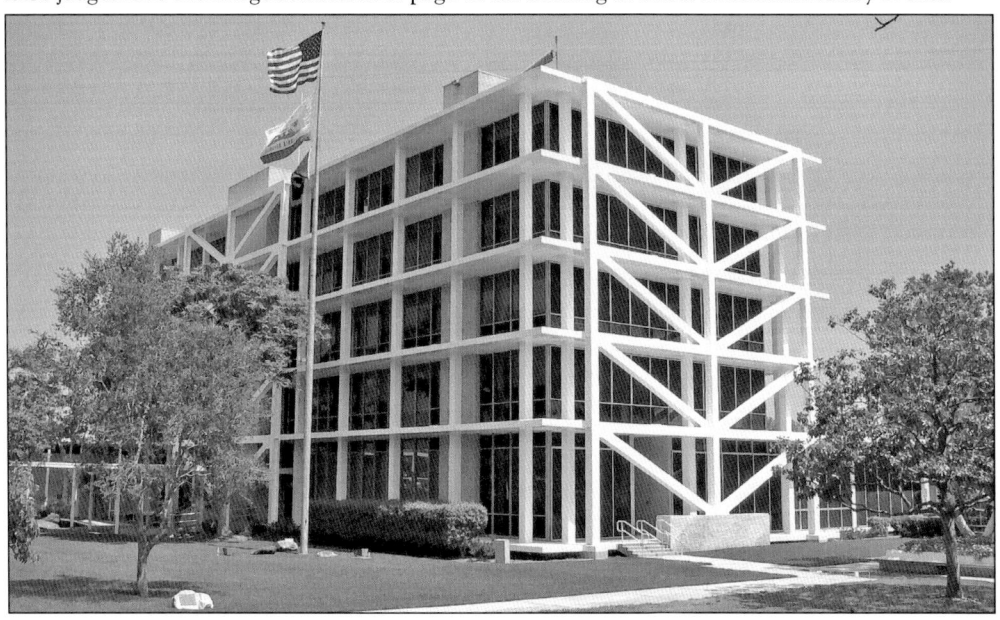

The kick-off for Costa Mesa's 50th anniversary took place at city hall, with an opening color guard ceremony and keynote speeches, followed by a public barbecue. When those events took place on June 30, 2003, city hall had received the X-Beam seismic retrofit shown here. (Compare this view to that at the bottom of page 68.) The retrofit gave city hall a solid framework for embarking on the next 50 years.

Epilogue

A dozen years have passed since the 2003 end date for this book. In those years, issues have emerged that will influence the content of the next book on Costa Mesa history. Yes, the next book will continue to document favorite activities, iconic places, and everyday life in Costa Mesa. But these memories will live on a foundation of planning, infrastructure, and urban growth that some will view as progress, others not.

Prominent among emerging issues is the next phase of water independence and reliability, which must consider desalination. Equally as significant is the density of new development and resulting infrastructure demands, mitigated by the as-yet unrealized promise of the co-located live-work-play concept. Also significant to Costa Mesa is future development not under the city's exclusive control at Banning Ranch, Fairview State Hospital, Orange Coast College, and the Orange County Fairgrounds. New development at these latter three sites brings into question the future of the central Costa Mesa greenbelt. Another factor not under Costa Mesa's exclusive control is the evolution of mass transit, including the Orange County Airport, Measure M2, and light rail.

A bit more under local control is the issue of charter city status. Costa Mesa is demographically more significant than its population or footprint would suggest, and is surrounded by charter cities willing to declare findings of "municipal affairs" when it is in their self-interest to do so. Also to be documented is progress in the arts post–Henry Segerstrom—not only the performing arts but also the visual and literary arts.

When Costa Mesans voted to incorporate in 1953, a strong community spirit and personality had already developed. In that sense, Costa Mesa got off to a running start. Still, the growth of Costa Mesa in the 50 years since incorporation was nothing short of "CostaMazing." In the process, the small-town vibe gave way to urban development and the emergence of South Coast Metro. From that, there would be no turning back. Costa Mesa had come of age. Now, only time will allow its journey towards maturity to be told.

Discover Thousands of Local History Books Featuring Millions of Vintage Images

Arcadia Publishing, the leading local history publisher in the United States, is committed to making history accessible and meaningful through publishing books that celebrate and preserve the heritage of America's people and places.

Find more books like this at
www.arcadiapublishing.com

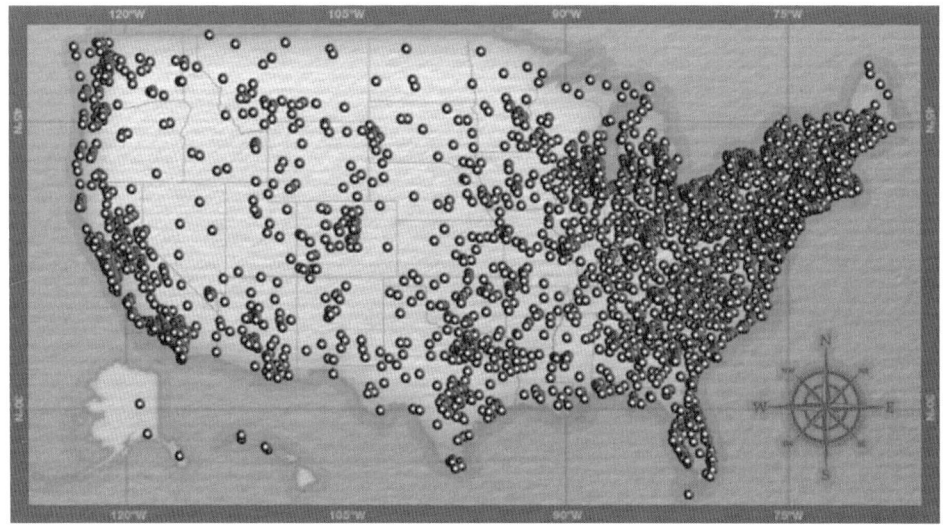

Search for your hometown history, your old stomping grounds, and even your favorite sports team.

Consistent with our mission to preserve history on a local level, this book was printed in South Carolina on American-made paper and manufactured entirely in the United States. Products carrying the accredited Forest Stewardship Council (FSC) label are printed on 100 percent FSC-certified paper.

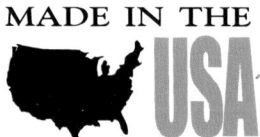